ROUTLEDGE LIBRARY EDITIONS: PEACE STUDIES

Volume 7

A LASTING PEACE

A LASTING PEACE

**MAXWELL GARNETT AND
H. F. KOEPPLER**

LONDON AND NEW YORK

First published in 1940 by George Allen & Unwin Ltd

This edition first published in 2020
by Routledge
2 Park Square, Milton Park, Abingdon, Oxon OX14 4RN

and by Routledge
52 Vanderbilt Avenue, New York, NY 10017

Routledge is an imprint of the Taylor & Francis Group, an informa business

© 1940 Maxwell Garnett and H. F. Koeppler

All rights reserved. No part of this book may be reprinted or reproduced or utilised in any form or by any electronic, mechanical, or other means, now known or hereafter invented, including photocopying and recording, or in any information storage or retrieval system, without permission in writing from the publishers.

Trademark notice: Product or corporate names may be trademarks or registered trademarks, and are used only for identification and explanation without intent to infringe.

British Library Cataloguing in Publication Data
A catalogue record for this book is available from the British Library

ISBN: 978-0-367-21777-8 (Set)
ISBN: 978-0-429-29830-1 (Set) (ebk)
ISBN: 978-0-367-26159-7 (Volume 7) (hbk)
ISBN: 978-0-367-26162-7 (Volume 7) (pbk)
ISBN: 978-0-429-29176-0 (Volume 7) (ebk)

Publisher's Note
The publisher has gone to great lengths to ensure the quality of this reprint but points out that some imperfections in the original copies may be apparent.

Disclaimer
The publisher has made every effort to trace copyright holders and would welcome correspondence from those they have been unable to trace.

A LASTING PEACE

by

MAXWELL GARNETT
C.B.E., M.A., Sc.D.
Sometime Fellow of Trinity College
Cambridge
Barrister-at-Law

WITH SOME CHAPTERS ON THE BASIS
OF
GERMAN CO-OPERATION

by

H. F. KOEPPLER
M.A., D.PHIL.(OXON)
Sometime Senior Demy of Magdalen
College, Oxford
Lecturer to the Delegacy of Extra-Mural
Studies in the University
of Oxford

LONDON
GEORGE ALLEN & UNWIN LTD
MUSEUM STREET

FIRST PUBLISHED IN 1940

ALL RIGHTS RESERVED

PRINTED IN GREAT BRITAIN
in 11-Point Plantin Type
BY UNWIN BROTHERS LIMITED
WOKING

TO ALL WHO HAVE HAD
A SHARE IN
THE GREAT ADVENTURE
OF
THE LEAGUE OF NATIONS
UNION

PREFACE

The origin and purpose of this book are described in the first chapter. I need only add here that Messrs. George Allen and Unwin, when they asked me to plan and edit the book, suggested that it might be the work of more than one author and that it 'should stress the absolute necessity of supporting the Democratic Leaders of the German people when the Nazis have fled.' To that suggestion I owe the pleasure and profit of collaborating with Dr. Heinz Koeppler who has written the chapters on the basis of German co-operation in building a new world order. He asks me to say that, although his essay is chiefly concerned with the conflict between German democracy and Prussian Junkerdom (as he defines it), he would have welcomed more space in which to treat of Church and State in Germany and to discuss the idea of *Mitteleuropa*. As Dr. Koeppler deserves all the credit so he assumes the whole responsibility for the statements of fact and the expressions of opinion in his chapters. And he does not necessarily approve all that I have printed in the earlier part of our book.

Dr. Koeppler was born and brought up as a German in Germany. After studying Law and History in the Universities of Berlin, Heidelberg and Kiel, he left Germany in 1933 when Herr Hitler became Chancellor of the Reich. Since then, Dr. Koeppler has studied and taught History in Oxford and has assisted the University in the work of adult education outside its walls; and his nationality is now British. He is therefore peculiarly well fitted to describe to British readers the ideals and hopes, often frustrated but never destroyed, of German democracy. He looks forward, in his last chapter, to the realization of these hopes in a new Europe where a secure France can be reconciled with an equal Germany.

J. C. M. G.

OXFORD,
14 February, 1940

NOTE ADDED ON 16 APRIL, 1940

Professor Sir Alfred Zimmern has done me the great kindness of reading the page-proofs of the first twenty chapters. His suggestions have enabled me to remove several faults. He has, of course, no responsibility for those that still remain.

M. G.

NETTLESTONE, I.W.

CONTENTS

CHAPTER	PAGE
INTRODUCTION	13
FRANCO-BRITISH DECLARATION	16
1. THE PURPOSE OF THIS BOOK	17
2. THE UNITY OF CIVILIZATION	20
3. TOWARDS POLITICAL UNITY	29
4. BEGINNINGS OF WORLD GOVERNMENT	41
5. THE DRIFT TOWARDS WAR	52
6. AN UNSTABLE EUROPE	61
7. THE WORLD WAR	65
8. MIXED MOTIVES AT PARIS	76
9. THE COVENANT OF THE LEAGUE OF NATIONS	88
10. TEN SUCCESSFUL YEARS	97
11. THE TIDE TURNS	105
12. APPEASEMENT	116
13. HOW HITLER'S WAR BEGAN	127
14. WAR AND PEACE AIMS	136
15. LAW AND ORDER	146

CHAPTER	PAGE
16. WELFARE AND ECONOMICS	161
17. COLONIES	167
18. THE FREEDOM OF THE AIR	179
19. INTER-STATE AND FEDERAL UNION	188
20. EDUCATION FOR CITIZENSHIP	201

CHAPTERS ON
THE BASIS OF GERMAN CO-OPERATION

21. THE BASIC TRIANGLE	215
22. HOW TO APPROACH THE GERMAN PROBLEM	223
23. ENTER THE JUNKERS	229
24. WHO THE PRUSSIANS ARE	236
25. UNITY, LAW AND LIBERTY	245
26. THE PRICE PAID FOR UNITY	254
27. LESSONS FOR A LASTING PEACE	265
INDEX	280

INTRODUCTION

The 'lasting peace' outlined in Chapters 14 to 20 of this book will strike some readers as based upon an over-optimistic view of the world of 1940. Does it not ignore, they will say, such plain facts as the political backwardness of the greater part of mankind, and the small-scale mind of the average man?

I would ask these critics to note that the union of States proposed in these chapters is to begin as a union of only part of the world and only for certain purposes; and that its subsequent development over many years is conceived as a psychological as well as a political process. Even such a partial uinon as is outlined in Chapter 19 would have been impracticable when Queen Victoria came to the throne and unimaginable in the days of Marco Polo. But the past century has seen man's planet become much smaller in proportion to man's mind. It is true that his habitat is no longer his village, nor yet his country, and is fast becoming the whole earth. Even so, two generations of education along the lines sketched in Chapter 20, would expand the mind of the average man to meet the shrinking globe. He would cease to be dwarfed by the world he lives in. World problems would be as well within his grasp as national politics are to-day. He would then be far better adapted to his environment, and far better able to enjoy the whole earth as his *Lebensraum*.

Other readers will complain that religion is mixed with politics in this plan for an international Commonwealth and for reaching it by way of education. I am not ashamed to seek a Christian civilization, nor do I see how it is to be reached if religion and politics are always kept apart. A recent writer* sees Utopia and Reality as 'belonging to two different planes which can never meet.' To me it seems that Reality (or the imperfect world about us) may approach Utopia (or the Commonwealth of God in which all nations are provinces) as a curve may draw ever nearer to a straight line until they meet and coincide at long last, infinitely far away.

But the approach of Reality to Utopia is not inevitable. It is only by sacrifice that man's free will can transform the existing order into a less imperfect world. Perhaps the hardest sacrifice of all will be the patrio-centric standpoint. A beginning has however been made during the past twenty years to increase world loyalty without

* Professor E. H. Carr in *The Twenty Years Crisis 1919–1939*, p. 118.

decreasing patriotism; and the last six months have seen a remarkable move by the Franco-British Allies to a Franco-British outlook, as is shown by the 'Solemn Declaration' of 28 March, 1940, printed on the next page. Why should not that progress, so apparently impossible a short time ago, continue in the future? And why need we despair of creating, by a gradual evolution already begun, an international Commonwealth where lasting *values*—liberty, justice, truth and friendship—count for more than the hard *facts* of the old 'sacred selfishness' and international anarchy?

Text of the
SOLEMN DECLARATION
issued on 28 March, 1940,
after the sixth meeting of the
SUPREME WAR COUNCIL

The Government of the French Republic and his Majesty's Government in the United Kingdom of Great Britain and Northern Ireland mutually undertake that during the present war they will neither negotiate nor conclude an armistice or treaty of peace except by mutual agreement.

They undertake not to discuss peace terms before reaching complete agreement on the conditions necessary to ensure to each of them an effective and lasting guarantee of their security.

Finally, they undertake to maintain, after the conclusion of peace, a community of action in all spheres for so long as may be necessary to safeguard their security and to effect the reconstruction, with the assistance of other nations, of an international order which will ensure the liberty of peoples, respect for law, and the maintenance of peace in Europe.

CHAPTER I

THE PURPOSE OF THIS BOOK

★

On Friday, 1 September, Herr Hitler attacked Poland in spite of the warning he had received from Great Britain and France. They had told him that they would stand firm in support of their pledges to the Polish Government and in resistance to further aggression by Germany. Two days later these pledges were fulfilled. The Western democracies entered the war when Herr Hitler refused to recall his troops beyond the German frontier.

On the following Monday, 4 September, *The Times* printed two letters on British war aims. The first read, in part, as follows:

> British war aims would, of course, be determined by the dual policy expounded by Lord Halifax on 29 June. Our first object would be to put an end to further aggression by Germany or her allies. Our second object would be to follow up this achievement by constructive peace. . . . The peace terms would, as I hope, include the all-round limitation of national armaments; the restoration of self-government to those non-German peoples who have lost it, or may yet lose it, as the result of German aggression; and Germany's participation in creating or adapting international institutions for two main purposes. The first of these would be to exercise supreme authority over certain matters of world-wide concern, such as the preservation of peace, the just settlement of international

disputes, and perhaps, also the administration of non-self-governing colonial territories. The second purpose would be to promote international co-operation in finance, economics and all those other fields of human welfare and social justice where . . . much valuable work has been done by the League of Nations and the International Labour Organization.

Resistance to aggression and then a general settlement would not, however, complete the building of world order on a lasting basis. A stable peace must be founded in the hearts and minds of men as well as upon the promises of Governments. . . . We who live where liberty is held in high regard are not likely to emulate the dictator States in the use of propaganda. But if, as we believe, truth is on our side when we try to translate the fatherhood of God, the brotherhood of man, and the unity of Western civilization into enough political unity to enable the human race to survive to-day's sudden changes in its material environment, it were madness to forgo the help of so powerful an ally as truth itself. In Christian education, properly conceived, the world may yet find the best bulwark of stable peace and the only sure foundation for world order.

The writer of this letter was asked by Messrs. George Allen and Unwin to plan a book which would emphasize the constructive aims of democracies and would lay down constructive suggestions of a lasting peace. The present volume springs from that suggestion.

When the World War ended in 1918, the clamour to 'hang the Kaiser' and make Germany pay for the war greatly increased the difficulties of the British peacemakers at Versailles. But for this outcry some of the worst features of the German treaty, notably the reparation clauses and the so-called war-guilt clause attributing to 'the aggression of Germany and her allies' the whole responsibility for

THE PURPOSE OF THIS BOOK

the war, might have been avoided. It is true that the defects of the treaty have been grossly exaggerated of late years. But if the matter of the treaty is not so bad as it is often painted, its manner could hardly have been worse. Had it not been for the desire of public opinion in the Allied countries to humiliate republican Germany as if it were still the Germany of the Kaiser, the peace terms might have been negotiated instead of being dictated.

If the mistakes of Versailles are not to be repeated after the present war, public opinion must be prepared for whatever apparent sacrifices may be needed in order to build world order on a lasting basis. The correspondence which began in *The Times* on 4 September showed how great a change of mind is still required.

It will not happen of its own accord. We need to find out from past experience what are the conditions of lasting peace, and how the foundation of a new world order may be well and truly laid in the convictions and sentiments, the thoughts and feelings, of individual men and women. We are not proposing a voyage to Utopia as a way of escape from the horrible realities of war. Rather is our task an essential part of the British and French war effort. Indeed, a *twofold* effort is needed if we are to win not only the war but also the peace. One is to stop aggression and make it possible to open negotiations for a world settlement. The other is to prepare public opinion for some measure of political unity among as many as possible of the nations of the world, for a common authority concerned with common needs, and for a common loyalty to that authority strong enough to ensure that selfish national interests have less influence than the well-being of the whole of our world.

CHAPTER 2

THE UNITY OF CIVILIZATION

★

The political unity of a number of nations, and a common authority for their common concerns, are not to be imposed by conquest upon unwilling peoples. Rather are they to be the outcome of a growing conviction that the uniting nations have certain common interests, that to conserve and extend these interests is a common purpose of them all, and that this common purpose can only be achieved by continued and organized effort.

But the political changes cannot wait until the psychological changes are complete. When Herr Hitler and his followers have been defeated by the British and French, or expelled by the Germans, the time will have come to create the nucleus of the organization, to frame the constitution, to establish the government that will regulate those matters of common concern which cannot be effectively handled by the national governments of independent sovereign States. This political change, when it takes place, will have a profound psychological effect. It will accelerate the psychological changes that will lead in turn to further political developments. For the evolution of a new world order resembles the opening of a stiff drawer with two handles. If the drawer is to open, both handles must be pulled together, or else there must be a succession of tugs, first at one and then at the other. We shall not see much of any new world order unless use is made of both handles, the political and the psychological.

Anglo-French co-operation in defence, commerce, finance and colonial administration has made a beginning at the political end.* The time has come for a tug at the psychological handle. Without it, that end may have become jammed when the war is over and peace terms have to be discussed. Indeed, there is no need to wait before beginning to persuade the nations, whether belligerent or neutral, that they do in fact share common interests. They are all concerned to preserve and extend the unity of civilization that is a common heritage of Europe, the Americas and the British Commonwealth of Nations.

Great Britain and France are at war with the Third Reich to-day because, if we do not fight, we must stand idly by while Herr Hitler's rule is gradually forced upon more and more of the peoples of Europe. We are satisfied that this would be a worse evil for us than war itself. One reason why we are so sure is that, were we left without friends in Europe, we should be less able than we are to-day to resist Herr Hitler's power. But there is another, and a more cogent reason. It is because the rule of National Socialism tends to destroy, and seeks to destroy, what we believe to be most valuable in our western civilization.

These priceless possessions are not things that can be seen or handled. Yet they are more precious than rubies. They form part of a rich inheritance that has come down to us from our fathers and from the old time before them: from the men who, twenty years ago, tried to make a world-wide League of Nations; from those who gave its present shape to our British Commonwealth that covers

* Relief has also been sent to Turkey and to Finland.

a quarter of the earth and governs a quarter of the human race; from the group of ex-Englishmen (notably Hamilton and Madison and Jay) who devised the American Constitution and so made possible the government of the people by the people for the people—in one word, democracy—on a vaster scale than ever before; from Simon de Montfort, the father of the Mother of Parliaments; from the Romans whose law and order gave Europe the longest term of peace she has ever enjoyed; from the liberty-loving Greeks whose City States were the birthplace and nursery of democracy (but whose wisest men, down to the time of Alexander the Great, had no notion of the unity of mankind); from the Hebrew prophets who first taught the oneness of all creation; and from a greater than any of them, the Founder of Christianity.

Jesus summed up the law and the prophets in two commands, to love God and to love one's neighbour as oneself. If we all love God above all else and seek first His kingdom, we all share our main purpose in life; and each of us is free to do as he wishes because what he wants most of all to do is what the others also want done; so that, from the first of these commands, springs liberty. And from the second flows justice; for if we all love our neighbours as ourselves, we shall treat their concerns as equally important with our own; and that is justice.*

To the Christian faith we owe our idea of the fatherhood of God and the brotherhood of man, the equal and infinite value of every human spirit, 'the eternal value of every human soul.'† The human race is also of infinite value. But there is nothing infinite about States or

---

* See below, Chapter 20.

† Lord Halifax, addressing the University of Oxford, on 27 February, 1940.

nations that wax and wane and cease to be. 'While States and nations are formal, men and mankind are essential.'

Don Salvador de Madariaga, who wrote the quoted words, goes on:

> No historical limitations can hold the destinies of man as they do the destinies of all nations. The humblest and obscurest citizen of the proudest Empire has in him that which no Empire however mighty can conquer—immortality either as a certainty or as a hope. But even in this life, which falls under our immediate observation, who can set a limit to what a man may be or become within a year? The sight of essential and immortal man under the sway of formal and ephemeral nations strikes us as monstrous when the victims of such an aberration are prominent exponents of the human spirit, but it is equally monstrous when its victims are obscure men. Every man is an incognita which only time and eternity can unfold. Every man has therefore a finality which we must deny to any nation.
>
> As for mankind, no historical limitations can hold its destinies either. These destinies, perhaps just beginning their painful ascent on our planet after many thousands of years of savage, almost animal, life, are evidently meant to be a unit, just as mankind itself is a unit. . . . The sphere of the human spirit goes as far as Bach went in music, as far as Shakespeare went in poetry, Velasquez in painting, Kant in philosophy, Newton in mathematics, St. John of the Cross in mystical experience, . . . but none of these men, however great in their specific genius, passed the line of the normal or even of the mediocre in other directions, powers and faculties, although there is a common enjoyment and perception of all of them by all men. This observation proves the profound unity of the human spirit and therefore of mankind. It suffices to establish for mankind a finality which it possesses

with individual man but which the nation does not possess.*

Once more

For what is a nation? It is a society of men animated by a feeling of solidarity of a special kind, which may or may not be rooted in common racial, linguistic, religious, historical, geographical and economic ground, and varies in intensity both with space and time from a burning flame of patriotism to total extinction. There is no permanency, no fixity, no definiteness in a nation. Some have been shaped by tradition, others against tradition; some by language, others against language; some by religious unity, others against religious unity. There are nations which melt together into one; others which split into several; and all have their span of historical life and are doomed to lie asleep in the Pantheons of history, hardly disturbed by the rumours of busy scholars disinterring scientific errors about what their life once was. Nations are then *forms of collective life*, vessels which at a given time and in a given place contain and therefore shape the flow of human life. They correspond in the realm of the human spirit to what the landscape is in that of nature. . . .†

Our quotation from Madariaga ends with the words:

Hasty minds would conclude from these premises that nations must be removed from mankind. This would not carry them very far, for, though nations are forms of life, they are natural and necessary forms and will stay despite any ideas which may be held to the contrary. We can no more remove nations from mankind than valleys and hills and the landscapes they compose from the face of the earth. They are, of course, invaluable assets to civilization.

* *The Price of Peace*, the Richard Cobden Lecture for 1935, pp. 9, 10.   † *Loc. cit.*, p. 9.

They provide between man and mankind a welcome intermediate setting, a background of traditions, ways and conventions, which has proved one of the most potent factors in the creation and enrichment of culture. It follows that, though we cannot recognize finality in the nation, we acknowledge its immense value both for man and for mankind and therefore we must be ready to guarantee its existence and the fulfilment of its aims.... We know now that the nation should claim no rights injurious to the higher liberties of the individual, since we have admitted that it has no finality and is but instrumental and formal in the scheme of human life, and what is more to the point, instrumental precisely towards the achievement of the higher aims of the individual. We now know also that nations have duties both towards man and towards mankind. Finally we know now that citizens have duties towards their nation, but that these duties cannot conflict with the higher interests of mankind, since if that were so, their nation would be exacting from them what it has no right to demand—co-operation in the violation of a moral law.*

In fact, *we* think of the State as existing for the sake of its citizens. It protects them against attack from outside. It preserves law and order among them. It looks after their education and their health. It tries to ensure that their hours of work are not too long or their pay too low. And it leaves them free to worship God in their own way.

The political doctrines of Herr Hitler, of Signor Mussolini, or of M. Stalin, have a very different scale of values for these three kinds of human life: the individual, the nation, and the whole world of men. These doctrines loudly and proudly assert that the nation has the claim to finality. In Herr Hitler's view, the German State is of

* *Loc. cit.*, pp. 10, 11.

far greater value than any German individual or than all the rest of mankind put together. Indeed, he would have his Germans fall down and worship the State that he, Hitler, has set up. Like Nebuchadnezzar, he is a little mad.

Again, *we* think of Great Britain as one of many States tied to one another by rules and customs as well as by treaties which we are bound in honour to observe. Herr Hitler does not feel like that about Germany. Dr. Rauschning, after a talk with him in October, 1933, wrote:

Hitler told me that morning what was his view of the value of treaties. He was ready, he said, to sign anything. ... Anyone who was so fussy that he had to consult his conscience about whether he could keep to a pact, whatever the pact and whatever the situation, was a fool.*

Once more, *we* know that our English blood connects us with the wider life of the whole human family. Defoe, the author of *Robinson Crusoe*, wrote a humorous and pungent poem on 'The True-born Englishman.' It was prompted by the foolish attacks on his friend and hero, William of Orange, for being a foreigner. Defoe pointed out, with historic proof, that one and all of us were mongrels, but that we were none the worse for that, but rather the better. The first element in our English make-up is, so far as we know, what we call Iberian. That mysterious race came from North Africa, spread over Spain and France, and populated our own island. The second element in our blood is Celtic. Then the Romans from three continents mixed their blood with that of Celt and Iberian. After that came the Anglo-Saxon invasions, then Danes, and then Normans. Since the Norman Conquest

* *Germany's Revolution of Destruction*, by Hermann Rauschning, p. 251.

driblets have been added to our blood from Flemings and Huguenots and, in the nineteenth century, from almost every people in the world. The result is that the true-born Englishman to-day is, as Defoe said, a mongrel.* But Herr Hitler would have the Germans believe that theirs is a special kind of blood, a Nordic blood, that makes them the greatest of mankind. They are taught at school that the history of Europe is the work of peoples of Nordic race. Even the history of the Greeks, and again of Italy, as taught in Nazi schools, must 'begin in Central Europe!'

The Nazi Government deplores what it calls 'the intrusion of alien elements,' not only into German blood but also 'into German speech, law, into the German idea of the State and into the general outlook upon the world.'† But we in Britain are free to acknowledge the debt we owe to other peoples. In our common western civilization there is, as Dr. Gooch has pointed out, a bond that unites us to the rest of the world. Of the founders of modern astronomy, Copernicus was a Pole, Kepler a German, Tycho Brahe a Dane, Galileo an Italian, Newton an Englishman and Einstein a German Jew. Or take wireless telegraphy. Marconi's father was Italian and his mother Irish. But he could never have reached his goal if Faraday the Englishman, Clerk Maxwell the Scotsman and Hertz the German had not prepared the way. Nor does any branch of natural science come only from one country.

* Cf. an address delivered by Dr. G. P. Gooch to the Conference of Educational Associations in University College, London, on 8 January, 1924.

† The above quotations are taken from a circular issued by the German Minister of the Interior, Dr. Frick, to all his education authorities (Circular No. III, 120/22. 6). The circular is summarized by Professor Seton-Watson in *Britain and the Dictators*, pp. 291-2. The full text was published in *Nature*, 24 February, 1934.

The same is true of philosophy, literature, history, art, economics and social service.*

That is what we mean by the unity of civilization. The human race is a single family. Our knowledge, our ways of life, our outlook on the universe, all our most priceless possessions have come to us, and continue to come, not from one branch of the family but from all. These things make up our common civilization. To-day this precious inheritance is menaced by Herr Hitler and his gang. When that menace has been removed the time will have come for the belligerents, and as many neutrals as are willing, to agree upon a treaty of peace. If that peace is to be grounded and rooted in the minds of men, so that it may continue to grow until the spread of its branches covers all nations, the soil must be prepared before the tree is planted. The unity of civilization, the common heritage and common interests, must be more widely understood and appreciated. More and more people must think of themselves as belonging to a single human family and must share a strong family feeling, a world loyalty that supplements without supplanting loyalties to lesser groups.

* Cf. Gooch, *loc. cit.* See also *The Unity of Western Civilization*, ed. F. S. Marvin (3rd edition, 1929).

CHAPTER 3

TOWARDS POLITICAL UNITY

★

The history of Europe begins with the tiny City States of ancient Greece. These small towns divided between them a country no bigger than Scotland and each was an independent sovereign State. They had, like us, a unity of civilization. Like us, they struggled hard to obtain a political unity. They practised arbitration. They formed Leagues and Communities of cities. But no member of any Greek League was prepared to sacrifice enough sovereignty to render possible the constitution of a Greek Commonwealth possessing effective authority for maintaining law and order among the rival City States or for defending all Greek territory against aggression from outside.

The strength of Greek civilization was sapped by frequent fighting. The war between Athens and Sparta gave it a shock from which it never recovered. Eventually the Greek cities fell an easy prey to the growing power of Rome.

Rome achieved unity by conquest and maintained it by good government, or at least good policy, for many centuries. The Roman power had a certain brutality; but it enforced law and order throughout the Mediterranean world and over a great part of Europe. By providing a soil in which the roots of our western ideas spread rapidly and easily, Rome made a great contribution to the unity of our civilization to-day. To the content of that civilization her greatest gifts were the theory and practice of law—and the belief that world unity is practical politics.

The notion of a political unity linked to a spiritual unity was bequeathed by Rome to later ages. During the thousand years which began with Augustine and ended with Machiavelli, the idea of the unity of civilization made a great advance. 'The idea of a *Republica Christiana*, a Christian family, subject to the supreme guidance of God, who was represented on earth by the Pope and the Emperor, was held consciously, or semi-consciously, by Christendom for a thousand years. The modern idea of sovereignty, the modern idea that each nation and each political unity is supreme, that it owes no allegiance to anything outside itself and no allegiance to anything above itself—that monstrous notion was unknown in the Middle Ages. The Middle Ages had a real conception of the unity, not of civilization as a whole, but of Catholic Christendom.'* True, the civilized world was again made up of many States. But, as each in turn accepted Christianity, it entered the great family of which the Pope was the visible head. Central and western Europe became, in theory at least, a single community, united by a common creed and common principles of conduct, and subject to Pope and Emperor who were responsible to God, the invisible King.

When the Middle Ages ended with the revival of Greek learning and the disruption of the Church—the Renaissance and the Reformation—the idea that the Pope had a right to obedience from all Christians was given up. Each country felt free to go its own way as if its neighbours did not exist, and there was no longer any formal link between the different States of Europe. The idea of the

* Gooch, *loc. cit.*, pp. 14, 15.

independent sovereign State appeared; and the Christian message of the fatherhood of God and the brotherhood of man was forgotten under a narrow and exaggerated nationalism.*

Religious conflicts added to the bitterness. Yet the international anarchy of the following centuries did not extinguish the sense that there was a law of nations which Princes should obey in their dealings with one another. There was, for example, the Grand Design of a Christian Republic, the work of Sully, Henri Quatre's Huguenot minister. And, moved by the horrors of the Thirty Years War, Hugo Grotius (1583-1645), a citizen of the Dutch Republic, wrote his great work, *De jure belli ac pacis*. He proclaimed that States ought to regard themselves as members of a society bound together by the universal supremacy of justice. At the heart of Grotius' system, writes Professor Brierly,

> lay the attempt to distinguish between lawful and unlawful war; he saw clearly that international order is precarious unless that distinction can be established, just as national order would be precarious if the law within the state did not distinguish between the lawful and the unlawful use of force. Yet . . . it was not until the foundation of the League of Nations in 1919 that any real attempt was made . . . to embody in actual law the cardinal principle of Grotius' system.†

Grotius supplied a philosophy of inter-State relations as they ought to be: it could be set against Machiavelli's brutal description of those relations or as they often were. To that philosophy additions were made by the founder

* Cf. the Report on International Relations presented to the Conference on Politics, Economics and Citizenship, held in Birmingham in April, 1924.
† J. L. Brierly, *The Law of Nations*, p. 26.

of Pennsylvania, William Penn, the Quaker son of an English admiral and his Dutch wife; by the man who first worked out a detailed scheme for a League of Nations, the Abbé St. Pierre, the diplomatist who went as a representative of France to the Congress of Utrecht; by Immanuel Kant, the German son of a Scottish mother; and by the Tsar, Alexander I, who conceived 'the Holy Alliance, which bound all the sovereigns of Europe to behave as Christians, not only in relation to one another but also towards their subjects.'* These men who have striven to keep alive the ideal of the unity of civilization are, as Gooch observes,† among the benefactors of humanity.

The French Revolution and the armies of Napoleon tried to give back to Europe her political unity, but at the price of French domination. That price the European nations were unwilling to pay. Encouraged by Britain and helped by her control of the seas, by her money, and (at last) by her expeditionary forces, the continental Powers combined with Britain to defeat Napoleon.

Their co-operation continued for some years after Waterloo. The alliance of Britain, Prussia, Austria and Russia, was reconstituted at the Congress of Vienna. For a time it was directed against the fifth Great Power, France. But 'before Europe could be organized for peace instead of war, a way had to be found to admit France as an equal.'‡ That was soon done, and the Quintuple Alliance—not to be confused with the Holy Alliance—was the result. The object of the allied Great Powers was to direct the affairs of Europe in the interests of peace. To the British Foreign Secretary, Castlereagh, the most important aspect of the Alliance was, perhaps, its plan for

---

* C. K. Webster, *The Foreign Policy of Castlereagh*, p. 58.
† *Loc. cit.* ‡ Webster, *loc. cit.*, p. 58.

TOWARDS POLITICAL UNITY

meetings of statesmen 'at fixed periods.'* Castlereagh hoped that the Alliance would found a new system of European diplomacy by bringing together 'the Councils of the Sovereigns' and so enabling them to look at their special interests from a common standpoint instead of 'through that cloud of prejudice and uncertainty which must always intervene when events are viewed at a distance.'† In this way the differences between the Great Powers might be composed and the greatest benefits conferred on humanity. 'How difficult,' adds Professor Webster, 'it was to be to ensure the success of such a system without formal interpretations or the driving power of public opinion, Castlereagh could not as yet be expected to realize.'‡

Before long the system failed. Not only did it lack the driving power of a common loyalty and common ideals among the citizens of the allied countries, but the Governments were too autocratic and too selfish, and the distances were too great, for the experiment to succeed. It came to an end when Canning succeeded Castlereagh, and insisted on recognizing the independence of the Spanish-American states against the frantic opposition of the other allied Powers. At the same time Canning in England, together with Quincy Adams and President Monroe in the United States, conceived the Monroe Doctrine as a means to stop any future European attempt at dominion over the New World which Canning claimed to have called into existence 'to restore the balance of the Old.' Like the Peace Front of 1939, the Monroe Doctrine was an example of pacific initiative designed to forestall and prevent possible aggression.

After 1823 nothing remained of the Quintuple Alliance

---

* Webster, *loc. cit.*, p. 55. † Webster, *loc. cit.*, p. 56.
‡ Webster, *loc. cit.*, p. 57.

but the feeble and intermittent Concert of Europe. But the standard of international duty was constantly growing during the nineteenth century. The principles of Gladstone or Salisbury would have seemed dangerously idealist to Queen Victoria's first Prime Minister, Lord Melbourne. In particular, the movement for arbitration was making progress. Between 1820 and 1840 there were eight cases of international arbitration; between 1840 and 1860, thirty; between 1860 and 1880, forty-four, including the famous *Alabama* case, when Great Britain accepted the award of the arbitrators and paid more than £3,000,000 to the United States for the damage done by that vessel and other commerce-destroyers in the American Civil War. Between 1880 and 1900 there were ninety cases.

This movement for the peaceful settlement of international disputes culminated, before the World War, in the two Hague Conferences of 1899 and 1907. The Hague Convention for the Pacific Settlement of International Disputes, made in 1899 and revised in 1907, created a permanent panel of arbitrators, miscalled the 'Permanent Court of Arbitration.'

Although the machinery and practice of arbitration increased during the nineteenth century, there was neither obligation to use the machinery nor means of enforcing the arbitral awards. War still remained the only final settlement of national differences. *Si vis pacem, para bellum* ('if you want peace, get ready for war') was inscribed in letters of gold on the Austro-Hungarian War Office in Vienna. So the nations of Europe prepared for war by piling up rival armaments. This policy was enormously and increasingly costly. The curve on page 35 shows how many hundreds of millions of pounds were spent on it by the six Great Powers of Europe in the twenty-five years before 1914. 'The enormous growth of armaments and the insecurity and fear caused by them—it was these made war inevitable.'*

Meanwhile in the English-speaking world new experiments were being tried and new experience gained. The

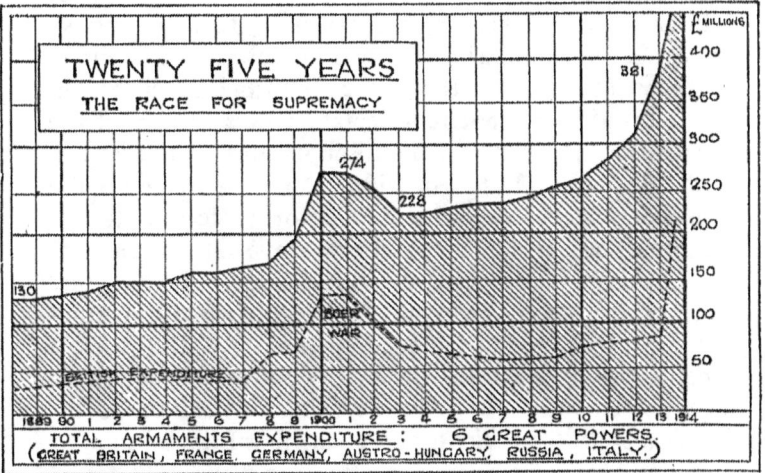

INCREASE, 11 YEARS, 1888–1899—£70 MILLIONS = £6⅜ MILLIONS PER ANNUM.

INCREASE, 9 YEARS, 1904–1913—£153 MILLIONS = £17 MILLIONS PER ANNUM.

Chart plotted from figures compiled by Arthur G. Enock out of British Statistical Abstracts and from his tables in *The Problem of Armaments*.

purpose of these experiments was to discover how government of the people by the people for the people might be conducted among larger or more scattered groups than any that had hitherto enjoyed parliamentary institutions. The result of the experience so obtained is to be seen in

* Viscount Grey of Fallodon, *Twenty-Five Years*, Vol. I, p. 92.

the United States of America and in the British Commonwealth of Nations.

When six or seven weeks of disagreeable ocean tossing still divided London from Boston, the representation of the thirteen American colonies in the Parliament at Westminster seemed to be out of the question. But George III insisted, with unbending stubbornness, that the English colonists must contribute something towards the military expenses incurred by the mother country on their behalf. 'No taxation without representation' was the cry of the colonists, who felt that the disappearance of the French flag from the North American Continent removed the danger which made them look for protection to the mother country. Yet they made no move to tax themselves for imperial purposes. 'A way out could have been found,' writes Professor Trevelyan, 'by men of good will summoned to a round-table conference. . . . But such a conference was outside the range of ideas on either side of the Atlantic. . . . And so things drifted on to the catastrophe,'* the disruption of the first British Empire.

The thirteen colonies became the United States of America. Their first 'Articles of Confederation and Perpetual Union' declared that

each State retains its sovereignty, freedom, and independence, and every power, jurisdiction, and right which is not by this Confederation expressly delegated to the United States in the Congress assembled. This Confederation . . . was rather a league than a national government, for it possessed no central authority except an assembly in which every State, the largest and the smallest alike, had one vote, and this authority had no jurisdiction over the individual citizens. There was no Federal executive, no Federal judiciary, no means of

* *History of England*, pp. 551–2.

raising money except by the contributions of the States, contributions which they were slow to render, no power of compelling the obedience either of States or individuals to the commands of Congress. . . .

Sad experience of their internal difficulties, and of the contempt with which foreign governments treated them, at last produced a feeling that some firmer and closer union was needed.*

A new Constitution was therefore prepared at Philadelphia in 1787. The acceptance of the new Constitution made the American people into a nation, although they still speak of themselves, and pray for themselves, as 'these United States.' The Constitution transformed what had been a League of States into a Federal State, by giving it a national government with direct authority over all citizens. But this national government did not supersede the governments of the uniting States. It was, 'so to speak, the complement and crown of the State Constitutions.'†

When the American Constitution came into force it had to contend with great difficulties: 'The sea was stormy in winter, the roads were very bad, it took as long to travel by land from Charleston to Boston as to cross the ocean to Europe, nor was the journey less dangerous.'‡ But the federal solution of the problem of democratic government overcame these geographical difficulties—greater than those of communication between the most distant States in the world to-day—as successfully as it reconciled the divergent interests and purposes of the thirteen States.

An alternative solution of the same problem has been

* Viscount Bryce, *The American Commonwealth*, pp. 17, 18.
† Bryce, *loc. cit.*, pp. 29-30.   ‡ Bryce, *loc. cit.*, p. 21.

discovered in the second British Empire which followed upon the disruption of the first. In 1837, two rebellions in Canada caused the British Government to suspend the constitution and to send out Lord Durham as a temporary despot. He was to act in place of the usual authorities of Upper (or English) and Lower (or French) Canada, and to report on the real state of affairs.

The selection of Durham (writes Trevelyan) saved Canada and the Empire. . . . The Durham Report of 1839, which took effect in . . . 1840, advised that the time had come for full responsible government to be given to Canada—that is, that the executive should in future be chosen from the ranks of the majority in the elected Assembly. This principle of responsible government was applied first to Canada, then to the rest of British North America, next to Australia, and finally to South Africa. It is acknowledged to have proved the cement of Empire.*

Subsequently the Irish Free State, or Eire, has been separated from the United Kingdom and been given its own system of responsible government. Thus the British Commonwealth now includes no less than six separate sovereignties; and Dominion government for India is on the way. The governments of the United Kingdom, of Eire, of Canada, of Australia, of New Zealand, and of South Africa are each responsible to their own electorates, even for the conduct of foreign affairs. By the Statute of Westminster, passed into law by the British parliament on 3 December, 1931, that parliament renounced all future right to legislate for the Dominions except at the instance of their own governments. Henceforward Great Britain and the self-governing Dominions were to be united in constitutional law only by the fact that the same monarch

* *British History in the Nineteenth Century*, pp. 260–1.

would officiate as head of each of each of these self-governing States. '*They are autonomous Communities within the British Empire, equal in status, in no way subordinate one to another in any aspect of their domestic or external affairs, though united by a common allegiance to the Crown, and freely associated as members of the British Commonwealth of Nations.*'*

'The question is,' as General Smuts told the South African Parliament on 8 March, 1928, 'How do they hold together?' His answer was:

There is a common kingship which . . . is naturally a very great bond, but of perhaps even greater force and importance is the invisible bond of ideals. . . . That, although it is no formal legal bond, and although judged by the ordinary terms and conceptions of law it means nothing at all, is probably the strongest bond of all which holds us together. . . . The old world was held together by sovereignty and those laws which could be translated into force. Here is an entirely new condition—no central force, but psychology, which is more powerful, the soul of a group of nations. And I am sure this will prove a more potent force in the future in holding this great group together than any central authority of force could possibly have done.†

Thus, while the separate European States were arming against one another, and so making war inevitable as soon as any nation or group of nations should become strong enough to challenge the might of the British Navy, the English-speaking peoples were developing two different systems of democratic government by means of which

* Lord Balfour's Report of Committee appointed by the Imperial Conference on 25 October, 1926.
† Speech delivered by General Smuts in the Union Parliament, Cape Town, on 8 March, 1928.

large areas of the world were firmly held together. In the American, or federal, system the supreme authority is directly elected by the citizens of the federation. In the British, or inter-State, system the supreme authority rests with the State governments which may combine, as in time of war, to appoint a Supreme Council. But these two systems—the federal and the inter-State—are not in any sense rivals. Not a gun, not a soldier, guards the three thousand miles of their common land frontier, between the United States and Canada.* The same 'invisible bond of ideals' unites the British and American Commonwealths. They are fundamentally at one on the issues that really matter. They are thus able to agree, quickly and easily, when any dispute threatens to divide them.†

* The same is true of the frontier between Sweden and Norway, where there is also an 'invisible bond of ideals.'

† When, for example, America went dry, there was a danger lest trouble with Canada might arise from smugglers, or 'bootleggers,' carrying the forbidden liquor across the Canadian border for thirsty Americans to drink. So Canadian and United States representatives met in Washington to talk things over. The United States proposed that their aeroplanes should patrol the south side of the border while Canadian planes watched the north side. A Canadian delegate asked if it would not be cheaper and better to use only one set of planes in which Canadians and Americans should sit side by side. The American President said 'Why, sure!' And so it was settled.

CHAPTER 4

BEGINNINGS OF WORLD GOVERNMENT

★

In the last chapter we traced a number of attempts to translate the unity of our western civilization into some measure of political unity. Although we completed a stage in the evolution of the British Commonwealth of Nations by continuing its story up to the Statute of Westminster, for the rest we paused before the outbreak of the World War in 1914. We saw how the separate sovereign States of Europe were preparing for that war, having failed to devise any system which would enable them to unite for the maintenance of justice in their dealings with one another while remaining free to manage their own internal affairs. Yet we observed that the English-speaking world was meanwhile working out two such systems. One was the federation of the forty-eight States of the North American Union, completed just before the war. The other was the still incomplete system of the British Commonwealth, the inter-State system of 'units within a larger Unity.'

We now turn from politics to economics. We are to think of the material conditions of human life and of the vast changes that have suddenly come about during the last hundred years or thereabouts. In that period the world has been shrinking rapidly. Discovery and invention—steam, petrol and electricity—have enormously reduced the time it takes to travel or to send news or goods about the globe. The most distant parts of Europe can now be reached from London in a shorter time than was needed to get from London to the furthest coasts of Great Britain a century ago. Wireless has linked London more closely with the world than it was linked with its own suburbs in 1800.

This metamorphosis is almost a thing of yesterday. In the days of Roman Britain it was possible to get from Rome to London in fourteen, or perhaps even in twelve, days. In the year 1834 Sir Robert Peel had to hurry home from Rome to become Prime Minister, and it took him, travelling as fast as possible, just twelve days. No appreciable change in seventeen hundred years! But in the summer of 1939 anyone who paid the fare and booked his seat could travel from New York to Southampton in a single day.*

The changes brought about in a hundred years are indeed unbelievable. Compare, for example, the food of a south-country household just after the war against Napoleon and the food of a comfortable English home

---

* Such journeys not only linked up distant countries but mixed up all sorts of people. Already in 1933, within a hundred years of Peel's journey, two Americans were returning from the Far East by the India Air Mail. When the machine reached Basra, at the top of the Persian Gulf, two Iraquis entered and seated themselves opposite the Americans, who invited them to play bridge. The play ended as the aeroplane approached Baghdad. There the aerodrome was beflagged, troops were paraded and bands were playing. The Iraquis got out and drove off in a large car, saluted by the troops. One of the Americans asked who they were. On learning that he had been playing with King Feisal and his aide-de-camp, he remarked: 'If I had been told, in my little home in Oklahoma, that I was going to fly over the garden of Eden playing cards with a reigning monarch who would take from me one hundred and fifty good American dollars, I would never have believed it.'

just before the war against Hitler. Apart from their sugar, tea and wines, Jane Austen's young people were fed, in the main, from their own parish or its immediate neighbourhood. A hundred years later their great grandchildren were eating bread made with flour from Canada and from Hungary; their butter and bacon might come from Denmark; some of their meat from New Zealand, Australia, Argentine or Chicago; their fruit from South Africa, California, Brazil, the West Indies, or the Mediterranean; their coffee from Brazil or East Africa; their chocolate from West Africa; their sugar from Czecho-Slovakia (but still in part from the West Indies); and the newspapers on their breakfast-table displayed last night's news from all the world printed on paper made from the forests of Newfoundland or Scandinavia.

Or take another example. The prosperity or distress of Lancashire cotton workers is bound up with those of the cotton growers in America, the coalminers of their own country, the people engaged in the shipping industry centred in Liverpool, and the wearers of cotton goods in tropical lands. An Indian boycott of English goods, or the growth of Japanese competition, may make all the difference between success and failure in the Lancashire cotton industry, which in turn affects Lancashire's demand for cotton and so the whole economic life of Egypt.*

From every point of view but that of the geometer, the earth is fast becoming smaller. Meanwhile the knowledge, if not the mind, of man is growing out to meet it. The scale of man and of his planet are becoming more commensurate. The material world is coming to be a much more manageable proposition.

* *Geography Teaching in Relation to World Citizenship* (a Report by the Geography Panel of the League of Nations Union Education Committee, 1934), p. 14.

The food problem will serve again as an example. A century ago the average respectable man believed that the Rev. Thomas Malthus had shown poverty, and eventually starvation, to be inevitable for the majority of mankind on account of the natural increase of population. Even forty years ago men of science were explaining to popular audiences that, while the total population which the earth could feed was limited and roughly ascertainable, the actual population was increasing fast enough to pass this limit within three or four generations, after which people must starve. In the 1930's, as we know, the difficulty has been all the other way: there is too much food, and the supply has increased so much faster than the demand for it that wheat land has been returned to grass in the United States and coffee has been burnt as fuel in Brazil. What is true of food is more or less true of minerals and other raw materials, including those out of which clothes are made. Man's habitat is well able to satisfy all his material needs.

But if he is to gain full advantage from the illimitable resources of the earth, he must use it as a whole, even as he uses his own body as a whole. 'All the earth for all the people' is the goal to aim at.* The more nearly any commonwealth of men approaches world-wide dimensions, the better will it be able to ensure that every person in it has a fair chance of leading a happy and useful life. The larger it becomes, the more material wealth will it produce, other things being equal, for each of its citizens. Imagine what would happen to the State of Nebraska if it broke away from the American Commonwealth, and its people had to live in economic isolation. How poverty-stricken would they soon become in comparison with their neighbours in the United States!

* 'Each country's "living room" is the entire world.' P. Reynaud (3.4.40).

The essential truth that concerns us here is that man's planet, like man's body, is different in different parts and most of them are necessary for his complete well-being. But it is perhaps worth noticing that, even if the parts were interchangeable, a world divided into very small parts would be less well off than if the parts were larger. A playing field of twenty acres may well suffice for a school of six hundred boys. But divide both figures by twenty and you find that one acre gives a village school of thirty boys no chance to play a proper game of football or hockey. Divide again by five, and your half-dozen boys at a private tutor's have only a small back yard in which to get fresh air and exercise.

Thus the laws of number join the facts of geography in offering men inducements to co-operate. Indeed Nature*—man's material environment—is not content merely to offer him prizes for co-operation. She threatens him with dire punishment if he refuses to walk in the paths of peace that she has marked out for him. We have only to look at the state of the world in the spring of 1940 to realize how severe that punishment may be.

If, on the other hand, we cast our gaze back over the past century, we see the natural forces at work compelling men to widen their narrow minds so as to encompass the earth. As the world has grown smaller the lives of men and women in different countries have come to touch one another far more frequently and closely than they did a hundred years ago.

In the eighteenth century (writes Leonard Woolf) the number of persons in these islands who had any relations with any inhabitants of Sweden could probably be counted on the fingers of two hands; to-day, any person

* Cf. Kant on *Nature's lead towards Perpetual Peace*.

who buys a box of matches is linked by an intricate chain of relationship with hundreds of Swedish woodcutters, factory workers, employers, railwaymen, and shippers. In the eighteenth century, therefore, because relations between the individuals of the two countries scarcely existed, interests common to Englishmen and Swedes did not exist, or, at any rate, could not become apparent to the people themselves; to-day, the continual intercourse between the two countries produces a network of Anglo-Swedish interests which affect the everyday life of hundreds of persons in the two countries. And a similar network of international intercourse and interest has been woven, mainly by the telephone, over the whole face of the earth.

It is impossible to have any highly organized system of human relationship without government—that is to say, without regulation of the relations through agreement or agreements. Man adapts his institutions to his needs, and, if he did not, he would have remained with the simple needs and under the simple institutions of his cousins of the jungle—the gorilla, the chimpanzee, and the ourang-outang Thus the system of International Government which has developed in the last one hundred years has not been the perverse invention of international cranks, but a spontaneous growth to meet international needs, and without which everyday life, as we know it, would have been impossible.*

From the days of the Quintuple Alliance and the congress system that followed the struggle against Napoleon it became the practice of sovereign States to arrange sporadic conferences between their diplomatic representatives whenever a new agreement was needed to decide an issue on which no country wished to fight. 'By the twentieth century we had reached a stage at which no

* Woolf, *International Government*, pp. 154–5.

year passed without several such conferences meeting and at which between fifty and a hundred treaties, embodying international legislation, were signed annually.'*

But these sporadic conferences could only pass isolated measures of international legislation. As a rule, they left behind them no machinery to administer their new laws. Many international interests had, however, become so permanent, intricate, and urgent as to require continual revision of the law relating to them and, in several cases, to need also some form of international administration. Indeed, the shrinking of the world had made it more and more difficult, and finally impossible, for the world to be managed by sovereign States acting independently. Some wider authority was fast becoming indispensable. So it came about that, while in 1815 there was no public international organization—not a single authority through which governments could join in looking after world affairs—no less than thirty-three public international organizations had been forced into existence by 1913.

They were 'forced' into existence because the creation of each of them required every participating State to sacrifice some of its independence, some of its sovereignty, some of its supposed 'national interests,' for the sake of international interests; and no State was willing to make such sacrifices until compelled to do so by conclusive evidence that the interests of their own bit of the world —their real national interests—could only be served by seeking first the interests of the world as a whole. So France refused at first to join the Postal Union, 'believing that it would involve a sacrifice of her peculiar financial interests.'* And 'Great Britain refused for some time to enter the Radio-telegraphic Union on the ground that it would involve the sacrifice of vital Imperial interests, just

* Woolf, loc. cit., p. 156.

as she refused for long to sign any general Sanitary Convention on the ground that it would involve the sacrifice of interests vital to her as a great maritime Power with a great carrying trade.'*

Let us look more closely at those two examples of public international organization. The best known example of all is the Universal Postal Union. We most of us take it for granted that, in times of peace, a two-pence-halfpenny stamp will take an ordinary letter to any foreign part. This was not always so. Until 1874 each country arranged its own postal charges with the aim of making the foreigner pay. The result was hopeless confusion. A letter from Germany to Austria could be sent at three different rates; and a letter from America to Australia might cost anything from 5 to 102 cents per half-ounce, according to the way it went.† At length the common sense of the world could bear it no longer; and the nations joined in the Universal Postal Union to regulate international posts from an office at Berne.

Again, when sailing ships gave place to steamships, cholera and plague as well as goods and passengers made the journey from Eastern Asia to Western Europe more easily and on a much bigger scale than before. Great Britain and other countries were threatened with dangerous epidemics. Each tried to protect itself with quarantine rules of its own. They did not succeed. Trade was delayed, but cholera continued to enter freely and frequently. Each epidemic after 1851 was followed by an international conference; and it soon became clear that only by having a single quarantine system, and an international body to administer it, could success be attained. Yet for forty years 'conflicting national interests' made improvement

* Woolf, *International Government*, p. 186.
† Cf. Woolf, *loc. cit.*, pp. 186-8.

impossible. At last, however, the logic of facts taught its lesson. When the epidemic of 1892 broke out, it was plain that all the interests of all the nations required common international action. There followed the first International Sanitary Convention of 1892 and the Dresden Convention of 1893, when Great Britain admitted that the freedom of international trade could not be secured without international control. There has been no cholera epidemic in Western Europe since that time.*

Thus there grew up the beginnings of international government for the control of public health, posts, telegraphs and wireless and other matters in which 'conflicting national interests' have been forced to give away before the interests of the world as a whole.

While the governments of sovereign States were creating several separate instruments of international government, the citizens of those States were welding their interests together by means of international conferences, and linking up some of those conferences by means of permanent secretariats. These bodies administered international societies or associations such as the International Federation of Trades Unions, the International Chamber of Commerce, or the Inter-Parliamentary Union.

The first 'International Congress, not of representatives of the Governments of States, but of individuals of different nations who realized that they had an interest to serve or an object to attain which was international rather than national,'† seems to have met in 1840. This was the World Anti-Slavery Convention, in London. The growing number of international conferences since that time is shown in the diagram on page 50.

* Cf. Woolf, *loc. cit.*, pp. 221-32.   † Woolf, *loc. cit.*, p. 165.

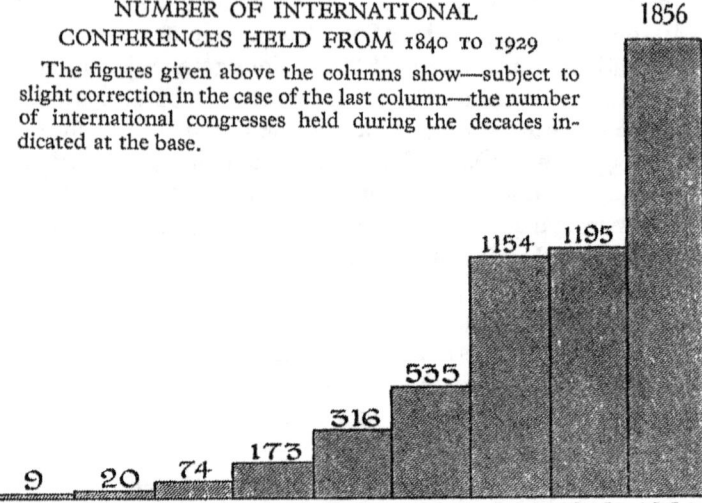

NUMBER OF INTERNATIONAL CONFERENCES HELD FROM 1840 TO 1929

The figures given above the columns show—subject to slight correction in the case of the last column—the number of international congresses held during the decades indicated at the base.

There is still another kind of international organization that was brought into existence by the shrinking of the world during the past century. Woolf writes:

Everyone has heard or read such phrases as: 'Capital is international,' or 'finance is international'; but few people realize the extent to which not only finance but industry has been internationalized in the last hundred years. A large part of the production and distribution of commodities throughout the world is regulated by agreement between the groups of producers and suppliers in the different countries; in other words, International Government has been extensively applied to national and international trade. . . . The organisms or organizations through which this government has been established take many different forms. In the simplest form there is merely an agreement between national companies or individual producers and traders—each an 'independent sovereign' commercial or industrial entity—to regulate competition or production or price or to divide the world into 'markets.' In other cases the national groups surrender some of their independence and sovereignty, and form international trusts and cartels, which may be very elaborate international organisms; in others, again, the groups merge their own individuality completely in one International Company* such as the *Compagnie Internationale des Wagons-Lits* (now associated with Messrs. Thos. Cook & Son, Ltd.), familiar to every traveller by train from Calais to Constantinople.

* Woolf, *loc. cit.*, p. 177.

CHAPTER 5

THE DRIFT TOWARDS WAR

After discussing (in Chapter 3) the political machinery and the psychological driving power needed to unite the world in a creative peace, we observed (in Chapter 4) that the physical structure of our planet and the laws of arithmetic combined to reward international co-operation and to punish the failure of nations to agree with one another. We have been looking at the prizes: freedom from epidemic disease, more and better food, increase of material wealth, cheaper communications, more rapid and reliable transit. We now turn our gaze from the rewards in heaven in order to take note of the punishments in hell.

Disputes between nations may be resolved in the same three ways as differences between one man and another. These ways correspond to the three methods—'conscious control,' 'displacement,' and 'repression'—of restoring harmony to a mind rent by conflicting tendencies.

The first way wholly avoids open conflict. Real agreement is the characteristic feature of this method. Both disputing nations, or persons, are persuaded that their fundamental aims are consistent with the proposed settlement. The arbitration of the *Alabama* dispute* between Great Britain and the United States resulted in a settlement of this kind. So also did Lord Durham's way of ending the Canadian rebellions of 1838.†

* See above, p. 34. † See above, p. 38.

THE DRIFT TOWARDS WAR

The second way to stop a quarrel also avoids open conflict. But it does not remove the cause. Latent conflict is thus the usual product of this method. It consists in the parties agreeing to differ. Each retains its own aims, which are not reconciled with those on the other side. But neither party tries to impose its will upon the other. This method has its value when the disagreement concerns matters of minor importance which ought not to be allowed to disturb the good relations between parties who are fundamentally at one; or when the parties are so far apart, as regards most of their interests, that they can afford to ignore, at least for the present, the one point where their interests clash. This mode of settlement is therefore better suited to a society of nations more or less united by a common purpose, or living in the spacious days of George the Third, than to nations which differ widely about the meaning and purpose of life or are as closely packed together as those of western and central Europe to-day. Indeed we are not likely to forget how attempts at 'appeasement'* or 'a patch-work peace' have failed to avoid open conflict between the Powers now at war. And, if we are right in likening this method to 'displacement' in Freudian psychology, we may expect to find in it many marks of a general ethical inferiority. An example of this method is the payment of Dane-geld by one set of our ancestors to another. Its ethical inferiority appears in Kipling's verse:

> It is wrong to put temptation in the path of any nation,
> For fear they should succumb and go astray,
> So when you are requested to pay up or be molested,
> You will find it better policy to say:—

* See below, Chapter 12.

'We never pay anyone Dane-geld,
  No matter how trifling the cost,
For the end of that game is oppression and
    shame,
  And the nation that plays it is lost!'*

The third way to end a dispute is to fight it out. 'War,' wrote von Clausewitz, 'is . . . intended to compel our opponent to fulfil our will';† and 'War is a political instrument, a continuation of political intercourse, a carrying out of the same by other means.'‡ And, until the Covenant of the League of Nations in 1920 and the Pact of Paris (or Briand-Kellogg Pact) of 1928 made of war an international crime, there was nothing in international law to prevent the use, although not the unrestricted use, of war as an instrument of national policy.

But war employed as an instrument of national policy has seldom ended the dispute out of which it arose. A victory followed by such a peace as Rome eventually imposed on Carthage would indeed avert all future risk of conflict between the combatants. But the obliteration of a defeated enemy is not now a possible outcome of a war won by the Western democracies. War, indeed, settles nothing unless it either wipes out the foe or ends in a peace that makes him into a friend. Other wars, most wars, have a wholly disintegrative effect. They merely sow seeds of future conflicts, as witness the long series of struggles between French and Germans from the time of Louis XIV or even since the death of Charlemagne.

There are then three ways of handling an international dispute: removing the cause of it, ignoring or dodging it,

---

* Fletcher and Kipling, *History of England*, p. 41.
† Von Clausewitz, *On War*, Vol. I, 1, 2.
‡ Von Clausewitz, *loc. cit.*, Vol. I, 1, 27.

and fighting it out. The first method results in no conflict, the second in latent conflict, and the third in open conflict. Disputes between a Great Power and a small State without allies do not as a rule result in war; and Great Powers can (and, even before the régime of the League of Nations, often did) combine to stop war between small States. But, in the absence of any effective international machinery to prevent it, war is the more likely to occur between Great Powers the smaller their world becomes; and there are still five Great Powers in Europe as there were at the time of the Congress of Vienna when, for political purposes, Europe was at least ten times larger than it is to-day.

One reason why the shrinking of the world makes war more likely is that it multiplies international contacts and therefore increases the possible causes of friction of the old kinds between the Great Powers. Another reason is that it creates wholly new sources of trouble. Independent sovereign States feel themselves to be fighting a losing battle against a natural movement towards international government. Only by creating artificial barriers between the twenty-five—or twenty-two while Austria, Czecho-Slovakia and Poland are, for the time being, submerged —States of Europe can they hope to preserve so absurd an anachronism as their complete independence of international control. So they seek to prolong their autarchy,* or sovereignty, by striving after autarky,† or economic self-sufficiency. They hope that, by making themselves independent of supplies of foodstuffs or other raw materials which they do not themselves control, they can avoid coercion by any lesser means than military defeat. So they compete for the ownership of sources of raw materials, particularly in tropical lands‡; for the control of markets

* From αὐταρχία, despotism, autocracy, or self-government.
† From αὐτάρκεια, self-sufficiency.   ‡ See below, Chapter 18.

where they can sell their exports to pay for their imports; for power over the currencies used in those markets; and for mastery of the seas, lest their imports and exports be cut off in time of war. They even strive to dominate the minds of their own citizens so that their country's natural frontiers (which may be non-existent, as on the north-east of Germany) and its tariff-walls may be reinforced by psychological barriers against the intrusion of alien ideas. Hence come ministries of propaganda, the printing and broadcasting of garbled facts, restrictions upon foreign travel, and bans upon personal contacts with citizens of other States. How great a change from the Europe of our great-grandfathers when, even while England was at war with Napoleon, wealthy Englishmen used to slip across to France for a little bit of gaiety!

But disputes between Great Powers are not only more likely to arise than they were a century ago. They are also harder to settle by real agreement, or even by agreement to differ. The main reason why real agreement between the five Great Powers of Europe is harder to come by in the confined Europe of to-day than in the spacious days of a hundred years ago, is that the only agreement now worth having is one that creates some sort of international government* and so limits national sovereignty. It is as if the nations which formerly lived, each a law unto itself, on their great estates amid the wide open spaces, had now moved into town. As town-dwellers, they feel the need of collective services to maintain law and order and to minister in other ways to the general welfare. But the

* Broadcasting on the Allied 'peace aims' on 26 November, 1939, the Prime Minister said: 'Conditions never cease to change and corresponding adjustments would be required if friction is to be avoided. Consequently, you would need some machinery capable of conducting and guiding the development of Europe in the right direction.' See also below, Chapters 15 to 20.

nations are inveterate individualists, and their governments even more so. They are as unwilling to yield further morsels of their sovereignty as they were, in the nineteenth century, to form a postal union or to sign a sanitary convention: as unwilling as were the Barons of the Wars of the Roses to give up at the behest of Henry VII their private armies and their walled castles and come under the protection of the King's peace. Thus real agreement between Great Powers is harder to achieve to-day than it used to be before Europe became a built-up area. At the same time lack of space leaves less room for agreement to differ.

The tendency towards war between Great Powers who have been squeezed tightly together but are loth to lose the least bit of separate identity is checked, but not checkmated (as the present war proves), by certain trends in the opposite direction.

The first of these is the growing power of defence in comparison with attack. We saw its effect early in this war, when the Allied and German armies sat facing one another like cats on a wall. It also makes the outbreak of war less likely because it holds back a would-be aggressor until he feels sure of possessing ample excess of power over that of his intended victim.

Another deterrent to war is the increase in its destructive power and, consequently, in men's horror of it. We need not go back to that 'vendetta of the country houses' known to English History as the Wars of the Roses in order to see how slight were the social and economic effects of old-fashioned war. Trevelyan's study of *England under Queen Anne* shows how little disturbed were the lives of most English people during that brilliant age by the fact that the greatest English soldier of all time was fighting and defeating the armies of Louis XIV. Marlborough, when he won his victory at Blenheim, was in command of no more than nine thousand British troops. A century later, the Napoleonic wars made very little difference to the even tenor of the lives in the South of England homes described by Jane Austen, although it is true that the Orders in Council deeply affected the mills and factories of the North. When, in the final battle, Napoleon

1704	1815
BRITISH FORCES	BRITISH FORCES
AT BATTLE OF BLENHEIM	AT BATTLE OF WATERLOO
9,000	35,000
▪	▣

BRITISH DEAD
IN THE GREAT WAR
1,090,000

was defeated by Wellington and Blücher, the British forces numbered only thirty-five thousand men. But the next century saw a vastly greater change. The British dead in the World War of 1914–1918 were more than one million. The scale of war had completely altered because modern transport could feed and clothe and supply with munitions the whole manhood of a nation in the field. The destructive power of war had also grown out of all knowledge. Even in this country, which escaped more lightly than some others, no one who has lived through the twenty years since the World War ended has not felt its economic consequences. Poison gas, aeroplanes, tanks and great guns added to its horror.

All the horrors (wrote Winston Churchill) of all the ages were brought together, and not only armies, but whole populations were thrust into the midst of them. . . . Every outrage against humanity or international law was repaid by reprisals, often on a greater scale and of longer duration. No truce or parley mitigated the strife of the armies. The wounded died between the lines: the dead mouldered into the soil. Merchant ships and neutral ships and hospital ships were sunk on the seas, and all on board left to their fate or killed as they swam. Every effort was made to starve whole populations into submission without regard to age or sex. Cities and monuments were smashed by artillery; bombs from the air were cast down indiscriminately; poison gas in many forms stifled or scarred the soldiers; liquid fire was projected into their bodies; men fell from the air in flames or were smothered, often slowly, in the dark recesses of the sea.*

The World War differed from all ancient wars in the immense power of the combatants and their efficient agents of destruction, and from all modern wars in the utter ruthlessness with which it was fought. That experience, shared, although not equally, by neutrals and belligerents, left no room for doubt that 'private' war—fighting out a private squabble between two or more States—ought to be banned as a crime by the society of nations. A 'vendetta of the country houses,' or the small-scale wars of the old spacious times, might perhaps be tolerated, like the rough justice of a North American mining camp in the days of Bret Harte, when it seemed simpler to allow people to settle their quarrels with pistols on the spot than to provide those sparsely inhabited regions with police and magistrates. But now that population has increased and distances have shortened in the

* *The World Crisis* (One Volume Edition), pp. 19, 20.

western United States, the safety of the community has made it necessary to treat private fighting as a crime and to suppress it by the machinery of law and order, which also gives people the means of settling their quarrels peacefully and justly. And, when the World War ended in 1918, it seemed to many people that the hammer blows of common suffering had welded mankind into an international community which would not tolerate private wars but could, and should, create machinery for the just and peaceful settlement of all disputes between nations. Here, it was felt, was yet another case where so-called 'conflicting national interests' must yield to the interests of the world as a whole, even as they had to give way when the spread of cholera epidemics to the western world was at last stopped by international action.

CHAPTER 6

AN UNSTABLE EUROPE

We saw in the last chapter how the shrinking of the world tends to multiply unsettled disputes between Great Powers which do not recognize any superior, or supreme, authority for the adjustment of their differences, the protection of their territories and the regulation of their armaments. Their many mutual grievances cause the peoples, and their governments, to feel increasing irritation against their rivals. This mounting irritation fosters the gradual growth of a sentiment of hatred. And this sentiment, when it is full-blown, makes for war.

We also saw how defence was coming to have an ever greater advantage over attack, and how the damage done by war was on an ever larger scale. On both these accounts there is a growing fear of war which deters sovereign States from fighting one another, and even from preparing to fight by increasing their armaments.

So long as armaments remain at a low level and none of the more powerful States embarks upon a policy of expansion, a stable equilibrium may be maintained between the forces that make for war and those that tend to preserve peace. But if one of the Great Powers increases its armaments beyond a certain point, or otherwise (as, for example, by aggressive acts or propaganda) makes itself feared overmuch, this new particular fear will counteract the fear of war in general until the equilibrium becomes unstable. Instability begins when other Great Powers are more deeply stirred by fear of their aggressive neighbour, and by anger and disgust at his behaviour, than by fear of war in general. An early fight with him may even appear a less appalling prospect than the war that begins to seem inevitable so soon as he shall have sufficiently strengthened himself by increasing his armaments, and perhaps also by absorbing, one after another, the potential allies of the Great Powers that feel themselves threatened. These Powers then begin to arm. Their growing strength produces a feeling of encirclement or persecution in the country that made the first move. Its armaments are therefore increased more rapidly than before. This development is felt by the other Powers to be a further threat to their security, and they accelerate their preparations for war. So the process goes on, and there is no end to it except war itself.

Thus the international equilibrium becomes unstable, and war is the inevitable result, when two or more Great Powers, brought into close proximity by the shrinking of their world, try to carry on the government of their respective countries as independent sovereign States owing obedience to no international authority capable of making the common interest of both prevail over the particular interests of either. But if to the deterrent effect of fear of war were added a fear of collective action backed by overwhelming force, ready to be used against any State whose armaments increased beyond an agreed limit, any growth of military preparations would be checked and reversed before that limit was reached. The international equilibrium would then become stable. There would be no drift towards war.

The rapid shrinking of the world began shortly before the Crimean War. But the European situation remained comparatively stable for fifty years and more. Does that disprove our theory? Not at all; for so long as Britain remained the unchallenged mistress of the seas there existed, on that element at least, the equivalent of collective action by an international authority. Sir Alfred Zimmern writes:

British sea-power in the nineteenth century was exercised so silently, yet so efficiently, with so complete a mastery yet with such characteristic reserve—a reserve as characteristic of the Service as of the people—that it is only in retrospect that its full significance and, still more, its undeveloped potentialities are coming to be realized. . . . For the essence of the Navy's achievement lay, not in what it performed but in what it prevented, not in its own acts and accomplishments but in its influence over the acts of others. It was a major factor underlying every diplomatic negotiation in the oceanic world—and in many of those outside it—a factor that could never be assessed with precision but which could always be counted on, if need be, to turn the scales. If its weight was seldom thrown in, it was because those who had it at their command, true children of the nineteenth century, believed in the virtue of sparing use, both in the economy of force and in the economy of advertisement. But both were available when they were needed. The British Navy carried out, under nineteenth-century conditions, tasks for which in some quarters appeal is to-day being made to an 'international police force.' It kept the seas open for traffic and closed for pirates, made the 'Open Door' a reality and, so far as international law allowed, suppressed the slave trade and rescued its victims. Thus, to use the words of a naval historian,* 'The White Ensign became the token of equal rights for all, a pledge of the brotherhood of all mankind.'†

* Callendar, *The Naval Side of British History* (1924), p. 237.
† *The League of Nations and the Rule of Law*, 1918–1935 (1936), pp. 87, 88.

British naval supremacy ensured, while it lasted, that such wars as did occur between Great Powers in Europe were easily isolated and did not lead to any widespread conflagration. But, when this supremacy was challenged by the growing might of the Imperial German Navy, the restraining influence was removed. Europe became unstable, and the World War followed as a matter of course.

CHAPTER 7

THE WORLD WAR

★

Before the World War began the general horror of war was much less acute than it soon became and afterwards remained. The effect of this fear, acting as a restraint upon the outbreak of war, was therefore greater after 1918 than before 1914.

Besides increasing the general fear of war, the World War had the effect, as we saw in Chapter 5, of convincing a great many people that an altogether new deterrent of war was needed: some sort of international authority which would settle disputes (and so remove the grievances, and the anger and hatred resulting from them), prevent aggression (and so put an end to the fears caused by the apparently aggressive intentions of another State), and limit armaments (and so avoid the armaments race which, once begun, must end in war). In fact, the world became full of schemes for a new international organization to prevent a recurrence of the catastrophe which had overtaken it. Most of these schemes originated in the Anglo-Saxon world where, as we have seen, the idea of uniting States with common interests was already familiar, and where the idea of 'a war to end war' appealed most strongly; but some of the smaller neutrals joined in the search, especially the Dutch and Scandinavians. How these schemes developed under the influence of the World War has been described by Webster:

So insistent was the pressure from below that the statesmen of the warring countries were gradually forced to take notice of it. Indeed, Mr. Asquith* and Lord Grey† had from the outset made a world organized to prevent war one of the objects of British policy. In the strain and hazard of the conflict, however, this object stood some chance of being relegated to a very subordinate position in the Allied councils had it not been for three men of lofty ideals.

By far the most important and influential was, of course, President Wilson,‡ who put the idea of a new world organization in the forefront of his wonderful speeches which echoed through the world and penetrated Cabinets and Foreign Offices, as well as Parliaments and public places. . . . In Britain the idea had warm advocates in General Smuts and Lord Cecil.§ It was the latter who caused an official Committee‖ to be set up by the British Cabinet to consider the proposal from a British point of view, and thus produced the draft which was the germ of the League of Nations. It was General Smuts who, at a later stage, extended and developed the idea of the League into an organization for peace, as well as a preventive of war. In France no statesman of first rank reckoned much of these ideas, so preoccupied were they in the immediate danger. But M. Bourgeois, a veteran of the Hague Conferences, was designated by them to draw up a French scheme. . . .

All these men were affected by the unofficial schemes of which a large number were being drawn up in Britain and the United States. In each country new voluntary

---

* Prime Minister until 1916.   † Foreign Secretary, 1906–1916.
‡ President of the United States, 1913–1921.
§ Then Lord Robert Cecil.
‖ The Chairman of the Committee was Lord Phillimore, then a Lord of Appeal, and among its members were Sir Eyre Crowe, afterwards Permanent Under-Secretary of State for Foreign Affairs, and two other Foreign Office officials.

societies, in accordance with precedent, had sprung up to advocate the new idea. In America the League to Enforce Peace . . . began to explore the possibility of a world organization long before America entered the war. In Britain a group led by Viscount Bryce early began an examination of the subject and produced specific proposals. Two League of Nations societies were formed which included many different liberal forces, and subsequently fused together to form the League of Nations Union. . . .*

While the scheme for a League of Nations was thus being evolved by such leaders as President Wilson, Lord Cecil and General Smuts, with the support of a growing volume of public opinion in the English-speaking world, the World War was having a very different effect upon other minds. As the hard-fought struggle wore on, masses of people came to feel a growing hatred for the enemy on whom they laid the blame for all the sorrows and losses they had suffered. That is not to be wondered at, since for four years the governments used every means to create what was called a 'war psychology' among their peoples. Their object was to instil hatred as an antidote to fear. In this way they hoped to give men the 'martial spirit,' and at the same time to creat a unity of purpose to win the war. When it was all over 'there were 7,500,000 men lying dead in Europe and 20,000,000 had been wounded; there were devastated cities, ruined mines and

* *The League of Nations in Theory and Practice* (1933), pp. 30–2. Webster adds: The word 'League' apparently was first used [by the Anglo-Saxons] in order to emphasize that the proposed body was confined to certain states for certain purposes. But as the [official] scheme developed the word became very inadequate to the conceptions of the authors and it is unfortunate that the word 'Society' was not adopted in English as in French. (*Loc. cit.*, p. 35.)

factories, stupendous debts.'* To hate the enemy had become natural enough.

Mr. Howard-Ellis has collected 'a few specimens of the war mind in England,' showing how people's thoughts were influenced by the sentiment of hatred. 'These samples,' he says, 'were drawn at random from a large number of similar utterances by persons far above the average in intelligence, education and liberality of view, but all conscious that they reflect the attitude of the great mass of their countrymen.' Indeed, they are but 'precise expressions—elaborate rationalizations—of the prevailing complex, which . . . was in other belligerent countries more violent, if possible, than in England.'†

The first of these specimens is an article in *The Hibbert Journal* for April, 1917, anticipating Mr. Lloyd George's election slogan of hanging the Kaiser and punishing the war criminals. The article is entitled 'Punishment and Reconstruction.' Its eminent author believed that 'any issue short of a clear vindication of the principles for which the Allies are fighting would be an irreparable disaster to the human race.' He went on:

For ages past the life of man has been darkened and blighted by the presence of a class of criminals who, under many names and disguises and by various arts, have first befooled and then exploited the nations who tolerated them. . . . Their chief representatives to-day are well known to the whole world. . . . They are responsible for the war, and for all the faithlessness, cruelty and moral imbecility which has surrounded the conduct of the war with the darkest crimes of history. . . . A vision begins to

---

* Ray Stannard Baker, *Woodrow Wilson and World Settlement*, Vol. I., Chapter IX.

† *The Origins, Structure and Working of the League of Nations* (1928), p. 45.

form itself . . . of punishment so solemn, so deliberate, so just, and so universally approved that it would shine to future ages as one of the most sacred deeds in the history of man. Let these malefactors, then, be informed, by methods which admit of no misunderstanding, that the time has come at last when their presence, and the presence of their likes, is no longer to be tolerated on this planet. Let them be called to account for their crimes, solemnly judged, and effectually disposed of by the human race. A victory which takes that form will be a victory for all mankind. . . . We might well be content to leave all other proposals in abeyance for the time being and to concentrate upon this as our essential aim in the war.'*

How well all this expressed and rationalized the prevailing sentiment of hate is seen in Article 227 of the Treaty of Versailles. It reads

> The Allied and Associated Powers publicly arraign William II of Hohenzollern, formerly German Emperor, for a supreme offence against international morality and the sanctity of treaties. . . . The Allied and Associated Powers will address a request to the Government of the Netherlands for the surrender to them of the ex-Emperor in order that he may be put on trial.

Fortunately the Dutch Government refused this request. The victorious Powers were thus saved from an act of vengeance which might indeed have pleased the haters by fulfilling their war-aims but would have darkened the hopes of those† who sought to create a new world so united as to render impossible the repetition of the Kaiser's 'supreme offence.'

* Quoted by Howard-Ellis, *loc. cit.*, p. 46.
† Their aims also found expression in the Treaty, notably in Part I (The Covenant of the League of Nations) and in Part XIII (The Labour Clauses).

When Herr Hitler repeated that offence in a worse form, the Kaiser was still living under the Dutch Government's protection. Had he been hanged, would his execution have made any difference to Herr Hitler's career? If, however, the Versailles treaty had not needed to compromise between the wishes of the haters who sought to hold Germany down and those seekers after real agreement who desired to raise her from defeat to equal partnership in rebuilding the world, if the latter opinion had been dominant when the treaty was made, it may be doubted whether the name of Adolf Hitler would ever have become known outside the cafés and clubs of Munich.

Another of Mr. Howard-Ellis's examples of the sentiment of hate, as it developed and expressed itself in England during the World War, is taken from *The Herd instinct in Peace and War* (1916) by W. Trotter. Professor Trotter compared 'German society with the wolf-pack and the feelings, desires and impulses of the individual German with those of the wolf or dog.' He saw the struggle between England and Germany as

a war not so much of contending nations as of contending species. We are not taking part in a mere war, but in one of Nature's august experiments. . . . To the socialized peoples . . . she has given substance to the creation of a nightmare, and they must destroy this werewolf or die.*

Trotter believed that he possessed an 'invigorating contact with reality' which was lacking in 'pacifist intellectuals,' and that it enabled him to see the biological difference between German nature and human nature—a phrase of Mr. Bonar Law's. Trotter proceeds:

* Howard-Ellis, *loc. cit.*, p. 49.

A psychological hint of great value may be obtained from our knowledge of those animals whose gregariousness, like that of the Germans, is of the aggressive type. When it is thought necessary to correct a dog by corporal measures, it is found that the best effect is got by what is rather callously called a 'sound' thrashing. The animal must be left in no doubt as to who is the master. And his punishment must not be diluted by hesitation, nervousness or compunction on the part of the punisher. . . . If there is any truth in the view I have expressed that the moral reactions of Germany follow the gregarious type which is illustrated by the wolf and dog, it follows that her respect is to be won by a thorough and drastic beating. . . .*

It was this kind of war mind that enabled Mr. Lloyd George to win his General Election, after the Armistice and before the Peace Conference, by an overwhelming majority on *hanging the Kaiser* and *making Germany pay for the war*. 'Squeeze the German Orange until the pips squeak' was the election cry of one Cabinet Minister. There were other members of Parliament, like Lord Balfour,† the Foreign Secretary, and his cousin, Lord Cecil,‡ who represented that section of public opinion which believed in preventing another great war, not by the destruction of Germany, but by the reconstruction of the world. Their influence, as we have seen, made itself felt at the Peace Conference. But the British delegation in Paris was never allowed to forget that the destructive element predominated over the constructive in the new Parliament at Westminster. When, for example, rumours

---

* Howard-Ellis, *loc. cit.*, p. 50.
† Then the Rt. Hon. A. J. Balfour, M.P.
‡ Then Lord Robert Cecil, M.P. He resigned from the Government just before the General Election.

reached London that Mr. Lloyd George was urging a moderate peace at the Conference, he received a telegram from 370 Members of Parliament who said:

> Our constituents have always expected that the first action of the peace delegates would be, as you repeatedly stated in your election speeches, to present the bill in full and make Germany acknowledge the debt.

The French delegation sided with the majority of the British Parliament and the American delegation with the minority. Indeed, the rival peace schemes, the destructive and the constructive, seemed to be embodied in the French and American leaders. The eighty-year-old realist, Clemenceau, *le Tigre*, stood for the one and Woodrow Wilson, the idealist, for the other.*

It is not therefore surprising that the treaty was a compromise between the destructive and the constructive tendencies of public opinion. To the latter it owed most of the Covenant of the League of Nations, the Labour clauses and the provision for protecting racial, religious and linguistic minorities of the population of Czecho-Slovakia and of Poland. To the former tendency may be attributed, *inter alia*, the treatment of the new German Republic as if it were no different from the old Imperial Germany; the fact that the treaty was wholly dictated to the German delegates, instead of being in part at least negotiated so that real agreement might be reached on as

---

* But 'Wilson's idealism was in line with a healthy *Realpolitik*.' Mr. Harold Nicolson (*Peacemaking 1919*, p. 86) quotes these words, from Dr. Charles Seymour's edition of the *Papers of Colonel House*. Dr. Seymour justifies this conclusion as follows: 'We sacrificed little in announcing that we would take no territory (which we did not want) nor reparations (which we could not collect). Our interest lay in assuring a régime of world tranquillity; our geographic position was such that we could advocate disarmament and arbitration with complete safety.'

many points as possible; the inclusion in the treaty of the so-called war guilt clause* and the exaction of reparations far beyond Germany's capacity to pay;† the exclusion of Germany from the League of Nations during its first six-and-a-half formative years; and the long delay in carrying out the pledge given by M. Clemenceau to the German delegation at the Peace Conference before they agreed to sign the clauses regulating the future armaments of Germany.

It is possible that, as Mr. Harold Nicolson has observed, either of these trends of public opinion might, in the absence of the other, have led to a settlement which would have averted the present war with Germany. Nicolson writes:

It is possible, and I now think probable, that if the Rhine frontier had really been given to France [as Marshal Foch and the French General Staff desired], Germany would thereafter have been deprived of the physical possibility of committing any further acts of aggression. It is possible and I now think probable, that if the doctrine of President Wilson had been applied in its entirety Germany would not have had the moral temptation to seek to upset the Versailles settlement. The fundamental error which was made was to compromise between these two opposites. Either there should have been a peace of force or a peace of justice. The peace which emerged from

---

* Article 231. It reads: 'The Allied and Associated Governments affirm and Germany accepts the responsibility of Germany and her allies for causing all the loss and damage to which the Allied and Associated Governments and their nationals have been subjected as a consequence of the war imposed upon them by the aggression of Germany and her allies.'

† The Treaty fixed no total for the reparation claim, but left the amount for subsequent investigation and settlement. The amounts proposed at different times and finally agreed are set out in the Note at the end of this chapter.

the Paris Conference was unjust enough to cause resentment, but not forceful enough to render such resentment impotent. Germany was neither conciliated nor suppressed. She was wounded, but not slain. It took her fourteen years and more to recover from her wounds.*

While, however, Nicolson may be right in thinking that the application of the French theory at Versailles might have staved off the Hitler régime and the renewal of German aggression, to 'suppress' or 'slay' Germany was not practical politics for victorious democracies in the twentieth century. Moreover, a purely French treaty could not have provided the basis for a world settlement or a lasting peace. The instability of Europe might have been diminished but it would not have been ended. The history of the next ten years showed that to avert the danger of German aggression only was not enough.

But if the American theory could have determined the settlement, the result would have been a just peace which neither Germany nor any other State would have wished to upset. And the peace would have been stable as well as just; for, if some adventurer had seized power in any country and tried to dominate his neighbours, his aggressive policy would have been frustrated by a united and world-wide League, ever ready to use 'the strength of all for the defence of each.'

* *Why Britain is at War* (Penguin Special), p. 147.

Notes continued from page 75]
claimed to be unable to pay her debt at the rate of some £30 millions a year to the United States at a time when she was planning to spend nearly ten times this sum yearly on rearmament.
¶ *Ibid.*, Chapter III.
** The Chancellor of the Exchequer, *The Times*, 15 May, 1923.
†† Present value on 1 April, 1929, interest being reckoned at $5\frac{1}{2}$ per cent per annum.
‡‡ This agreement is conditional upon the general cancellation of war debts.

A NOTE ON REPARATIONS
SIXPENCE IN THE POUND!

'PRESENT VALUE' AT THE DATE INDICATED OF THE PROPOSED TOTAL REPARATIONS LIABILITY OF GERMANY MEASURED IN MILLIONS OF GOLD POUNDS

Date		£ millions
1919	At Peace Conference:	
	Britain proposes	11,000*
	United States proposes as maximum figure	7,000†
	Mr. Keynes proposes	2,000‡
1920	Allied and Associated Powers' Bills amount to	11,300
1921	German Government proposes	2,500§
	Reparations Commission fixes Germany's liability at	6,600‖
	Germany agrees to make periodic payments equivalent to	2,500
	plus (some day perhaps)¶	4,100
1922	Germany fails to maintain periodic payments equivalent to	2,500
1923	Britain proposes	1,975**
	Germany offers at most	1,500**
	or, at least, just under	800**
1924	Germany agrees to pay under the Dawes Report	2,445††
1929	Germany agrees to pay under the Young Plan	1,806††
	conditional payments	1,167††
	unconditional payments	639††
1932	At Lausanne, Germany agrees ‡‡ to pay after 3 years	150

* *Woodrow Wilson and World Settlement*, R. S. Baker, Vol. III, p. 396.
† Memorandum by N. H. Davis to President Wilson, *ibid.*, p. 395.
‡ *The Economic Consequences of the Peace*, p. 186.
§ *A Revision of the Treaty*, J. M. Keynes, pp. 25 and 32.
‖ *Ibid.*, p. 36. This is the figure described on p. 73 above as far beyond Germany's capacity to pay. It may be true that Germany has spent some two-thirds of this sum in five or six years on her rearmament. But there is a great difference between internal spending and international payments. That is why the United Kingdom

[*Continued on page* 74

CHAPTER 8

MIXED MOTIVES AT PARIS

★

Ruskin has described the blue stream 'not of flowing but of flying water' that pours from Lac Léman under the Geneva bridges and past Rousseau's island. A little lower down, the clear Rhône is joined by the grey and turbid Arve, thick with the dust of the glaciers around Mont Blanc. For some distance the two rivers flow side by side in the same channel, without seeming to mix their waters: a strange sight which patriotic Genévois are never tired of pointing out to strangers.

But the two streams of public opinion which met at Paris did not keep apart. The elements of hate and distrust mingled with those of faith* and hope, the vindictive with the conciliatory, the destructive with the constructive, the 'realist' with the 'Utopian.' The result was that those parts of the Versailles treaty which aimed at coercing or wounding Germany were milder than they might have been—far milder, for example, than the treaty dictated by the German victors to the vanquished Russians at Brest-Litovsk on 3 March, 1918. On the other hand the mixed motives of the peacemakers impaired the working and, to some small extent, marred the actual structure of the League of Nations. Some of these harmful effects are to be noticed in this chapter.

* Sir Arthur Salter wrote in *Allied Shipping Control* that morally the League of Nations was 'a great effort of faith.' Cf. Zimmern, *loc. cit.*, p. 150.

The last of President Wilson's Fourteen Points which*
formed the basis of the Armistice between Germany
and the Allied and Associated Powers proposed:

A general association of nations must be formed under specific covenants 'for the purpose of affording mutual guarantees of political independence and territorial integrity to great and small States alike.'

The principle of a League of Nations as an integral part of the peace settlement was therefore already accepted by the principal States taking part in the Conference as well as by Germany. But Germany was excluded from the negotiations until the Covenant—the Constitution of the League of Nations—was complete. Not only did Germany take no part in drafting the Covenant, but, by its first Article, she was excluded from Membership of the League until, *inter alia*, 'she should give effective guarantees of [her] sincere intention to observe all [her] international obligations'. When, therefore, the Peace Treaty, with the Covenant as its first chapter, was handed to the German delegates who had come to Versailles to receive it on 7 May, 1919, they protested against being forced to accept it unless Germany were allowed to become a Member of the League. Webster writes:

They had drawn up an elaborate scheme of their own which they forwarded with other criticisms to the Allied and Associated Powers. But it was of course impossible to make changes in the Covenant at this time. The criticisms of the Germans received but little attention.†

* Together with the 'Four Principles' and the 'Five Particulars' contained in his speeches of 11 February, 1918, and 27 September, 1918. The 'Fourteen Points' were made in his speech of 8 January, 1918. See Harold Nicolson, *Peacemaking 1919*, pp. 38–41.
† *Loc. cit.*, p. 61.

The hostile feelings which excluded Germany from the drafting of the Covenant and, at first, from the League itself, were so strong that they still persisted in odd places when Germany was at last admitted to the League seven years later. At that time a country branch of the League of Nations Union ceased to show any signs of life. Enquiries were made; and the answer came from a leading lady member: 'Did you not know? We always said, "If Germany comes in, Edenbridge goes out." '

That the Covenant should form an integral part of the Treaty of Peace had always been President Wilson's intention. By this means the League became at once a body with definite duties* which could not be postponed. This was 'one of the causes why it survived the difficulties of its early years.'† And it is very unlikely that the League plan would have been accepted by some of the nations who were to benefit from the Peace Treaty if the Covenant had been separated from the Treaty.

But neither President Wilson nor Lord Cecil wished the League's main business to be the enforcement of the Treaty. They refused, for example, a proposal by M. Clemenceau's financial minister to make the League supervise Germany's payment of reparations. Nevertheless, the League did become so closely associated in German minds with the hateful Versailles *Diktat* that the German people could hardly be expected to give the Covenant their loyal support. It was chiefly for this reason that the German *Liga für Völkerbund*, or League of Nations Union, despite its many distinguished patrons

---

* Danzig was placed under its protection. It administered the Saar basin. It supervised the government, under League mandate, of the ex-German colonies and certain territories formerly belonging to Turkey. It had to decide a number of questions left unsettled by the Peace Treaties. And the Minorities Treaties with the new States depended on the League. † Webster, *loc. cit.*, p. 53.

and the backing of the Republican Government of Germany, never succeeded in persuading the mass of German citizens that their best interests were bound up with the growth of the League in might, majesty and power.

The original purpose of the League, as laid down in President Wilson's fourteen points* and as contemplated by the first draft of the Covenant made in the British Foreign Office,† was to prevent further acts of aggression from impairing the territorial integrity or political independence of the Member States. With this essential aim the British plan linked up the peaceful settlement of international disputes. Mainly under the inspiration of General Smuts,‡ this negative idea of a League to preserve peace—and, incidentally, the world order established by the Peace Conference—was widened into that of a League to create justice, both international and social. Thus the new organization became endowed with positive and creative functions. It was given the task of promoting international co-operation over a wide field. Opium, the White Slave Traffic, Health, and Labour Conditions, whether at home or in colonial territories controlled by League Members, were specifically mentioned in the Covenant as coming within the purview of the League. And Lord Cecil saw to it that the clause§ aimed against attempts to alter treaty rights by force was balanced by another¶ authorizing the League to advise changes in treaties and 'the consideration of international conditions whose continuance might endanger the peace of the world.' In this way it was hoped to enable the defects of the Treaty to be remedied by a process of peaceful change.

* See above, p. 77 † See above, p. 66.
‡ See above, p. 66. § Article 10.
¶ Article 19. See below, pp. 92, 93, and Chapter 15.

Yet the League continued to be looked upon in France and in the new States as primarily a means of preventing change. This preoccupation with its negative aspect helped to discredit the League, and not only among Germans or their former allies.

The problem of disarmament shows perhaps better than any other how the two streams of public opinion interacted at the Peace Conference. While, in the long view taken by the Anglo-Saxons, an all-round limitation of national armaments was an essential condition of stable peace, the short view of those in whom the hatred and fear of Germany was most strongly developed pointed only to the need for Germany's armaments being immediately reduced and rigidly limited. The all-round limitation of armaments was accordingly deferred: none at all was to be obligatory until the League should formulate plans which should be adopted by the several governments. But the military clauses of the Treaty forthwith reduced the German army, which had been the greatest in the world, to one hundred thousand men without tanks or heavy guns; forbade her navy to include any surface ships larger than ten thousand tons,* or any submarines whatever; and wholly suppressed her air force—she was not to own military aeroplanes.

But before Germany accepted these restrictions, the German delegation told the Peace Conference that

> Germany is prepared to agree to the basic idea of the army, navy and air regulations . . . provided that this is a beginning of a general reduction of armaments.

It was to this observation that M. Clemenceau, in the name of the Allied and Associated Powers, made the answer which Mr. Ramsay MacDonald afterwards said†

* *Cf.* below, p. 147.   † In the Albert Hall on 11 July, 1931.

should be displayed on every hoarding in Britain in order to remind the British people of their pledge:

> The Allied and Associated Powers wish to make it clear that their requirements in regard to German armaments were not made solely with the object of rendering it impossible for Germany to resume her policy of military aggression. They are also the first step towards the reduction and limitation of armaments which they seek to bring about as one of the most fruitful preventives of war, and which it will be one of the first duties of the League of Nations to promote.

Not much was ever done to carry out this pledge. It is true that the Naval Conferences at Washington in 1921 and London in 1930 limited the greatest navies in the world until 1936. So long as this limitation lasted, it prevented the cost of armaments from rising far above the minimum figures of 1930–31. The official figures for armaments when at their lowest were:

	Average 1909—13 Millions £s (gold)	1930 Millions £s (gold)	Percentage Increase since 1909–13
Great Britain	64·0	95·0	48
France	60·0	94·0	57
Germany	70·0	35·1	— 50 (decrease)
Italy	25·0	53·6	114
Russia*	76·0	118·9	56
U.S. of America	61·7	145·4	135
Japan	19·7†	48·0	143
Total, Great Powers	376·4	590·0	57

* With pensions.   † Average 1910–1914.

A Lasting Peace

These figures are taken from the *Economist* for 18 July, 1931. They show the expenditure on armaments (effective services only without pensions) in millions of gold £s, both before the World War and again in 1930, when stable currencies on a gold basis still made comparison possible. It will be seen that, as the Prime Minister (Mr. Ramsay MacDonald) said in the House of Commons on 10 December, 1931, 'the ratio of British armaments in 1930 to British armaments before the War is less than the corresponding ratio for any other Great Power, except of course Germany.' While, however, a golden sovereign would buy far less in 1930 than during the five years before the war, these figures give very little support for the view that any step was ever taken to reduce the armaments of the Great Powers substantially below their pre-war level. And, as we shall see, the all-round limitation of armaments foreseen in M. Clemenceau's pledge never happened at all.*

The problem of disarmament was intimately linked with that of security. France and the other nations with most reason to fear a renewal of German aggression consistently maintained that they could not rely upon other League Members, and notably upon Britain, coming to their rescue if they were attacked, and that, until reliable guarantees were forthcoming, they dared not join in an all-round reduction of armaments to the German level. But, with America holding aloof, the short view prevailed over the long view in Britain. The British people failed to understand that their interests were bound up with those of France and other Members of the League, and they did not feel enough loyalty to the League to make them as ready to protect its covenants as they were to defend the British Empire.

* See below, p. 115.

This lack of League loyalty was most noticeable in that class of British citizens where its absence had worst results. Had long views predominated in Britain when the Peace Conference opened, the Prime Minister would have sat with the American President on the Committee that drafted the Covenant. The French Premier would then have joined them. In that case British (and French) officialdom would have felt a paternal interest in the League. The League would have been their 'show.' As it was, there was no great enthusiasm for it among the principal British and French representatives at Paris.* Lord Cecil, the chief British delegate on the Committee, was not even a member of the Government.† While the Covenant gained immensely from Lord Cecil's long vision and wide experience, the League suffered untold harm from the feeling in Whitehall and Downing Street that the Geneva institution was not a major British interest and that the lives of British sailors, soldiers and airmen ought not to be risked on its behalf.

On one issue there was no difference between the two streams of public opinion represented at Paris. Whatever constitution the Peace Conference might devise for the League of Nations, the delegates must be able to assert that it did not impair the 'sovereignty' of their several States. The League would never be accepted by the nations or by their governments if it were thought to be a 'Super-State.' In fact, however, membership of the League did and does impose very considerable restrictions upon the right of a State to be, in all things, a law unto itself. By accepting the Covenant, a State undertook its

---

* Cf. Webster, *loc. cit.*, p. 46.
† He had resigned the office of Assistant Foreign Secretary in November, 1918, on an issue unconnected with international affairs.

share of responsibility for safeguarding 'the peace of nations'* and renounced its freedom to remain a disinterested spectator of a distant war; it surrendered its sovereign right to break the peace suddenly without first trying to get peace through the League;† it lost its right to be judge in its own cause on any and every issue;‡ it gave up its right to be neutral if an act of aggression should be committed against a Member of the League§ or if certain other of the main rules of the Covenant were broken.‖

Thus authority of the organization designed by the makers of the Covenant was not confined to that of its sovereign State Members when, with its help, they managed to agree upon the action to be taken in regard to any particular matter. The Covenant was in fact the Constitution of an international authority which could, and often did, act *as if* it had been entrusted with sovereign power over 'any matter within the sphere of action of the League or affecting the peace of the world.'¶ 'What the League *is*, at any given moment,' writes Zimmern, 'is determined in fact by the degree of willingness of the powers to co-operate with one another.'** And the League *worked*, not by means of new machinery operated by delegated authority, but (like the Allied Shipping Control during the World War, or like the Allied armies in France in the autumn of 1939) by 'national organizations linked together for international work and themselves forming the instruments for that work.'††

Looking back now on the drafting of the Covenant

---

* Article 11.   † Article 12.   ‡ Article 13.
§ Article 10.   ‖ Articles 16, 17.
¶ Articles 3 and 4.   ** *Loc. cit.*, p. 282.
†† See *Allied Shipping Control*, by J. A. Salter (Sir Arthur Salter, M.P., at one time Secretary of the Allied Maritime Transport Council).

and on the early years of the League of Nations we can see how much the League suffered from the worship of the fetish of sovereignty. Lest the same mistake be repeated after Hitler's war, it is time this image be dislodged from the public mind and that people come to see the old idea of sovereignty as no less a fiction than the unicorn. Sovereignty, according to Austin, is 'that power which is possessed by a body to which the mass of the people are habitually obedient and which itself is obedient to no one.' Such a power mere men never had, nor will any merely human institution ever wield it.

None of the early Caesars (wrote Professor Dicey) could at their pleasure have subverted the worship or fundamental institutions of the Roman world, and when Constantine carried through a religious revolution his success was due to the sympathy of a large part of his subjects. . . . Parliament might legally establish an Episcopal Church in Scotland . . . but . . . widespread resistance would result from legislation which, though legally valid, is in fact beyond the stretch of Parliamentary power.*

What power there is in the British Parliament, or was in the Roman Caesars, is conditioned by the sympathy of a large part of the people whose obedience they have a *legal* right to command. And this power may be subdivided between more than one authority, as in the federal union of the United States, or as in the inter-State system of the British Commonwealth when, for certain purposes, supreme authority is exercised by a War Cabinet or an inter-Allied High Command. The essential question is not whether one body or another possesses legal sovereignty

* A. V. Dicey, K.C., *Introduction to the Study of the Law of the Constitution.* Eighth Edition (1938), pp. 75–7.

to deal with this or that matter, but which body the mass of people (or of States) are prepared to obey in any given matter at any given moment. The main issue that will have to be decided when the time comes for the next world settlement is not merely whether sovereignty (and how much of it) should be transferred from the uniting States to an international body, or whether that body will be a Super-State or a Federal Union or a restored and reconstructed League of Nations. The crucial question is whether the people of the uniting States and their governments are prepared loyally to follow the common authority's lead in certain matters of common concern. It is the will of the people and their will alone that can make their Union a living reality.*

The answer to this crucial question will depend upon the growth, between now and then, of a sentiment of loyalty to the international community—'an invisible bond of ideals,' such as holds the British Commonwealth together—coupled with a clear conviction in the uniting States that a stable peace is only to be attained by sacrificing the conflicting interests of each to the common interests of all. The breakdown of the League of Nations in its second decade was directly due to the feebleness of League loyalty in France and Britain combined with the failure of public opinion in those two countries, and notably among their officials, to understand that aggression in China, Abyssinia, Spain, Austria, Albania and Czecho-Slovakia threatened French and British interests hardly less than direct attacks upon French or British territory. This vital fact was only grasped after the last of these acts of aggression on the Ides of March, 1939. Then indeed Britain and France promised to make common cause with the next victim on the list. But, after all that had

* Cf. Zimmern, *loc. cit.*, p. 284. Cf. also below, p. 196.

happened, their promise to Poland was so heavily discounted by Herr Hitler that it failed to avert war. He believed that, if he could achieve a lightning victory over Poland, Great Britain and France would acquiesce almost as readily in his latest conquest as in his earlier alterations to the map of Europe.

CHAPTER 9

THE COVENANT OF THE LEAGUE OF NATIONS

'What we seek is the reign of law, based upon the consent of the governed and sustained by the organized opinion of mankind.' That is how President Wilson described the purpose of the League of Nations as he conceived it on 4 July, 1918. It was due to his immense influence and his stubborn insistence, when he came to Paris six months later, that the Covenant was framed and the League created.

It was, indeed, a more ample League than he had planned. It was concerned not only with law and order but also with social justice and human welfare. But, without Woodrow Wilson, that section of public opinion which stood solidly behind his winged words and his 'lapidary' English would never have prevailed over the unwillingness of most governments and most peoples to renounce any of the privileges of independent sovereignty as they understood it. They wished to remain as free as possible to act exactly as they pleased. But, when they accepted the Covenant, they 'sacrificed,' as we have seen,* a certain amount of national sovereignty. They did not, indeed, abandon it on principle; but they opened the

---

* See above, pp. 83, 84.

THE COVENANT OF THE LEAGUE OF NATIONS   89

way to further 'sacrifices' of a like kind; and more changes did in fact take place in this direction.*

The American President came to the Conference with a clear vision of the need for most sovereign States to make the peace of nations their common concern. He perceived that only so could the stability of peace be assured. He also saw that, as the principle of 'self-determination' was applied to create a string of new States† from the Arctic to the Adriatic, and as 'the reign of law' throughout this central zone of Europe came to be 'based upon the consent of the governed,' so did it become more than ever necessary for that 'reign of law' to be 'sustained by the organized opinion of mankind.' As he foresaw, and as the events of 1938 and 1939 have abundantly proved, the new small States would be at the mercy of their great neighbours to the West and East unless great and small States alike combined to establish and enforce the new reign of law.

Moreover, General Smuts‡ had persuaded the other framers of the Covenant that there could be no stable peace unless there was much more than mere absence of war. A stable peace must be positive and constructive. It must provide social justice as well as international justice. Accordingly the Covenant was concerned with the co-operation of nations in a wide field extending far beyond the achievement of peace and security.

The Covenant was approved by the Peace Conference

---

* For example, His Majesty's Governments in the United Kingdom and in the self-governing Dominions agreed, in 1929, to be bound by the optional clause of the Statute of the Permanent Court of International Justice, with the result that any other country similarly bound could for ten years thereafter summon any of His Majesty's Governments before the World Court on any issue concerning such of their legal rights as were disputed by the foreign State.

† See the maps on the next page.   ‡ See above, p. 66.

on 28 April, 1919. Its inclusion as the first chapter in each of the Peace Treaties—with Germany, with Austria,

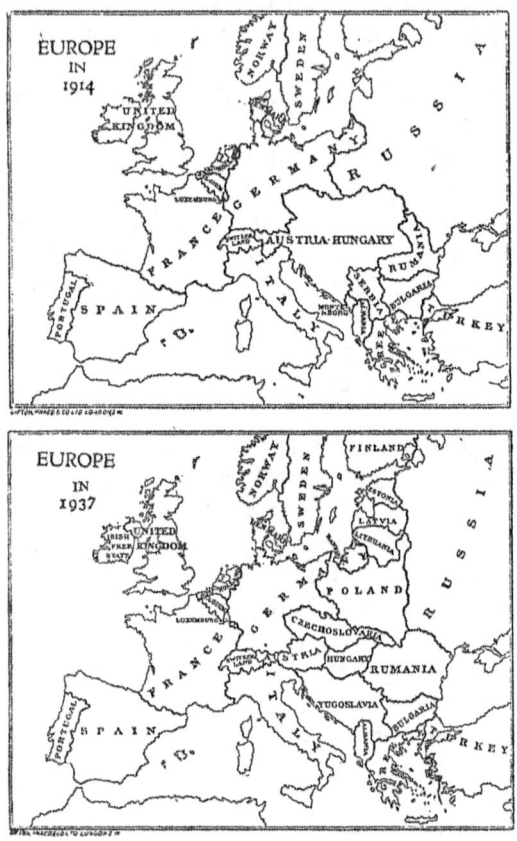

with Hungary and with Bulgaria—led to its being accepted within a year by forty-two States, and afterwards by twenty more.* So it became not only a *Declaration of*

* The largest number of Members of the League was sixty, including practically every country in the world except the U.S.A.

Interdependence but also a first attempt at a *World Constitution*.

In the opening words, or Preamble, of the Covenant, the nations thus set forth the purpose of their League:

THE HIGH CONTRACTING PARTIES,
In order to promote international co-operation and to achieve international peace and security
> by the acceptance of obligations not to resort to war,
> by the prescription of open, just and honourable relations between nations,
> by the firm establishment of the understandings of international law as the actual rule of conduct among Governments, and
> by the maintenance of justice and a scrupulous respect for all treaty obligations in the dealings of organized peoples with one another,

Agree to this Covenant of the League of Nations.

The Covenant consists altogether of twenty-six articles or sections.

The first seven describe the League's constitution.

The next two are concerned with 'disarmament'—the reduction and limitation of national armaments by international agreement—as the first step towards peace and security.

But the only hope of 'disarmament' lay in all the heavily armed nations 'disarming' together. Nor was there any prospect of the nations greatly reducing their armed forces unless the others promised to help them if they

(which, however, became a Member of the League's International Labour Organization in August, 1934), Saudi Arabia, Costa Rica (admitted in 1922, retired in 1927) and Brazil (an original Member, retired in 1928, but remained a Member of the I.L.O.). It reached that total in September, 1934, after the admissions of that year and before Germany and Japan retired in 1935.

were attacked. This principle of 'collective security'—the strength of all for the defence of each—is the concern of the tenth, sixteenth, and seventeenth articles.

The eleventh article aimed at forestalling an attack and so preventing an outbreak of war. It enacts that 'any war or threat of war . . . is . . . a matter of concern to the whole League, and the League shall take any action that may be deemed wise and effectual to safeguard the peace of nations. . . .'

If, however, nations are not to attack one another in defence of what they conceive their rights to be, or fancy that they ought to be, the international community must make itself responsible for deciding what these rights are; for ensuring that they are respected so long as they do not conflict with justice as interpreted by impartial persons backed by world opinion; and for altering legal rights when they are incompatible with international justice. Peaceful means are needed for settling international disputes on these lines. Except for the important case* when the settlement of a dispute would require the alteration of the legal rights of one of the parties against its will, these means—including conciliation and arbitration as well as decision by a court of law—are provided by the remaining articles up to the fifteenth. Their use would not, however, rule out all possibility of war. This 'gap in the Covenant' was closed in 1928 by the Pact of Paris, or Briand-Kellogg Pact.†

Then follow four articles concerned with preserving and altering treaties. Among them is Article 18, enacting that no future treaty made by a Member of the League shall be binding unless it has been registered with the League and published. And Article 19 authorizes the

* See below, Chapter 15, pp. 157-160.
† See below, p. 114.

League to 'advise the reconsideration' of out-of-date treaties. This is as far as the Covenant goes towards asserting the principle that it is as much a part of the League's business to bring about the alteration of unjust treaties by peaceful means as to prevent any State from using force for the purpose of altering its legal rights to suit itself. The Covenant, as we shall see in Chapter 15, does not solve the problem of adapting the existing order to changing conditions.

After that come three articles (22 to 24) about international co-operation, especially in the interests of human welfare and social justice. This, together with the maintenance of international justice, is the positive and constructive side of the League's work as contemplated in the Covenant.* It includes the handling of all sorts of business (such as protecting 'minorities,' securing fair and humane labour conditions, suppressing the traffic in women, and supervising the traffic in arms and in dangerous drugs) that concern all nations but cannot be managed by separate governments. These articles include one designed to help certain backward races by making them a 'sacred trust for civilization' and placing them, by means of 'mandates,' under the supervision of the League.

Two more articles, one promising support for Red Cross organizations and the other dealing with amendments, complete the Covenant.

The diagram on page 94 shows the machinery of the League of Nations. Its instruments are not confined to the Assembly, the Council and the Secretariat of the League.

---

* A large part of this positive and constructive work for human welfare and social justice is performed by the International Labour Organization: see below, pp. 95, 96 and 98.

They also include the International Labour Organization and the Permanent Court of International Justice.

The Assembly, created by Article 3 of the Covenant, consists of not more than three Representatives of each Member of the League. Each State Member has one vote. Ordinary meetings of the Assembly took place in

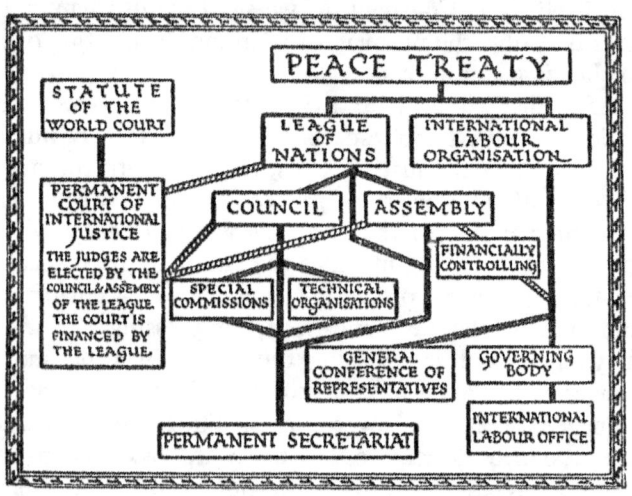

December, 1920, and thereafter annually for eighteen years, in September of each year. At the League's Sixth Assembly every European Member, except Italy and Spain, was represented by its Prime Minister or Foreign Minister or both. The League's Tenth Assembly was attended by eight Prime Ministers and twenty-one Foreign Ministers.

The Council, created by Article 4 of the Covenant, is a smaller body and has met much more often: latterly three times a year. It consists of permanent members and temporary members. The permanent members are those Great Powers who are Members of the League. The temporary members, originally four but eventually eleven in number, are Member States chosen by the whole League.

The Secretariat is the international Civil Service that forms the League's permanent staff. It is appointed by the Secretary General with the approval of the Council.

The Permanent Court of International Justice was set up in accordance with Article 14 of the Covenant. Its separate Statute was approved by the League's First Assembly in December, 1920. The first eleven judges—among them an American judge and a former British Lord Chancellor—and four deputy judges were elected* in September, 1921. In September, 1924, the number of judges was increased to fifteen and they were required to live at the Hague. In the first fourteen years of its existence the Court had before it sixty-four cases, delivered twenty-two judgments, and rendered twenty-seven advisory opinions. In no instance did any party to the litigation defy the authority of the Court by refusing to give effect to its decisions.

The International Labour Organization was set up by a separate section (Part XIII) of the Treaty of Versailles, the first peace treaty to recognize that the peace of the world may be in peril if its workers suffer 'injustice, hardship and privation.' At the annual conferences of the Organization, each State is represented by two government delegates as well as by one representative of its

* The main obstacle to setting up a permanent court of law in 1899 (see above, p. 34) was that the nations could not agree on the method of electing judges. The creators of the present Permanent Court of International Justice got over this difficulty. They worked out a compromise between the political doctrine of State equality and the political fact of the hegemony of the Great Powers. In the first fourteen years of its existence the Permanent Court handled three times as many cases as the old Hague Arbitration Court had handled since 1899.

employers and one of its workers. Employers and workers also sit on the Governing Body of the Office along with delegates from sixteen governments, including the eight States of chief industrial importance. Great Britain, Canada and India are among this number.

To sum up:

The authors of the Covenant, even though they sometimes, as was only natural, were not aware of all they were doing, had made a wonderful structure. . . . It has provided the greatest experiment in political machinery that the world has known. By its mere existence it has taught more about international co-operation and the prevention of war than all the theorists of the previous four hundred years of modern history.*

* Webster, *loc. cit.*, pp. 54–5.

CHAPTER 10

TEN SUCCESSFUL YEARS

From the first meeting of the League's Assembly in December, 1920, until its eleventh ordinary meeting in September, 1931, the Covenant worked well. There was rapid progress towards a real international organization. From time to time there dawned at Geneva a feeling for the whole society of nations, strong enough to unite the delegates in the conviction that the national patriotism of each was best served by working for the common interests of all. This feeling, and this impulse to put world interests first, were described by Lord Balfour as a 'collective sentiment.'

The advance towards world order took place in spite of great handicaps. Without the power and idealism of America the League could never have been created. The American President signed the Covenant which he had helped to draft, and a majority of the United States Senators voted for its ratification. But the majority was less than the two to one required by the American Constitution, and the United States kept out of the League. Then came a change of feeling towards Geneva; and, by the time the League began its work, a hostile government had been installed at Washington.

Nor did the League Great Powers give the Covenant full support. Among the smaller States, the ex-Allies saw it as a means of preserving the *status quo*, and the ex-neutrals tended to revert to their neutrality. Post-war Europe, war-weary though it was, retained the passions which excluded Germany from the League and extracted harsh peace terms. It thus became impossible to use the League machinery, as General Smuts and other framers of the Covenant had intended that it should be used, to revise the territorial settlement of the treaties. And, despite the efforts of Lord Cecil, the limitation of armaments was inevitably delayed.

Yet during this period the League achieved considerable success. Its institutions gained authority. It settled many international disputes of which some fifteen or twenty were serious. Its technical work for refugees was effective.* Financial and economic co-operation developed under its guidance. Its machinery was used to increase human welfare by fighting disease and other insidious enemies of mankind. The International Labour Organization† became the world focus of social progress. Germany entered the League. Russia co-operated, although she did not become a Member until 1934. The United States came to take part in most of the League's activities and her money payment to Geneva was almost as large as that of Great Britain.

Various elements combined to make the early success of the League possible. The whole system was based upon the rule of law. Not only the Covenant but treaties and customary international law were regarded in League deliberations as normally binding. Except for armaments, all vital inter-State relations were subjected to these rules. Third-party judgment was accepted in disputes con-

* For a brief and authoritative account of their work, see *The Refugee Question* by Sir John Hope Simpson, Oxford Pamphlet, No. 13.

† See *The International Labour Organization* by Harold Butler, Oxford University Press (1939).

cerning existing legal rights; and many changes were made in international law. The conception of justice began to have real power at Geneva. The publicity of League meetings enlisted public opinion in its support. The regularity of its proceedings enabled Member States to claim their rights. Such principles are essential to any working international system.*

It is not the function of this book to describe in detail either the nature or the working of the League of Nations. We do, however, desire to learn from the Geneva experiment such lessons as we can usefully apply to planning the lasting peace which we hope will follow the end of Hitler's War. We therefore add some further particulars of typical examples of how the League worked, and how it was meant to work, in the fields of social service, economics, settling disputes and averting war.

We have seen that the League was meant to extend the reign of law beyond national frontiers into the world of nations. It was not, as we said, to supplant but to supplement and support State governments. It was not empowered to intervene between the government and the citizens of a State whenever the interests of justice or liberty demanded, but only when authorized to do so by special treaties (such as those governing the relations of certain States to the religious, racial or linguistic minorities of their citizens), or if conditions became so bad as to threaten or cause war. Yet the League was available to help the local (national or State) government if it needed

* I am indebted to the League of Nations Union and to the Delegates of the Clarendon Press for permission to use the four preceding paragraphs: see *World Unity* by Maxwell Garnett, Oxford University Press (October, 1939).

and asked for such help in order to promote the welfare of its citizens.

When, for example, in 1930, the national Chinese Government found itself unable to cope with a number of problems of internal administration—involving public health, communications, economics and finance, education and flood-relief—the League selected and appointed expert advisers for each of these departments. China paid their expenses and they reported to the Chinese Government. Here are some of the results:

> Under the direction of a doctor from Yugoslavia, the Chinese Government established a Central Field Health Station, giving courses for sanitary inspectors and post-graduate courses for doctors. Sanitation and veterinary work was done in certain provinces of the interior.
>
> A campaign against malaria in the Yangtse valley was begun.
>
> A new Central Hospital was opened in 1933. Doctors chosen to serve on its staff were given travelling fellowships by the League's Health Organization to study hospital management in European countries; and the School of Nurses attached to the hospital trained its first class in 1933.
>
> Three League officials helped to form a quarantine organization.
>
> With the advice of the Communications and Transit Organization of the League, the Chinese Government made a road-building programme for seven provinces and many roads were already complete by 1936.
>
> League experts advised the Chinese Government on financial, agricultural, social and educational questions. There has followed a steady growth of the number of Chinese citizens fit to serve in the reconstruction and the government of their country.
>
> After the Yangtse floods of 1931, the League appointed Sir John Hope Simpson as High Commissioner for Flood Relief. He organized the work of re-embanking the river, gained the co-operation of the river provinces not then

ruled by the Government at Nanking, and saved many lives by feeding the people engaged in the work of reconstruction.

The rescue of Austria in 1922 is another example of the League's intervention to help a national government solve local problems which had got out of control. Austria was at that time threatened by bankruptcy and ruin, due to the fact that the new Austria, surrounded by enemies and with barely one-eighth of the inhabitants of the old empire of Austria-Hungary, was quite unable to support itself. Its money became worthless. A sum which in 1914 would have purchased a small house, in 1922 would only pay for a light luncheon. Vienna as the metropolis of a mighty State had acquired a population exceeding 2,000,000. Under the new conditions many of these people had little to do and were in danger of starving. Misery was making them dangerous and the country was threatened with revolution, which might have meant invasion and fighting between its neighbours. Five years later, thanks to the League, Austria had been saved and Vienna was fairly prosperous once more. How was it done?

On 6 September, 1922, after the leading countries of Europe had tried their hand at helping Austria and failed, the League set up a Committee with Lord Balfour as Chairman. That Committee solved the problem. Within a month (on 4 October, 1922) the League's scheme was accepted by the governments principally concerned, including that of Austria, and drew from the Austrian Chancellor the exclamation, 'Thank God, we can say to-day the League of Nations has not failed us!' The scheme was put into operation under a Commissioner appointed by, and responsible to, the League. After sixteen months' work the result was to balance the

Austrian budget, to fix the value of Austrian money, to produce a twentyfold increase in the amount of savings in the Austrian banks, to lower the cost of living, and to keep down unemployment within manageable limits.

Early in 1924 there was a sharp economic setback, which other countries also felt. But, with the help of the League's scheme, Austria was able to weather it. And on 1 October, 1936, Austria took over the reins and assumed responsibility for her national finances after fourteen years on the economic leading strings of the League of Nations.

Take next a sample of the settlement of an international dispute on a question of law. When the Permanent Court of International Justice was first established, Lord Reading, who had lately been Lord Chief Justice of England, observed that the Court could not function because 'No judge would ever give a decision against his country.' A year later his prophecy was contradicted by the event.

In the autumn of that year (1922) a dispute arose between Great Britain and France. Certain men of British nationality, but of Maltese race, living in the French protectorates of Tunis and Morocco, had been forced into the French army as conscripts. The British Foreign Office complained, and asked that the men might be allowed to return to their homes and to their work. The French replied that, according to their law, the men were Frenchmen. The British thereupon suggested arbitration; but the French rejected it on the ground that the British Government's curious rules of nationality could not be allowed to interfere with French internal jurisdiction. When, however, the British representative on the Council of the League of Nations mentioned the dispute there, the French readily agreed to ask the World

Court to decide the question of jurisdiction. Meanwhile the conscripts were allowed to go home.

The Court met on 8 January, 1923. The British case was put by the Attorney-General, Sir Douglas Hogg (now Lord Hailsham), who observed how great a thing it was that now, at long last, there was a World Court to which disputing nations could go for the settlement of disputes which they were unable to settle for themselves. After four weeks the Court gave a unanimous decision, the French judge voting with the others. The judgment went against the French claim to jurisdiction, and made the question of nationality one of international law. The French advocate thereupon offered to ask the Court to decide it. The British representative could not agree without consulting his government. But three weeks later the whole matter was amicably settled on the basis that, while these conscripts were not to be recalled to the colours, the British nationality laws should, for the future, operate differently in the French protectorates.

Our last example shows how the League worked, and was meant to work, for the prevention of war. One Monday in October, 1925, a Greek sentry was shot on the Bulgarian frontier. Three days later Greek troops invaded Bulgaria. The Bulgarian General Staff telegraphed to the officer commanding their forces:

> Make only slight resistance; protect the fugitive and stricken population; prevent the spread of panic in the Struma Valley; and do not expose the troops to unnecessary losses in view of the fact that the incident has been laid before the Council of the League of Nations, which is expected to stop the invasion.

The Bulgarian appeal to the League to intervene reached Geneva at half-past six the next morning, Friday. By half-past eleven telegrams had been sent out from Paris (since M. Briand was Acting-President of the League's Council) summoning a meeting of the Council for the following Monday. Other telegrams reminded Greece and Bulgaria that they were Members of the League, and called upon them to stop their armies until the Council of the League should meet. The telegram to Athens was just in time to prevent what would have been the first battle of the war.

When the Council met on the Monday, all but one of the members were present. They included the British Foreign Secretary, the French Foreign Minister, and the Foreign Minister of Sweden. The Council ordered the Greek armies to be withdrawn within three days. By Friday of that week the last Greek soldier had left Bulgaria. The League had stopped the invasion.

But this was not all. The Council was not content with stopping the fighting. It was determined, if possible, to remove the cause. So it sent a neutral Commission under Sir Horace Rumbold to examine on the spot the origin of the quarrel, fix the blame, and suggest how to prevent the same thing from happening again. All this was done without a hitch. When the Council met again in December, Greece agreed to pay £45,000 in damages, and both governments accepted the League's plan for preventing a similar explosion. And, when a frontier dispute did occur a few months later, there was no serious trouble.

CHAPTER 11

THE TIDE TURNS

★

In the autumn of 1931 the tide turned. In the following years the League failed to prevent the conquest of Manchuria, Abyssinia, Austria, Czecho-Slovakia and Albania, or the outbreak of Hitler's War.

During the League's early years the general peace had been secured by the dominant strength of its loyal Members. On each occasion when its authority was challenged—between the first* and the eleventh annual meetings of the Assembly, and notably when Yugoslavia attacked Albania in 1921, when Italy landed troops in Corfu in 1923, and when Greece invaded Bulgaria in 1925 †—Members of the League were ready to defend its covenants with an immense preponderance of power.

But in 1929 came the calamitous break in prices on the New York stock exchange. From Wall Street the slump spread to Europe. The flow of American loans, particularly to Germany, came to a sudden stop. Prosperity ceased to rise and began to decline. Unemployment and unrest increased. Germany was again unable to make her reparations payments to France and Great Britain, and this fact disturbed international relations. In the summer of 1931 the crisis became a catastrophe. In September

* General Zeligovski's Polish Army seized Vilna two months before the Assembly's first meeting.
† See above, pp. 103, 104.

the United Kingdom was forced off the gold standard: the Bank of England ceased to export gold. Foreign governments, who had treasured British paper in the belief that it would always retain its face value, were hard hit by the sudden drop in the gold value of the pound sterling. Thus all the Members of the League, and particularly the European Members, preoccupied as they already were with the economic crisis, found themselves further weakened overnight by the financial crash.

A body of Japanese conspirators chose this moment— the week-end when Britain abandoned the gold-standard —to strike the first blow against the League system. They invaded Manchuria on the night 18 September, 1931, against the orders of their Government. They tried to assassinate their own Foreign Secretary. The League's Assembly was in session at the time. By acting vigorously with the Japanese Government, the League could probably have nipped this conspiracy in the bud. But the statesmen at Geneva and their governments at home had their private troubles to think of when the Assembly met on that Monday morning.* They felt little inclination to act vigorously in so remote a region as the Far East. The moment passed. The Japanese Government fell and was replaced by another, more careless of its international obligations. The invasion continued; but gingerly, stage by stage, with a pause between each to see whether the League and the United States were going to move. Nothing of the sort happened. Eventually four great provinces were wrested by Japan from China.

In looking back upon these events, we must remember that neither the U.S.A. nor, at that time, the U.S.S.R. were members of the League. Without the co-operation of the United States, the Japanese aggression could not

* 21 September, 1931.

be stopped. But the British Government did not believe that they could rely upon American help. They therefore refused to take the lead in economic or financial measures to restrain Japan. The Americans,* however, claim that they were ready to join in collective action for the protection of China, and that the unwillingness of the British made such action impossible.

The failure to restrain Japan in 1931 and 1932 had disastrous consequences. One was that it helped to kill the Disarmament Conference.† When that Conference opened in February, 1932, Japanese bombs were falling on a suburb of Shanghai. The nations represented at the Conference doubted whether the League system of collective security could, after all, be relied upon when the aggressor was a Great Power. Their consequent unwillingness to reduce armaments put an end to the German policy of fulfilling the Versailles Treaty. It contributed to the fall of the last German Government that might fairly be called Republican, and to the rise of Herr Hitler to supreme power in Germany.

Another result of Japan's success on the continent across the water was Signor Mussolini's desire to follow suit. But whatever excuses there may have been for the League's failure to stop Japan's aggression in Manchuria, they did not apply to Italy's attack upon Abyssinia. In particular it was plain from the start that the Members of the League were amply strong enough to stop Italy. The knowledge that Britain would rather fight, unassisted

---

* *The Times* of 18 September, 1936, reviewing a new book on *The Far Eastern Crisis*, by Mr. Henry L. Stimson, Secretary of State at Washington in 1931, wrote:

'Significant is the proof he provides of the Administration's willingness, not only to collaborate with the League of Nations in decisive action, but also to act in advance of the League.'

† See below, p. 115.

if need be, than permit the occupation of Malta or Egypt, caused Signor Mussolini to look further afield for a less attractive but perhaps more easy prey. Had he known for certain that Britain and France would rather fight than allow him to annex Abyssinia, he would have 'renounced any offensive action.'*

Here, it seemed, was a heaven-sent opportunity for the League to recover the ground lost since September, 1931. A better test of the League's war-preventing machinery could not have been devised or desired. But the Great Powers chiefly concerned wanted Italy's co-operation against the growing might of Germany;† and they refused to let the test be made. The unfortunate statement by a Cabinet Minister in the House of Commons that 'we are not prepared to see a single ship sunk in a successful battle in the cause of Abyssinian independence' showed how slight was the value he attached to collective

* *Anno XIIII* by Emilio de Bono. On p. 202 the Marshal writes: 'In a strictly confidential note he [the Duce] informed me [in September, 1935, shortly before de Bono's troops were ordered to cross the frontier from the Italian Colony of Eritrea into Abyssinia] that in case we should find ourselves engaged with the British we should be obliged, of course, to renounce any offensive action, and content ourselves, at first, with restricting ourselves to a defensive which would assure the integrity of the Colony.'

† Signor Mussolini talked with M. Laval, the French Prime Minister, in January, 1935. In the same month he inquired of the British Foreign Secretary whether Britain 'had any interests' in Abyssinia. But neither then, nor when the British Prime Minister and Foreign Secretary had a full discussion of policy with him at Stresa in April, 1935, did he receive any clear warning that England or France had any objection to his Abyssinian plans. Much less was there any hint that France or Britain would fulfil their obligations under the Covenant 'to preserve, as against external aggression, the territorial integrity and existing political independence' of Abyssinia. After his experience at Stresa, nothing would persuade the Italian dictator that the League really meant business. He felt sure that, so far as the League was concerned, he was free to fight, to conquer and to annex.

security; but it did less than justice to the real British motives. There could, however, be no mistaking the fact that a great British fleet was brought home from the Mediterranean after being compelled, through no fault of the sailors, to stand idly by during a gross breach of a multilateral treaty to which Britain was a party. And yet it was only a few months since another British Foreign Secretary had assured the League's Sixteenth Assembly that

The League stands, and my country stands with it, for the collective maintenance of the Covenant in its entirety, and particularly for steady and collective resistance to all acts of unprovoked aggression.*

If the League's failure to prevent Italy from conquering and annexing Abyssinia was plain for all to see, so also were the reasons for that failure. It was not due to any fatal flaw in the Covenant. But it followed from the principal League Powers lacking any adequate 'collective sentiment,'† from the feebleness of their 'world loyalty,'‡ from their narrow conception of national interests as something different from (and more vital than) the interests of the world at large, and from their consequent reluctance to run the same risks for the protection of the covenants of the League as for the defence of their own territories. While the representatives of the governments were *talking* internationalism at Geneva, they were mostly *thinking* undiluted nationalism. The League's machinery,

---

* Sir Samuel Hoare, in a speech made in Geneva on 11 September, 1935. Sir Samuel had succeeded Sir John Simon as Foreign Secretary since the Stresa talks with Signor Mussolini. Sir Samuel resigned in December, 1935, and was followed by Mr. Anthony Eden. He, in turn, resigned the office of Foreign Secretary in February, 1938.
† See above, p. 97. ‡ See below, Chapter 20.

as G. K. Chesterton said of Christianity, had not been tried and found wanting: it had been found difficult and not been tried.

It is true that some minor inconveniences were found in the application of the Covenant. Most of them were described and remedies were suggested by the British Foreign Secretary* addressing the League's Assembly on 25 September, 1936. There was, for example, a series of questions relating to the power of the Council or the Assembly to depart from the normal rule of unanimity and proceed by a majority vote. Failure to resolve these questions, by reference to the Permanent Court of International Justice or in some other way, constantly hampered the League's work. This source of trouble became serious after Japan's insistence in 1931 that a unanimous vote, including that of the Japanese aggressor, was needed in order to exercise the League's power under Article 11 of the Covenant to 'take any action that may be deemed wise and effective to safeguard the peace of nations.' There was also the problem how to make Article 19 fully effective for the revision of treaties.†

All these obstacles to the smooth working of the League might be removed by changes of procedure such as Mr. Eden suggested. The amendment of the Covenant was not indispensable. But it was indispensable to strengthen the foundations on which the whole League structure rested in the minds of the citizens of its States Members. Much more might have been done in this field during the League's first ten years, when it was successfully averting war and helping to increase prosperity. If only the governments had then known the time

* Mr. Eden: see last footnote but two.
† See below, pp. 157 to 160.

of their visitation and understood the things which belonged to their peace!

As it was, the education of public opinion to understand the League of Nations, and how peace depended upon the whole-hearted support of the League by governments and peoples, was left, in most countries, to voluntary effort. In the United Kingdom most of this effort was directed by the League of Nations Union. Similar, but smaller, voluntary societies worked in some thirty other countries including all the larger States whether Members of the League or not, Soviet Russia alone excepted.

It is true that the League of Nations Union received a Royal Charter from the King in Council; that it worked under the patronage of leading members of all political parties, including every Prime Minister and ex-Prime Minister save only Mr. Ramsay MacDonald; that it had the co-operation of all the Churches,* teachers associations, associations of Local Education Authorities, the Trades Union Congress, and almost every organization of women; and that the public subscribed in twenty years approximately one million pounds to pay for its work. But its precarious receipts, including both capital and income, seldom exceeded £60,000 in any one year. This was less than the annual expenditure of many a school or college. It was not nearly enough for the education of all classes of British people to realize that their peace and prosperity depended upon the maintenance and development of the League system, to look upon the League as a vital British interest, and to feel bound to the League by a sentiment of loyalty and an invisible bond of ideals such as holds the British Commonwealth together. In parti-

* On one of its Committees, concerned with work through the Churches, Roman Catholic priests sat side by side with officers of the Salvation Army, with Ministers of the Free Churches, and with Clergymen of the Church of England.

cular, little impression was made upon the official classes and the older generation of naval and military advisers to His Majesty's Government: men who were in any case apt to look askance at voluntary organizations.

When, in 1931, the League's decline began and the danger of general war gradually appeared above the horizon, the League of Nations Union was tempted to try a short cut in the race between education and catastrophe. Realizing that the danger could best be averted by firm and far-seeing British leadership at Geneva, the Union sought to promote this result by adding agitation to education. The ship of State may indeed be born along by a tide of public opinion; but the forward movement will be less on a rough sea where the agitation goes but a little way below the surface of the water than on 'such a tide as moving seems asleep.' The agitation of the public mind may be made to look as though a deep impression had been made upon the people, but it does not take the place of education in fundamentals. Both processes may sometimes be needed; but they should be kept distinct. The educational effort of the League of Nations Union certainly suffered in the later 1930s because it was supposed to come from a tainted source where it might have been contaminated by agitation or 'propaganda.'

In most other countries, the League of Nations societies had an even harder task and more limited resources than the League of Nations Union in Great Britain and Northern Ireland. What a different story the historians might have had to tell of the 1930s if, during the 1920s, every League government had spent upon the education of its people in international affairs one-tenth of one per cent of the sum it spent on national armaments!

But instead of thus strengthening the foundations of

the League system, the governments devoted much attention to the improvement of its superstructure. Instead of grasping the fact that the League could do,* and could only do, what enough public opinion sufficiently desired it to do, many of the governments supposed that the effective working of the League could be assured by further commitments. They sought to bind the future, not by the increase of understanding and loyalty in the minds of men, but by pacts and promises on paper.

France took the lead in these efforts.

It had been in return for the offer of Anglo-American guarantees of her security that France had agreed at the Peace Conference not to press her demand for the Rhine frontier as a protection against a repetition of German aggression. When the guarantees were not forthcoming,† France sought compensation in military alliances with Poland, Czecho-Slovakia and Yugoslavia. But that was not enough. In order to satisfy France and other nervous nations, further guarantees were devised at Geneva and embodied in a Draft Treaty of Mutual Assistance; but it was rejected by the British (Labour) Government in 1924. So the League's Assembly made a new plan, the Geneva Protocol, with the same object in view; but it was rejected by the British (Conservative) Government in 1925.

Later in the same year, the British Foreign Secretary, Sir Austen Chamberlain, with the cordial co-operation of the French and German Ministers of Foreign Affairs,

* The restrictions imposed by the Covenant on what the League could do were less rigid than the checks put upon the Federal Government by the Constitution of the United States. Yet President Franklin Roosevelt, backed by public opinion, has been able to use the Federal Government for purposes, such as unemployment insurance, for which it was never intended and which certainly infringed States' rights as previously understood and described by constitutional lawyers.

† See below, Chapter 21.

A Lasting Peace

M. Briand and Herr Stresemann, attacked the problem of European security from a new angle. They produced the Locarno agreements. In these treaties, Britain and Italy joined with Germany, France and Belgium to ensure the defence of Germany's western frontier against aggression *from either side*. The Locarno treaties came into force in September, 1926, when Germany joined the League.

'Locarno,' said Sir Austen at the time, 'is only a beginning.' It was followed, in 1928, by the Pact of Paris for the Renunciation of War.* By this treaty, sixty-three States, including all the principal countries in the world, renounced war as an instrument of national policy and pledged themselves never to seek the settlement of their disputes except by pacific means. A queer result of the treaty has been the shyness of subsequent aggressors to declare war or to acknowledge the existence of the wars for which they have been responsible. A more solid consequence of the pact was foreseen by Senator Borah when he said: 'It is not conceivable that America will stand idly by in case of a gross breach of a multilateral treaty to which it is a party.' When gross breaches of the treaty were committed by Japan (in 1931), and afterwards by Italy (in 1935), the Administration of the United States did not 'stand idly by.'

While the scope of the Pact of Paris was worldwide, the Locarno treaties were primarily concerned with the security of a particular region. They were, however, intended to be followed by similar regional pacts covering, between them, the whole of Europe. But nothing came

* The Pact is better known as the Briand-Kellogg Pact, after the French Foreign Minister and the American Secretary of State who took the initiative in negotiating the treaty. But the original suggestion came from a private citizen of the United States, Professor James T. Shotwell.

of this idea except the Franco-Soviet treaty* by which France and Russia undertook to consult and, consistently with the Covenant, to support each other if either were threatened with aggression by any European State.

Meanwhile the World Disarmament Conference assembled in Geneva in February, 1932, while Japan was making war on China. Not only the States Members of the League, but the United States of America, Soviet Russia and other non-member States helped to prepare for this Conference and took part in it from the outset. The Conference achieved no disarmament at all. By neglecting the need for a change of mind that would have won public support for their security pacts and so made collective defence every bit as dependable as national defence, the nations, or their governments, had made it impossible for the more nervous among them to reduce their armaments. By their slowness to begin reducing armaments to the German level, the victorious Powers convinced Germany that she could only attain equality of rights by levelling up: it was no use waiting for an all-round levelling down. In October, 1933, Herr Hitler's eight-months-old Government announced that Germany would leave the Disarmament Conference forthwith, and would retire from the League itself in two years' time. From then on, by the extent and duration of her secret re-armament, Germany increased the reluctance of the other nations to reduce their own strength. So the Conference failed. And, since 1936, when Italy's annexation of Abyssinia showed that the hope of collective security was also at an end, Europe followed Germany's lead and re-armed with a swiftness and on a scale that again made war inevitable.

* This treaty was signed in May, 1935, and came into force on 27 March, 1936.

CHAPTER 12

APPEASEMENT

The rearmament of Europe in general and of Great Britain* in particular lagged behind that of Germany. That was mainly because the British people did not yet know what to make of Herr Hitler, his violent acts and his specious promises. Great Britain was at first disposed to accept his assurances that Germany aimed only at equality with the other Great Powers, at being mistress in her own house, and—though this came a little later—at applying the principle of self-determination to incorporate in the Reich the German districts just beyond her borders.

Herr Hitler's first flagrant violation of the public law of Europe occurred on Saturday, 7 March, 1936, when he moved his troops into the demilitarized zone on both sides of the Rhine. This was an outrageous and ostentatious breach, not only of the dictated treaty of Versailles, but also of the freely negotiated Locarno pact. On the same day he offered the world, in somewhat vague terms, a new peace pact to last twenty-five years, an air pact, and Germany's return to the League of Nations. In view of this offer the British Government refrained, and persuaded France to refrain, from the military intervention

---

* It was on 17 February, 1937, that the British Government announced that they intended to spend on rearmament the sum of £400,000,000 in the first instance, and up to a possible limit of £1,500,000,000 in five years.

prescribed by the Locarno treaty. Germany would not have been able to resist prompt military action by France and Britain at that time. But two months later, when the German troops had occupied and begun to fortify the frontier, the Führer did not even trouble to reply to His Majesty's Government's enquiry what exactly his peace offer had meant.

A few weeks afterwards, on 4 July, 1936, the prestige of France and Britain suffered a further blow, when they acknowledged the final and complete failure of the League's half-hearted attempt to stop Italian aggression in Abyssinia.

There then occurred a revulsion of public opinion against the League system. The smaller nations hastened to repudiate their obligations. In Britain and France the public were partially persuaded that peace could be better preserved by ignoring the distinction between peaceful change, which the League approved in principle, and violent change, which the Covenant forbade; and by confining the activities of the League to non-contentious matters.

It was, however, plain enough that, if the League's preponderance of power was not going to be used to prevent violence, the aggressively minded or 'hungry' States—notably Germany and Italy and Japan—would satisfy their appetites by devouring the League's weaker Members one at a time. The only doubt concerned the size of their appetites and whether they would grow as they were fed. Many people in the United Kingdom chose to assume that Germany's ambitions were so limited that it would be safe for Britain to take refuge with France behind her Maginot line* while Germany sated

---

* The line of fortifications recently built by France on her eastern frontier from Luxemburg to the Rhine.

herself with the prey she could seize across her eastern and south-eastern borders. As for Italy, it was generally felt that, so soon as the danger from Germany disappeared, it would be easy to cope with Signor Mussolini. This policy had the great advantage of being purely negative. Nothing needed to be done about it. It was merely necessary to wait and see.

An alternative positive policy was advocated in some quarters: for example, by the present writer in a letter published in *The Times* on 24 July, 1936. This alternative policy* involved an effort to restore collective security. The international community, said the letter, must be stronger—spiritually as well as materially—than any likely aggressor or group of aggressors; and the Members of the League, including Britain, must be as ready to use their strength in collective action 'to protect the covenants of the League' as in defence of their own territories.

But the positive policy was not confined to guarantees against aggression. 'In order to preserve law and order in Europe during these next critical years' a new attempt should be made to revise unjust treaties and remove national discontents by a process of peaceful change. The letter from which these quotations are made insisted, however, upon the need for avoiding any appearance of the League Powers 'whose superiority of military power over Germany is incontestable' having been frightened into making concessions.

Britain and France were not yet ready for this alternative dual policy of combining resolute resistance to aggression with the rebuilding of world order. They preferred inaction. They had yet to be convinced that, if

---

* See also an article on 'Germany and Geneva,' in the *Contemporary Review* for March, 1937.

APPEASEMENT

they did not make a common front against aggression while they and their fellow Members of the League still possessed preponderant power and while the League's system of collective security was still capable of being restored, they would have to make their stand at a less favourable moment when the forces of aggression were relatively far stronger.

The lesson which Britain and France had yet to learn had, however, been expounded with amazing frankness by Herr Hitler in *Mein Kampf*. Describing the technical method of the Viennese Socialists, from whom he professed to have learned the ways of terrorization and gangsterism which he himself adopted and afterwards perfected, Herr Hitler wrote:

> They would select the adversary whom they thought most formidable, and on a signal given would bombard him with a regular drum-fire of lies and calumnies. They kept it up till the nerves of the other side broke down, and to regain some peace they sacrificed the victim of the odium.
> Only, they never got their peace, the fools!
> Repeat the same performance over and over again; and dread of the mad dogs exercises through suggestion the effect of paralysis.*

But Mr. Eden, the British Foreign Secretary, refused to be paralysed as he watched the German and Italian dictators sharpening their claws in Spain† and preparing to pounce upon their next victims. Already, in the autumn

---

* One Hundred and Eighty-first German Edition, p. 45, quoted by R. C. K. Ensor in Oxford Pamphlet, No. 3 (1939), p. 7. Ensor adds: 'You could scarcely want a better description of how Herr Hitler himself has dealt with his opponents—first in internal German politics, and later in the international field with such men as Schuschnigg and Beneš.'

† The civil war in Spain began in Spanish Morocco on 17 July, 1936. Italy and Germany helped with men and material. So also did Soviet Russia on the other side.

of 1936, Mr. Eden had declared that 'because there has been one failure' to apply the principles of the Covenant and stop aggression 'that is not a reason why the world should turn its back upon an endeavour which is the only alternative to catastrophe and chaos.' In September of the following year he took the lead in calling a conference of the Mediterranean Powers at Nyon when agreement was quickly reached on counter-measures against submarine piracy in that sea. The counter-measures applied the League's principle of collective resistance to aggression; and the menace vanished at once. Again on 12 February, 1938, Mr. Eden reiterated his conviction that the League way was the right way: 'The world—I say "the world" deliberately—will be built again on the same foundations.'

Eight days later he ceased to be responsible for British foreign policy. His going was deplored at home by his late colleagues no less than by the political opponents of the Government. Other nations loyal to the League received the news with consternation. This was particularly true of those statesmen who, like the French Foreign Minister, had worked most intimately with Mr. Eden at Geneva. In Washington his loss was felt as a grievous blow to the Roosevelt doctrine (announced by the President at Chicago in October, 1937) that 'The peace-loving nations must make a concerted effort to uphold the laws on which alone peace can rest secure.' Only the avowed enemies of the League and of international order, notably in Germany and Italy where Mr. Eden's dismissal had been demanded by the Dictators, were left to triumph over the fall of the British Foreign Secretary.

Mr. Eden resigned rather than abandon the policy of collective resistance to violent aggression. 'We must stand by our conception of international order without which

APPEASEMENT

there can be no lasting peace,' he told his constituents on 26 February, 1938. He would not be responsible for a policy of acquiescence. But no sooner had he left office than 'appeasement'—the 'Chamberlain experiment' as it was called at first—became the order of the day. It provided the hungry Powers, particularly Germany, with a succession of victims. Austria was the first to be pounced upon: she was seized on 14 March, 1938. By that move Herr Hitler secured his southern frontier, just as his western frontier had been secured two years earlier by his occupation of the demilitarized zone on either side of the Rhine. At the same time, by incorporating Austria in the German Reich, he added ten per cent to the population, and eighteen per cent to the area, of Germany.

The next victim was Czecho-Slovakia. The same, the invariable, technique was followed. On 1 March, 1936, a few weeks after his troops entered the Rhineland, Herr Hitler had declared that possible attacks on Austria or Czecho-Slovakia were 'foreign lies.'*

When the day came for the first of these attacks, the Führer assured the Czecho-Slovak Minister in Berlin that Germany had no aggressive designs against Czecho-Slovakia: the German troops which were to occupy Austria on that day had received strict orders to keep at least fifteen kilometres from the Bohemian frontier. But no sooner was Herr Hitler in possession of Austria than he began to stalk his next prey.

He had to move warily. France was allied to Czecho-Slovakia besides being bound to her by the League Covenant which also bound Great Britain. And Great Britain could not allow France to be defeated by Germany. Moreover, there was Soviet Russia to consider. Herr Hitler feared to go far until he could be sure that Britain

* *Britain and the Dictators* (1938), by R. W. Seton-Watson, p. 263

would not fight in defence of Czecho-Slovakia. When he discovered that appeasement was still the order of the day in London,* he hesitated no longer. He began his 'regular drum-fire of lies and calumnies.'† He prepared to 'repeat the same performance' as in March, 1936, and in March, 1938. Gradually he made up his mind that it was safe for him to invade Czecho-Slovakia. By the end of September this conviction could not have been shaken by any threat from Mr. Chamberlain. It may well be that Czecho-Slovakia and the other victims of German aggression would have survived in peace if Mr. Eden's policy of collective security had not been abandoned in February. But war must have resulted from a sudden return to this policy in September. For this reason, although we may condemn the policy of appeasement—and it is easy to be wise after the event—we can hardly blame Mr. Chamberlain for accepting its inevitable result at Munich.

The Munich Conference met on 29 September, 1938. 'Dread of the mad dogs' had, as Herr Hitler had foreseen, 'the effect of paralysis' on the British and French Premiers who had come there to meet the German and Italian Dictators. 'To regain some peace,' as *Mein Kampf* has it, Mr. Chamberlain and M. Daladier 'sacrificed the victim of the odium'; and when the Czech representatives were at last admitted to the Conference (at 1.30 a.m. on 30 September) they were told that the decision had already

* 'At a luncheon party in London Mr. Chamberlain assured the American journalists who were present that neither Great Britain nor Russia nor even France would fight for the independence of Czecho-Slovakia. An account of these assurances was published by Mr. Joseph Driscoll in the *Montreal Daily Star* of 14 May. It was at once relayed to Berlin. Herr Hitler thereupon prepared for action.' (Harold Nicolson, *Why Britain is at War*, pp. 79, 80. See also *Munich and the Dictators*, by R. W. Seton-Watson, p. 39).

† See the quotation from *Mein Kampf* on p. 119 above.

been taken.* Britain and France were 'disinteresting themselves.' The Czechs felt compelled to acquiesce. Early the next morning, 1 October, German troops entered the Sudeten lands† of Bohemia. The military frontier of Czecho-Slovakia—'a fortress created by God Himself,' as Bismarck had called it, together with their own Maginot line by which the Czechs had sought to make it impregnable—was in Herr Hitler's hands. 'We have suffered total and unmitigated defeat' was Mr. Winston Churchill's verdict upon these proceedings.‡

Meanwhile Herr Hitler was busy with assurances to his next victim but one. On 26 September he said 'The Sudetenland is the last territorial claim which I shall have to make in Europe.' On 30 September he signed with Mr. Chamberlain a declaration 'of the desire of our two peoples never to go to war with one another again.' On 9 October Herr Hitler stated: 'We want nothing; no people can need peace more than we.' On 6 November: 'We only want our quiet and the right to live.' On 1 January, 1939: 'We have but one wish, that in the coming year we may be able to make our contribution to the general pacification.' And on 30 January: 'I think there will be a long period of peace.'

The old technique succeeded yet once more. On 15 March Herr Hitler entered Prague. A week later he annexed Memel.§

That was the end of 'appeasement.' Britain had learned her lesson. Henceforth the country was united in its

* Seton-Watson, *Munich and the Dictators*, p. 104.
† In these border regions lived some 3,500,000 German-speaking citizens of Czecho-Slovakia. For three centuries before 1918 they had been ruled from Vienna; but never from Berlin.
‡ In the House of Commons on 6 October, 1938.
§ Cf. Lord Lloyd's pamphlet, *The British Case* (1939), pp. 45, 47.

determination to resist further acts of German aggression. That this change of mind extended to the Cabinet was indicated by the speech of the Foreign Secretary* on 20 March, 1939, and proved by the British guarantee to Poland eleven days later.

The British and French Governments had been re-arming rapidly before,† and more rapidly after, the 'total and unmitigated defeat' of Munich. The guarantee to Poland began the effort to build up a 'Peace Front' against aggression. On 13 April, after Signor Mussolini had pulled down Albania during the Easter week-end, Great Britain extended her guarantee to Roumania and Greece, and a few days later opened negotiations with both Russia and Turkey. The Peace Front was, of course, purely defensive. It did not contemplate any attack upon the aggressive Powers. And it did not imply any control over the smaller States, which it sought to protect from domination by Germany.

On 29 June Lord Halifax explained the Peace Front policy at the annual dinner of the Royal Institute of International Affairs. The Foreign Secretary declared that 'Our foreign policy must constantly bear in mind the immediate present and the more distant future. . . . Our immediate task is to resist aggression.' When there is no more danger of aggression his Majesty's Government would 'be ready to pool their best thought with others in order to end the present political and economic insecurity' and 'reach a settlement which the world can trust.' But 'the first resolve is to stop aggression'; and again, 'In the event of further aggression we are resolved to use at once the whole of our strength in fulfilment of our pledges to resist it.'

---

* Lord Halifax had succeeded Mr. Eden at the Foreign Office in February, 1938.   † See the footnote on p. 116 above.

This dual policy—of stopping aggression and then rebuilding world order as part of a general settlement—united all but a small minority of British public opinion. The supporters of the Government, some of whom (like Mr. Eden, Mr. Winston Churchill and Mr. Duff Cooper) had distrusted the policy of appeasement long before the Ides of March, were all now convinced that the Empire was threatened by German aggression. The Labour Party had for a long time regarded Nazi Germany and her Axis partner, Fascist Italy, as hostile to the Left in general and to Trade Unions in particular. The Liberal Opposition loathed the suppression of free institutions at both ends of the Axis and especially the whole horrid system of secret police, concentration camps and licensed brutality employed by the National Socialist régime for the persecution of the Jews and for the suppression of liberty of thought or speech about political affairs. Even Communists supported a policy of which the immediate object was to resist aggression by the originators of the Anti-Comintern Pact. And the friends of the League of Nations, of all parties and of none, rejoiced in both aspects of the dual policy: in the knowledge that a basic principle of the Covenant was to be applied immediately, and in the hope that eventually the League would be reconstructed and restored for the purpose of conducting and guiding the development of the new world order in the right direction.*

The dual policy did more than win the support of public opinion in the United Kingdom. It secured the co-operation of all the British Dominions, save one, with Great Britain and France and Poland in resistance to Herr Hitler's next act of aggression.

Had Britain and France been united in support of the

* See footnote on p. 56 above.

same dual policy two or three years earlier, Austria, Czecho-Slovakia and Poland might never have been overrun. But, as we have seen, the British people and their government needed to have the same performance repeated, as Herr Hitler had written, 'over and over again' before they learned their lesson. This lesson was that, in a close-knit society of nations, the defence of each may well be a vital interest of all. That was part of the truth which the League of Nations Union, with its limited resources and in the limited time available, had failed to impress upon the British nation as a whole. But the effect of the lesson, when at last the British nation did learn it from so many tragic repetitions, was not at all what Herr Hitler had foreseen. He expected 'paralysis.' What he got was grim determination of the sort that made Mr. Eden resign office on 20 February, 1938, and that confounded the captain of the *Admiral Graf Spee* off the River Plate on 13 December, 1939.

CHAPTER 13

HOW HITLER'S WAR BEGAN

The dual policy was adopted too late to save Poland from invasion.

Anyone who cares to turn over the leaves of a historical atlas will observe that Poland and Danzig formed no part of the Holy Roman Empire during the Middle Ages. In modern times, down to the first partition of Poland in 1772, the lands ruled by German princes were divided into two parts by the Polish corridor. On its eastern boundary the Vistula flows down from Warsaw to the sea at Danzig. On the west side of the corridor lay the Holy Roman Empire which, by the middle of the eighteenth century, had become 'neither Holy nor Roman nor an Empire.' On the east side, beyond the Vistula, stretched the territory conquered from the Slavs by the Teutonic Knights in the thirteenth and fourteenth centuries. At one time these lands formed the Baltic coast from Danzig north-eastwards as far as the Russian border on the southern shore of the Gulf of Finland. By the middle of the eighteenth century all this region, except for a small East Prussia, belonged either to the Kingdom of Poland or to the Russian Czar. East Prussia was still outside the Empire, separated from it and from the rest of Prussia by the Polish corridor.

Then came the partitions of Poland between Russia, Austria and Prussia. Poland and the corridor disappeared from the map of Europe until they were restored, nearly a century and a half later, by the Treaty of Versailles.

Before Germany laid down her arms at the end of the World War, she agreed that the future Poland 'should include the territories inhabited by indisputably Polish population, which should be assured a free and secure access to the sea.' This was President Wilson's thirteenth point.

The only sea (writes Harold Nicolson) to which Poland could possibly be given access was the Baltic. The only means by which she could obtain this access was along her great river the Vistula. Yet at the very mouth of the Vistula was situated the German city of Danzig. How, therefore, was such access to be not only 'free' but 'secure'? It was . . . decided that Danzig should be created a free and unarmed city under a High Commissioner appointed by the League of Nations with a Senate and constitution of her own.*

Poland also obtained the use of Danzig harbour under certain conditions. But the population of the old Polish corridor was still predominantly Polish although some of the towns were German. So the new Poland, like the old, included the corridor. Without being allowed to annex the city of Danzig, Poland obtained what promised to be 'free and secure access to the sea.'

For many years the peace of Europe seemed more likely to be disturbed by the Polish corridor than by any of the other territorial settlements that followed the World War. It is true that East Prussia could be reached from Germany by sea (as easily as Northern Ireland from England) without crossing Poland; and that passenger trains, with the carriage doors locked, made Polish visas unnecessary

* *Why Britain is at War*, p. 108.

HOW HITLER'S WAR BEGAN

for travellers between western Germany and Danzig or East Prussia. Even so, Danzig and the corridor were a perpetual source of irritation to the German people.

Herr Hitler put an end to the squabbles between the Polish and German Governments. Within a year of becoming Chancellor of the Reich he devised the German-Polish Agreement of 26 January, 1934. By this treaty the two Governments agreed 'to base their mutual relations on the principles laid down in the Pact of Paris,'* and guaranteed peace between the two countries for a period of ten years. The treaty had survived for half this period when it was denounced by the Führer on 28 April, 1939.

Meanwhile the German-Polish agreement served to keep Poland quiet until it was her turn to be the next victim of German aggression. On 7 March, 1936, just before marching his troops into the Rhineland, Herr Hitler declared in the Reichstag:

> I would like the German people to understand the inner motives of National Socialist foreign policy, which finds it painful that the outlet to the sea of a people of 35 millions is situated on territory formerly belonging to the Reich, but which recognizes that it is unreasonable and impossible to deny a State of such a size as this any outlet to the sea at all.

Again, on 20 February, 1938, within three weeks of seizing Austria, Herr Hitler spoke in the Reichstag of his

> sincere gratification to be able to establish that, in our relationship to the State [Poland] with which we had perhaps the greatest differences, not only has there been a *détente*, but that . . . a constant improvement in relations has taken place.

Once more, on 26 September, 1938—on the eve of Munich and of his occupation of the Sudeten district of Czecho-Slovakia—the Führer told the Reichstag:

* See above, p. 114.

> The most difficult problem I had to face was that of our relations with Poland. . . . A people of 33 millions will always strive for an outlet to the sea. A way of understanding then had to be found; it has been found; and it will ever be further extended. . . . It was a real work of peace, of more worth than all the chattering in the League of Nations Palace at Geneva.

Finally, on 30 January, 1939, six weeks before seizing Prague and destroying what was left of Czecho-Slovakia (with some little help from Poland in the neighbourhood of Teschen), Herr Hitler reminded the Reichstag of the value of the German-Polish agreement. He added:

> During the troubled months of the past year the friendship between Germany and Poland was one of the reassuring factors in the political life of Europe.

But when, in March, 1939, German aggression had wiped Czecho-Slovakia off the map. Poland came next on the Führer's list of victims. On 21 March he proposed to Poland that Danzig should return to the Reich and that an extra-territorial railway and motor road should link up East Prussia with the Reich across the Polish corridor. On 28 April he repeated this demand in a formal memorandum to the Polish Government and coupled with it his denunciation of the pact of non-aggression. Since it was no longer of any value to him, he tore it up.

As we have seen, the events of March put an end to the British policy of appeasement. On 20 March, five days after the German occupation of Prague, Lord Halifax announced in the House of Lords that 'His Majesty's Government have not failed to draw the moral from these events,' since

> in all quarters there is likely immediately to be found a very much greater readiness to consider whether the acceptance

of wider mutual obligations, in the cause of mutual support, is not dictated, if for no other reason than the necessity of self-defence.

The British guarantee to Poland followed eleven days later. The British and French Governments undertook that 'in the event of any action which clearly threatened Polish independence, and which the Polish Government accordingly considered it vital to resist with their national forces, His Majesty's Government would feel themselves bound at once to lend the Polish Government all support in their power.' On August 25—two days after the signing of the Russo-German pact—these guarantees to Poland were translated into formal treaties of mutual assistance.

We have seen how the British and French guarantees to Poland were followed by guarantees to Roumania and Greece and by efforts to extend the Peace Front to Russia and Turkey. The negotiations with Russia failed completely. They had hardly begun when M. Litvinov was suddenly dismissed from office. As Russian Commissar for Foreign Affairs he had become well known at Geneva where he had been a good friend of the League of Nations and a vigorous advocate of collective security. The Peace Front against German aggression met with his warm approval. But after he had fallen the negotiations with Russia made little or no progress. They came to a sudden stop on 21 August with the amazing* news of the Nazi-

* In the British Blue Book the first suggestion that anything of the kind might be afoot is contained in Sir Nevile Henderson's despatch of 15 August, quoted on p. 133 below. But, according to the French Yellow Book, the French Ambassador in Berlin suggested the possibility of a German-Soviet Agreement on 13 June; and, as early as 16 December, 1938, the French Minister at Sofia reported that the Prime Minister of Bulgaria did not 'exclude the possibility' of a Russo-German pact and a fourth partition of Poland. (*Yellow Book*, pp. 54, 66.)

Soviet pact. When it was signed in Moscow two days later, Herr Hitler thought he had checkmated the Peace Front. Poland would now be at his mercy, not only because it would be impossible for her to receive any effective military help from the Western democracies but also because, as the Führer at first supposed, the British and French guarantees would now be withdrawn.

In fact, however, the effect of the Nazi-Soviet pact of non-aggression was not at all what Herr Hitler expected. A personal letter addressed to him by the British Prime Minister on 22 August assured him that Great Britain's obligation to Poland would certainly be fulfilled. If the case should arise, declared Mr. Chamberlain, the British Government 'are resolved, and prepared, to employ without delay all the forces at their command, and it is impossible to foresee the end of hostilities once engaged.'

While the Nazi-Soviet Pact failed to destroy the Peace Front it had other far-reaching effects most damaging to the National Socialist régime. It shook the Berlin-Rome axis almost, if not quite, off its bearings: the Italian end of the axis was not ready for such a violent change of direction. It destroyed the prospect that Japan might help Germany against the Western Powers: Japan still believed in the principles of the anti-Comintern Pact. It spoiled the hope of a *Drang nach Osten*: a purely German drive through Poland to the Ukraine and the Black Sea. It gave Russia a free hand in the Baltic so far as Germany was concerned and so restricted Germany's supremacy in that sea. It antagonized Spain, Portugal and the Latin American peoples who saw in Soviet Russia the worst enemy of all good Catholics. It strengthened the bonds between the United States and the Western democracies of Europe. And, because of its reversal of the policy of *Mein Kampf*, it shocked those German people who were not prepared to follow blindly wherever their Führer might choose to lead.

Meanwhile a 'regular drum-fire of lies and calumnies' had marked out Poland as the next victim on Herr Hitler's list. It began with the accusation, in the German memorandum* of 28 April, that, by accepting the British guarantee, 'the Polish Government have subordinated themselves to a policy inaugurated from another quarter aiming at the encirclement of Germany.'

There followed a violent anti-Polish agitation in Germany. As its intensity increased, the local situation at Danzig rapidly became worse. By the end of June the British Consul-General in Danzig was reporting military preparations in the city. After a lull in July the British Ambassador in Warsaw told Lord Halifax, on 9 August, of the German Press campaign against Poland and of 'the daily military and civil violation of all the treaties on which Poland's rights are based.' The same day the German Government intervened directly with a threatening note to Poland about the Danzig problem. A week later, on 15 August, the permanent head of the German Foreign Office told the British Ambassador in Berlin that the German 'Government did not, would not and could not believe that Britain would fight under all circumstances whatever folly the Poles might commit.' The German State Secretary, reported the Ambassador,

> seemed very confident, and professed to believe that Russian assistance to the Poles would not only be entirely negligible, but that the U.S.S.R. would even in the end join in sharing in the Polish spoils. Nor did my insistence on the inevitability of British intervention seem to move him.†

The Nazi-Soviet Pact was announced within a week

* See above, p. 129.
† *Documents concerning German-Polish relations* (Cmd. 6106), p. 91.

of this interview. When Sir Nevile Henderson* conveyed Mr. Neville Chamberlain's letter† on that subject to Herr Hitler at Berchtesgaden on 23 August, the Führer was 'excitable and uncompromising'; his language was 'violent and exaggerated both as regards England and Poland.' Herr Hitler observed, in reply to the Ambassador's repeated warnings that direct action against Poland would mean war with Great Britain, that 'Germany had nothing to lose and Great Britain much; that he did not desire war but would not shrink from it if it were necessary; and that his people were much more behind him than last September.'‡ In a second interview with the Ambassador on the same day, Herr Hitler declared his determination to attack Poland if 'another German were ill-treated in Poland.' He was, he said, fifty years old: he preferred war now to when he would be fifty-five or sixty.§

He started his war nine days later. During the interval attempts had been made to avert it by the President of the United States (on 23 and 24 August), by the King of the Belgians (on 23 August), by the King of the Belgians and the Queen of the Netherlands jointly (on 28 August), by the Pope (on 24 August), and by Signor Mussolini (on 31 August). None of these efforts was of any avail. At dawn on 1 September, the Führer's troops invaded Poland and his aeroplanes began their bombing raids on Warsaw and other Polish towns. At 5 a.m. on Sunday, 3 September, Lord Halifax telegraphed to the British Ambassador in Berlin instructing him to hand the following note to the German Foreign Secretary at 9 o'clock that morning:

* British Ambassador in Berlin. † See above, p. 132.
‡ *Documents concerning German-Polish relations*, p 100.
§ *Loc. cit.*, p. 100.

Sir,—In the communication which I had the honour to make to you on the 1st September, I informed you, on the instructions of His Majesty's Principal Secretary of State for Foreign Affairs, that unless the German Government were prepared to give His Majesty's Government in the United Kingdom satisfactory assurances that the German Government had suspended all aggressive action against Poland and were prepared promptly to withdraw their forces from Polish territory, His Majesty's Government in the United Kingdom would, without hesitation, fulfil their obligations to Poland.

Although this communication was made more than twenty-four hours ago, no reply had been received but German attacks upon Poland have been continued and intensified. I have accordingly the honour to inform you that, unless not later than 11 a.m., British Summer Time, to-day 3rd September, satisfactory assurances to the above effect have been given by the German Government and have reached His Majesty's Government in London, a state of war will exist between the two countries as from that hour.*

The Prime Minister read this out to the House of Commons later in the day. And he added: 'That was the final note. No such undertaking was received by the time stipulated, and, consequently, this country is at war with Germany.'

* *Documents, loc. cit.,* p. 178.

CHAPTER 14

WAR AND PEACE AIMS

That is how Britain and France came to be at war with Germany for the second time in a generation. Herr Hitler chose to fight rather than give up the use of force as a means to enlarge Germany at the expense of his weaker neighbours. But Britain and France chose to fight rather than allow Germany's aggression to continue unchecked. Who then was responsible for the war?

That is a question that must be left to the jury: the public opinion of mankind. *Securus judicat orbis terrarum.* What the world as a whole says goes. Apart from Russia who has been paid a big price by Germany for her favour, and with the doubtful exception of Italy where the government and the people seem to be divided on this issue, the whole world is practically unanimous in laying the blame on Herr Hitler. This consensus of opinion owes a great deal to the fact that Britain and France acquiesced three times in violent acts by the Führer (when he marched into the demilitarized Rhineland, when he seized Austria and when he took possession of the Sudeten lands) before still another act of violence (his occupation of Prague) finally destroyed the Allies' confidence in his promises to abstain from further acts of aggression. It was only then that they decided to fight rather than allow Herr Hitler to proceed unchecked on his way to dominate Europe and the world. Anyhow, in a moral judgment of this kind, the world is unlikely to be wrong. The war is Hitler's War.

In Chapter 13 we traced the last steps that led to war. We know how it began. We cannot be sure how it will end. But it is likely to finish as the Allies wish because they have the advantage over Germany in all, or almost all, the sinews of war. Their man-power is the larger and their material resources are greater. They are supported by the moral judgment of the majority of mankind and, particularly, of the United States. As these words are written it certainly looks as though the British and French Empires have only to persevere in order to succeed.

Let us then assume that the war will end as the Allies intend. What do they mean the finish to be? And what is to follow it?

The aims of the Allies have not altered since Lord Halifax explained British foreign policy on 29 June, 1939. In that speech he stated boldly and plainly what are 'our aims in the immediate present, and our aims in the future; what we are doing now, and what we should like to see done as soon as circumstances permit.'

The immediate aim of this dual policy* was originally, as we have seen, 'to stop aggression.' It is now also to repair, so far as we may, the damage already done by Germany's aggression against her weaker neighbours.†
The remoter aim is 'to get on with the constructive work of building peace.' Speaking after nearly three months

---

* On 28 March, 1940, the British and French Governments agreed to a 'solemn declaration' of their common aims: in effect, the same dual policy. See above, p. 16.

† See Lord Halifax's broadcast in *The Times* of 8 November.

of war, the British Prime Minister described these aims our 'war aim' and our 'peace aims' respectively.*

On Sunday, 3 September, a quarter of an hour after we entered the war, the Prime Minister broadcast to the nation. These were his final words:

> It is the evil things we shall be fighting against—brute force, bad faith, injustice, oppression, and persecution —and against them I am certain that the right will prevail.

That the right will prevail is the conviction of the whole nation for whom, and to whom, Mr. Chamberlain spoke. But it will not, it cannot, prevail simply because the Allies overcome the armed forces of Germany on land, at sea, and in the air. As Lord Halifax put it: 'The things of the spirit can only be finally conquered in the spiritual sphere.'

'We are fighting,' said Lord Halifax earlier in his broadcast, 'in defence of freedom; we are fighting for peace; we are meeting a challenge to our own security and that of others; we are defending the right of all nations to live their own lives.'†

These aims are not to be realized merely by winning the war. In order that the right may prevail the peace must also be won. It is not enough for the Allies to achieve as their war aim the stopping of German aggression (whether by defeating Herr Hitler or by carrying on the war until he is ejected by the people of Germany), the enabling of the people of Austria to decide for themselves whether or no they will continue to be governed from Berlin, and the restoring of political independence to all

---

* See the report of Mr. Chamberlain's speech in *The Times* of 27 November. Cf. above, p. 56.
† See *The Times* of 8 November for Lord Halifax's broadcast.

other victims of German aggression. It must also be part of the Allied war aim to ensure that the essential principles of the settlement which will be negotiated afterwards shall be agreed before the fighting ends. And these principles ought to be of a magnanimous and even generous character.

It is time to look more closely into the nature of our peace aims. Any attempt to define them with legal precision at this stage would be a waste of effort, or worse. We cannot lay down now the terms of a general settlement to be negotiated in the future under conditions which cannot be foreseen. Moreover, a multiplicity of comparatively unimportant detail would distract attention from the principles that are essential.

But it is important to make up our minds what these essential principles really are. And for two reasons.

In the first place, the more these principles are thought about and discussed in the Allied countries, the better will their public opinion be prepared for whatever apparent sacrifices may be required in order to pass from the old world order to the new, and the less danger will there be of repeating the mistakes that were due to the mixed motives of those responsible for the Treaty of Versailles.* We must do better this time. This time we must not seek to benefit ourselves at Germany's expense, or permanently to disable that great and vigorous nation, or even to interfere with her liberty to model her own internal political institutions on her own lines, so long as her internal government does not pursue an external policy injurious to its neighbours,† is willing to co-operate with other countries in matters of

* See Chapter 8 above.
* Cf. Mr. Neville Chamberlain's speech on 26 November, 1939.

common interest to them all, and does not permit the practice of cruelty or other vices degrading to mankind. There can be no question of a Carthaginian peace. But war, as we said in Chapter 5, settles nothing unless it either wipes out the foe or makes him into a friend. It can therefore be no part of our peace aims to put the German people into a subordinate position. Western civilization owes them a great deal, particularly for their music, philosophy, literature, natural science and technology. Their help is needed to repair the damage our world has suffered from the selfish nationalism of the twentieth century. Germany has an essential part to play in laying the foundations of a just and lasting peace, and in building upon those foundations when they have been laid.

Secondly, there is the effect of our peace aims upon the neutrals and, through them, upon the Germans. The outline of a peace plan can have both a political and a psychological effect. Reverting to the simile used in Chapter 2, it may open the drawer by pulling both handles at the same time. On the political side, the more clearly the German people understand the principles on which our ultimate aims are based, the less reason will there be to fear that they will prolong the war from a mistaken notion that its end will mean hardship for themselves and retribution for their country. On the psychological side, a generous peace policy is perhaps the best means of ridding the German mind of its aggressive purposes. If the peace aims of the Allies hold in store for the citizens of Germany an equal share in returning prosperity and equal opportunities in the great adventure of rebuilding peace, the sooner they know it the better. 'To proclaim always, and to persist in our desire to establish, a peace which is based upon intrinsically reasonable foundations and not one which is based upon the will of a victor and distorted by the passions of war, will not distract our effort. It will sustain it, and help, not hinder, us in securing the sympathy and aid of others.'*

The Allied Governments must agree upon their peace aims before these can be published or produce the political and psychological effects that we desire. Such a plan is outlined here in the hope that it may simplify the task of the Allied Governments by helping to move public opinion in the right direction. In order to leave ample room for freedom to negotiate with Germany when the time comes, this plan of a general settlement avoids detail, as it is sure to be avoided in any peace aims that may be published with 'the full authority of a deliberate Government statement.'†

Here then is the plan in outline.

A. The War Aim

The terms of the armistice must—

(*a*) put an end to all immediate danger of further aggression by Germany.

> The circumstances of the time will decide whether for this purpose it is necessary to insist on the unilateral disarmament of Germany and upon the temporary occupation of fortified areas on German frontiers or other parts of Germany.

(*b*) Provide for the restoration of political independence to the Polish, Czecho-Slovak and Danish peoples, and also to the Austrians if a plebiscite should show that a majority of them would prefer to be governed from Vienna rather than from Berlin.

---

* *Security*, by Sir Arthur Salter (1939), p. 316.

† The phrase is Sir Arthur Salter's: *Loc. cit.*, p. 343. The Anglo-French 'solemn declaration' of 28 March, 1940, appeared after this chapter was in print. See above, p. 16.

The frontiers of the restored Czecho-Slovakia and Poland, and all arrangements for the Austrian plebiscite, would be determined by the subsequent settlement. The decisions might come from neutral Powers in the event of the Allies and Germany failing to agree. Meanwhile the armies of the Reich would have to retire from all the countries they have invaded to the German frontier as it existed before 14 March, 1938.

(c) Ensure that Germany is willing to join with the Allies and such neutral Powers as may also be willing to take part in negotiating a general settlement on the lines of the following Peace Aims (on pages 142 to 145).

A provisional treaty of peace between the belligerents should be concluded as soon as possible after the armistice. The terms of this provisional treaty should be settled after discussion with all the directly interested parties. These terms could be altered at the subsequent Peace Conference.

B. THE PEACE AIMS

The subsequent Peace Conference, consisting of ex-belligerents and of as many ex-neutrals as are willing to join them in negotiating a general settlement, should have the following objects in view:

1. World anarchy must be prevented by some form of international organization* in which Great Britain,

---

* Lord Halifax, in his *Dual Policy* speech of 29 June, spoke of 'the reconstruction of the international order on a broader foundation'; and of 'a workable system of international organization.' And Mr. Chamberlain, distinguishing our peace aims from our war aims on 26 November, said: 'It would be impossible to set a time limit upon [the process of establishing a new Europe], for conditions never cease to change and corresponding adjustment would be required if friction is to be avoided. Consequently you would need some machinery capable of conducting and guiding the new Europe in the right direction' (*The Times*, 27 November, 1939).

France and Germany must collaborate with other States. This organization need not begin by being, but must aim at becoming, world-wide.* In it all participating States, whether former belligerents or neutrals, must have equal rights. And it must be habitually obeyed by them all in certain matters of common concern. How much further the limitation of national sovereignty can be carried is a matter for negotiation as part of the general settlement.

> In so far as sovereignty consists in being habitually obeyed by the mass of people over whom it is exercised, the national sovereignty of the participating States would be limited by the transfer to their international Union, or Commonwealth, of supreme authority over these matters of common concern. Britain and France have set the example.
>
> The Union or Commonwealth may well be the League of Nations revitalized, reinforced and reformed. But the League is associated in German minds with the rest of the Versailles Treaty, including the clause which implies war guilt† and which the new settlement should repeal. It seems wiser, therefore, to describe the international organization by a word—*Commonwealth*—with other connotations including not only a federal union in the American Commonwealth, in Canada, and in Australia, but also, in the British Commonwealth of Nations, a lighter kind of inter-State system covering a quarter of the earth.

The matters of common concern regulated by the international Commonwealth must include:

(*a*) The use of force between nations; and, until the Commonwealth has become world-wide, its protection against aggression from outside. Within the Commonwealth and except with its approval, 'nation shall not use force against nation.'

* Cf. Lord Halifax on 7 November: 'To this order that we shall seek to create all nations will have their contributions to make.'
† Article 231 of the Treaty, quoted on p. 73 above.

(b) The settlement by means of third party judgment —judicial decision, or arbitration, or authoritative mediation involving if need be the revision of treaties*—of all international disputes that are not settled by the parties themselves.

(c) The limitation of national armaments, so that no State will retain the means to enforce its own judgment in its own cause. Until the Commonwealth is world-wide, the level of national armaments within it must depend upon the level to which outside nations will agree to reduce their armaments.

2. In other matters of common concern the Commonwealth must promote co-operation between its Member States and, so far as it may, between them and other States not yet Members of it. Among such matters are:

(a) *Economics*, including such problems as:

(i) Freeing international commerce with due regard for standards of labour and wages.

(ii) Promoting increased consumption and better distribution of the world's resources. The higher the standard of living is raised within the Commonwealth, the more will its membership attract those peoples who have not yet joined it. The larger it becomes, the more material wealth will it produce, other things being equal, for each of its citizens.†

(iii) Post-war demobilization.

(b) *Finance*, including the granting of loans, especially reconstruction loans, on easy terms.

---

* Compare Lord Halifax on 29 June, 1939: 'It is not enough to devise measures for preventing the use of force to change the *status quo* unless there is also machinery for bringing about peaceful change.' See also the quotation from Mr. Chamberlain in the footnote on page 142.

† Cf. Chapter 4, above.

(c) *Health* and other *Social Services* concerned with human welfare and social justice. (It is in this field that the League of Nations and the International Labour Organization have been most successful. Here especially the Commonwealth should employ and extend the existing machinery.)

(d) *Minorities, Refugees* and '*Staatenlosen.*' The protection afforded by the existing Minorities Treaties should be extended to the racial, religious and linguistic minorities of all countries, and be made more effective. Commonwealth citizenship should be accorded, under suitable conditions, to all its inhabitants including those who are without nationality.

(e) *Communications and Transit*, particularly with a view to freeing air communications as far as possible from national restrictions.

(f) *Colonies.* The principle that colonies inhabited by peoples not yet able to stand alone should be administered as a trust for the well-being and development of their inhabitants and should be open on equal terms to the commerce of all nations, should be applied to all such colonies whether or not their sovereignty was affected by the World War. Consideration should be given to the problem of gradually opening colonial services to suitable nationals of all co-operating States.

Some of the many questions raised in this outline of peace aims will be discussed in the next five chapters.

CHAPTER 15

LAW AND ORDER

★

We have first to remind ourselves why some sort of international Union or Commonwealth plays so large a part in the peace aims we have outlined.

Limitation of Armaments

In Chapters 5 and 6 we traced the drift of Europe towards general war from the moment when, at the outset of the twentieth century, the British Navy began to lose its unchallenged supremacy at sea. Eventual war became inevitable unless some new factor of overwhelming strength could be brought in to check the growth of national armaments.

That is why the conception of a Society of Nations began to take shape during the World War primarily as a means to enforce peace. And, when the Covenant assumed its final form in Paris, the first duty which it laid* upon the League of Nations was the reduction and limitation of national armaments by international agreement.

And that is also why the general settlement outlined in our peace aims must include the creation, or restoration,

---

* Articles 8 and 9 of the Covenant. The first seven articles are concerned with the constitution, not the functions, of the League. See above, p. 91.

of a Union or Commonwealth of nations with authority and power to ensure the effective limitation of armaments of all the uniting States.* The Commonwealth must not allow the armaments of its Members to exceed the agreed limits. What those limits ought to be will depend upon the willingness of States outside the Commonwealth to reduce their national armaments to the proposed level. But even if some of the outside States would not agree, the use of mutual assistance or 'collective security' in the manner discussed below would enable the uniting States to enjoy much relief from the burden of armaments without jeopardizing their Commonwealth.

How exactly that relief is to be obtained, what armaments are to be limited and to what extent, are problems that must await the general settlement before they can be solved.† It is, however, worth noting that one of the questions then to be considered will have to be whether the common interests of all States, inside the Commonwealth or outside it, might not well be served by altogether abolishing national air forces,‡ and by severely limiting the maximum size of ships, guns, tanks and other weapons of navies and armies. For example, the maximum size of all warships might be reduced to 10,000 tons, or to 15,000 tons, at most.§

* Including at least Great Britain, France and Germany. See below, p. 197 and Chapter 21.
† These problems are discussed by Lord Davies in *The Problem of the Twentieth Century* (1930).
‡ See Chapter 19 below.
§ The case for limiting future construction of warships so that no new capital ship shall exceed 10,000 tons (or, at most, 15,000 tons) is ably presented by Admiral Richmond in *Sea Power in the Modern World* (1934). He argues that this change would benefit Great Britain and all other Powers. 'Nor can there be any doubt that the fleets themselves of all the Powers would be better instruments regarded as a whole, than those composed of a lower number of extremely costly vessels' (*Loc. cit.*, p. 219). *Cf.* p. 80 above.

If the nations outside the Commonwealth would not agree to get rid of their military aeroplanes, the uniting States might yet see their way to pool their air forces, or at least unite them as nearly as the naval forces of the British Commonwealth which fly different 'Jacks' but the same white ensign.*

The control of armaments is not, however, the only means by which the Commonwealth should preserve law and order within its borders. Two other functions of the Commonwealth are also essential for this purpose as well as for extending the reign of law more widely over the earth. The first is collective protection against aggression. The second is the removal of grievances and the peaceful settlement of disputes.

Collective Defence

Collective defence is, as we saw in Chapter 9, a necessary corollary to the limitation of armaments. Many countries would refuse to enter a Commonwealth which compelled its Members to limit their military, naval and air strength but did not defend them if they were attacked. Collective security was, therefore, a basic principle of the League of Nations. It is no less indispensable in the new Commonwealth or in any other system of world order that is to avert war.

'The strength of all for the defence of each' is perhaps

* 'Australia maintains a substantial navy which in wartime would come under unity of command with the British Fleet in the Pacific and the Indian Oceans; and New Zealand maintains at her own charge a miniature division of the Royal Navy.' India and Canada also have small naval forces. See *The British Empire*, by H. V. Hodson (Oxford Pamphlet, No. 2), p. 16. H.M.S. *Achilles* which distinguished herself in the action off the River Plate on 13 December, 1939, belonged to the New Zealand Division.

COLLECTIVE DEFENCE

the simplest expression of the principle of collective security. But it is not to be found in the Covenant. Article 10 comes nearest to it.:

> The Members of the League undertake to respect and preserve as against external aggregation the territorial integrity and existing political independence of all Members of the League

But the article goes on to say:

> In case of any such aggression or in case of any threat or danger of such aggression the Council shall advise upon the means by which this obligation shall be fulfilled.

So long as France and Britain had the will to work the Covenant and their combined power could not be challenged in Europe, the collective security guaranteed by the first of these two sentences was a reality. But when financial troubles* combined with the remoteness of Manchuria to make the Western democracies unwilling to take up Japan's challenge to the League in 1931, the second sentence of Article 10 was used to defeat the purpose of the first. The Council did not advise how the obligation should be fulfilled and the Members of the League felt free from any duty under Article 10.

We saw, in Chapter 9,† that Article 16 of the Covenant is also concerned with collective security. That article provides that if any Member of the League‡ resorts to war in defiance of certain of its obligations under the Covenant, the other Members will at once cut off its trade with the rest of the world. The next sentence reads:

> It shall be the duty of the Council in such a case to recommend to the several Governments concerned what

---

* See above, p. 105. † See above, p. 92.
‡ Article 17 in effect extends the provisions of Article 16 to non-Members of the League.

effective military, naval or air force the Members of the League shall severally contribute to the armed forces to be used to protect the covenants of the League.*

Thus the Covenant recognized that economic measures might not suffice to stop an aggressor unless supported by overwhelming 'military, naval or air force' in the background. But the Members of the League chose† to regard the raising of armed forces, not as an indispensable part of economic measures, but as an alternative to be considered if the aggressor did not yield to economic pressure. This departure from the Covenant had fatal results when Signor Mussolini defied the League in the autumn of 1935.

Article 11 of the Covenant is also concerned, although less directly, with collective security. It enacts that

> Any war or threat of war, whether immediately affecting any Member of the League or not, is hereby declared a matter of concern to the whole League, and the League shall take any action that may be deemed wise and effectual to safeguard the peace of nations.

But when the Japanese generals invaded Manchuria in 1931, the representative of Japan in Geneva claimed that the League could not take 'any action that might be deemed wise and effectual' except after a unanimous vote of the Council which Japan would be able to veto!‡

---

* Before Germany joined the League she asked, at Locarno, for certain explanations in regard to Article 16. Those explanations were given in Annex F of the Locarno treaties. The representatives of Belgium, Great Britain, France, Italy, Czecho-Slovakia and Poland who initialled this Annex said that, according to their interpretation of Article 16, 'each State Member of the League is bound to co-operate loyally and effectively in support of the Covenant and in resistance to any act of aggression to an extent which is compatible with its military situation and takes its geographical position into account.'

† By accepting the Report of the International Blockade Committee, dated 9 September, 1921.   ‡ See above, p. 110.

This formal difficulty was allowed to stultify Article 11. But it might easily have been overcome if France and Britain had been determined to use the League machinery, as they had already often used it, to prevent a war.

These three examples show how easy it is to make the written word of none effect unless it continues to represent the will of the governments and peoples who are bound by it. No paper plan, standing by itself, will be any more reliable in future.* That is why the need for collective security must be understood by the peoples of the Commonwealth and why the determination to use 'the strength of all for the defence of each' must be firmly fixed among the purposes of the uniting States. Collective security will not be a basic principle of the Commonwealth unless the citizens of the uniting States are as firmly resolved to defend the Commonwealth against aggression as they are to protect their own territories.

If the combined power of the Members of the Commonwealth is to enforce law and order within it and, until it becomes world-wide, to secure it against aggression from outside, the collective strength of the Commonwealth—spiritual as well as material, its common purpose combined with its military and economic resources—must sufficiently exceed that of any opposed alliance.† It follows that, as we said on page 143 above, the Commonwealth must include Germany as well as the French and British empires.‡ Presumably§ it would also unite the

* Cf. Lord Halifax's broadcast on war aims: 'No paper plan will endure that does not freely spring from the will of the people who alone can give it life' (*The Times*, 8 November, 1939).

† Cf. *Security*, by Sir Arthur Salter, p. 163.

‡ Eire, neutral in Hitler's War, is unlikely to stand out; but she should be free to do so if that is her wish.

§ See below, pp. 197 to 199.

Polish, Czech, and Slovak peoples, the Scandinavian Powers, the Dutch and Belgian empires, Switzerland, Turkey and most, if not all, of the Balkan States. No conceivable combination could challenge such a Commonwealth in Europe. Together with the United States, it would control a high proportion of the world's raw materials; and this economic power would add to the deterrent effect of its military power upon any State contemplating aggression. And if, as seems likely, China becomes a Member of the Commonwealth, the goodwill of America would enable the Commonwealth's authority to prevail in the Far East. Whether or no Canada was at first the only American country in the Commonwealth, there would then be no question but that it would have nothing to fear from any quarter of the globe.

The principle of collective defence does not, of course, imply that the Commonwealth would use any more force than might be needed in any particular case. If some of the uniting States were to bind themselves more closely to each other than to the Commonwealth as a whole, thus forming federations of a closer kind, these regional groups would serve as a first line of defence against aggression. If one of the members of such a group were threatened, the others might be able to give it all the aid it needed without asking the whole Commonwealth to come to the rescue. If the American nations were to join the Commonwealth, their Pan-American union might form one of these regional groups. Another would consist of the French Republic and the United Kingdom, since their governments undertook, on 28 March, 1940, 'to maintain, after the conclusion of peace, a community of action in all spheres for so long as may be necessary to safeguard their security.' Yet another group might comprise the Scandinavian countries; and the Balkan States, with Turkey, might link up in the same way.

Regional groups of this kind need not be mutually exclusive. Any Member of the Commonwealth might belong to one or more, or to none, of these groups.

Such a system of regional groups would make collective defence easier for nations who have not yet learned to think of themselves as parts of a world-wide whole. They would be quicker to realize the need for resisting aggression in their own neighbourhood than to understand how their own interests also required them to 'safeguard the peace of nations' anywhere on earth. The obligation to join in a local system of collective defence, being less onerous, would also be more likely to be honoured than a pledge to take part in a more comprehensive scheme.

While, however, local groups within the Commonwealth could reinforce its security, they would only form a first line of defence against aggression. They would need the support of the Commonwealth as a whole. In every case it would exert diplomatic and economic pressure to restrain an aggressor. But it would not use force unless the aggressor did so, and then only if the combined forces of the regional groups directly affected were not strong enough to stop the aggression. Moreover, the policy pursued by the American Administration for the past ten years makes it safe to assume that the Members of the Commonwealth, when giving each other mutual assistance against aggression, will be able to count, if not upon the active help, at least upon the benevolent neutrality of the Great Republic.

The religious views or political pacifism of certain persons would make them deplore the inclusion, among the Allies' peace aims, of a system of collective security maintained, if need be, by the use of armed force. Some of these people fail to see how the international enforcement of peace differs from 'war' as hitherto known: war as an instrument of national policy.* The enforcement of peace is a limited enterprise, being only concerned to prevent armed force from being used on behalf of the national policy of any State. 'War,' on the other hand, was by its nature unlimited and often involved grave difficulties with neutrals. Then again, the enforcement of peace seeks not the death of an aggressor but rather that he may turn from his wickedness and live. 'War,' however, aims at victory over a defeated foe. Once more, the enforcement of peace is essentially preventive rather than punitive: it tends to prevent future wars from breaking out by convincing the aggressor that he cannot hope to succeed against the overwhelming force arrayed against him. But 'war' breeds further wars. Finally, the enforcement of peace requires no propaganda of hate. With international law (and, as a rule, justice also) on its side, it differs morally from 'war' lawlessly undertaken in pursuance of national policy.

Indeed, readiness if need be to take part in collective defence against aggression marks a high order of political altruism, at least for those who have not yet attained a clear vision of their country as part of a larger whole. In any case, it is the price of peace. In words used† by the Archbishop of Canterbury on behalf of a number of leading Churchmen and Free Churchmen in England, Scotland and Wales:

> The chief obstacle to the attainment of security which the world needs, as also to recovery from economic depression,

* Cf. Lord Halifax: 'Always it is the spirit behind the application of force which makes or mars its value' (*Address to the University of Oxford* on 27 February, 1940).
† In a statement issued on 15 May, 1934.

is the spirit of a narrow and self-seeking nationalism, which refuses to pay the price whereby alone security and recovery can be achieved. The price is willingness to accept the principle of the collective action of nations as members of one great commonwealth.

If, then, the Commonwealth must be ready to use force for the maintenance of its internal law and order and for its protection against aggression from outside its borders, does it need to have its own army, navy and air force? Some people in England believe that it does. Since, however, national armies and navies are needed to maintain order within each nation's territory—in Germany, for example, during the change over from National Socialism; or in India while communal quarrels are apt to end in fighting—and territorial waters, it is likely that many nations will wish to retain substantial land and sea forces for a long time to come. In order to be effective, an international army or navy would have to be stronger than any of these, and to be so placed geographically as to be promptly available wherever it might be wanted. Afghanistan might, for example, wish to see quartered in the Himalayas a contingent so large as to be able to protect it against the whole military power of British India. The creation of such an international army, or navy, is therefore administratively impracticable and politically undesirable at the present time. By land and sea,* collective security must be guaranteed by contingents

* Cf. Admiral Sir Herbert Richmond, Master of Downing College, Cambridge: 'It is incorrect to say that joint international naval action is an impossibility. The ships blockading Crete [in 1898] and preventing the spread of the disturbances were French, Italian, British and Russian. The fleet which destroyed the Turks at Navarino [in 1827] was composed of British, French and Russian ships. The vessels employed in the Mediterranean in the war of 1914–1918 were Italian, French, American, Japanese and British. Co-operation and co-ordination are moreover easier afloat in a fleet than ashore in

from the forces of the Members of the Commonwealth; or, in the first instance perhaps, from those of regional groups of these States.

It will not be enough for mutual assistance of this kind to be promised in the constitution of the Commonwealth. The need for it must be grasped by public opinion. In particular, the personnel of the armies and navies of the uniting States must recognize that the main function of these forces in war-time is joint action with other armies and navies of the Commonwealth in order to defend it—or any part of it, including their own country—against aggression. In peace-time as well as in war-time much of the work of the Commonwealth navies could be jointly done. Admiral Richmond writes:

> The duties of a navy in peace are of a police or a philanthropic character. Those, for example, which are performed by the naval forces of various nations in the China seas and rivers* are for the common purpose of suppressing piracy and banditry: services as international in their nature as those conducted by the Ice Patrol in the North Atlantic against the common enemy of the shipping of all nations, the iceberg. The cruising ships of all the Powers perform acts of humanity on such occasions of great natural catastrophes as earthquakes at Jamaica, Messina, Hawke's Bay, in Greece, or a hurricane at Honduras. . . .†

Further, in time of peace there should be joint manœuvres of the Commonwealth forces. The presence of units from abroad in the general manœuvres of every Commonwealth army or navy would mark the acceptance of this principle, demonstrate it to the world, and prepare for its

an army; and yet the army which fought under Wellington at Waterloo was successful, though it was composed of British, Belgian, Hanoverian and Dutch troops, and was opposed by an army of one nationality' (*Sea Power in the Modern World*, pp. 194, 195).

* Admiral Richmond was writing in 1934. † *Loc. cit.*, p. 193.

application, thus increasing both the reliability and the efficiency of collective defence.

The air problem is different. National air forces are not needed to maintain internal order, at any rate in Europe. And, even if national air forces are the cheapest and most effective means of policing the wild fringes of civilization, there is no reason to suppose that any government would allow this consideration to stand in the way of collective security or disarmament. The British Government, in particular, have adopted this position. The questions of an Air Police Force for the Commonwealth, and of the Commonwealth's control of civil aviation, are reserved for Chapter 18.

Peaceful Change

We have seen[*] that the preservation of law and order within the Commonwealth depends upon its being able to remove grievances and settle disputes by a process of peaceful change. The stability of the Commonwealth, so far as internal forces are concerned, is conditional, as we have seen, upon its having the power to control the armaments of its Member States. Stability is further increased by collective security. But stability is not assured unless the Commonwealth is able to relieve and remove intolerable grievances. The Commonwealth will only be certain to avert war among its Members if it can settle peacefully and justly whatever disputes may arise between them.

The machinery of the Covenant of the League of Nations sufficed for the settlement of international

[*] See above, p. 148.

disputes concerning legal rights,* and also many disputes which involved the question whether the legal rights of one of the parties ought not to be altered in the interests of justice.† But the League's machinery could never be relied upon to settle a dispute when justice demanded an alteration of legal rights against the will of the State which benefited from the injustice. The Commonwealth will therefore need to improve upon the League's machinery for handling this most important and most difficult class of dispute. For the rest, there is no need to change the mechanism of Geneva and the Hague in order that, when the Commonwealth becomes world-wide, mankind may be able, by a process of peaceful change, to adapt its political institutions to its ever-changing environment.

We have said that the League has generally been unable to alter the existing legal rights of nations unless all concerned could be persuaded to agree. It is true that nations have sometimes been prevailed upon to give up peacefully rights which were undoubtedly theirs and which they regarded as important. For example, at the Montreux Conference in July, 1936, Turkey asked for and obtained relief from obligations not to fortify the zone of the Straits between the Black Sea and the Mediterranean. These obligations were binding upon Turkey under the Treaty of Lausanne (1922). Turkey urged that circumstances had materially changed since 1922, the other Powers concerned eventually agreed, and the Treaty of Lausanne was revised accordingly. But despite this and other examples of the peaceful revision of

* See, for example, the case reported on pp. 102 and 103 where such a case was settled with the help of the Permanent Court of International Justice.

† Such disputes were commonly settled by conciliation with the help of the League's Council. Sometimes they were disposed of by friendly discussion between delegates at the League's Assembly.

treaties, no nation has felt sure that it will obtain justice —what the impartial world would regard as justice—by bringing its discontents to the notice of the League. A remedy for this state of things has been proposed on the following lines:

1. When any member of the League desires the Assembly* to advise, under Article 19† of the Covenant, the reconsideration by Members of the League of a treaty (on the ground that it has become applicable) or the consideration of specified international conditions (on the ground that their continuance might endanger the peace of the world) a Commission of Inquiry should be appointed to discover the facts and to recommend what, if any, action should be taken.

2. After considering the report or reports of the Commission, the Assembly should 'advise' by means of a 'Recommendation' not requiring a unanimous vote;‡ and, if the Members of the League who are parties to the treaty or are responsible for the international conditions in question, do not act upon the advice within a reasonable time, the Council should consider the matter under Article 11 without counting the votes of the States immediately affected.§

* All the States Members of the League are equally represented on the League's Assembly.

† Article 19 reads: 'The Assembly may from time to time advise the reconsideration by Members of the League of treaties which have become inapplicable and the consideration of international conditions whose continuance might endanger the peace of the world.'

‡ Compare the British Foreign Secretary (Mr. Eden) at Geneva on 25 September, 1936: 'A clear expression by the League on the need for revision or on a grievance . . . would contain a strong element of moral pressure. We must strive for a balanced world in which justice is done to all and where grievances can be remedied. Unless we can set up peace on this basis, our work is useless. His Majesty's Government do not deceive themselves on this point, and, without its being achieved, they cannot hope to revitalize the League.'

§ If there is any danger of war, the League must, under that article, take any action which might be deemed wise and effectual to safeguard the peace of nations (see above, p. 92). The action which might be taken against a recalcitrant State would include

3. The Assembly should invite non-Member States to take part in the consideration of the Commission's report or reports, and to join in the consequent 'advice.'

4. In the event of a non-Member State desiring to avail itself of Article 19 thus interpreted, it should be invited to do so upon its undertaking to accept and act upon any 'advice' from a sufficiently large majority of the Assembly.

By such means as these a revitalized League of Nations might exert sufficient pressure to bring about peaceful change even against the will of a Member State whose legal rights needed to be altered in the interests of justice.

economic and financial measures and, at a later stage, withdrawal from that State of the collective protection guaranteed by Articles 10 and 16 against the employment of force by the aggrieved State or States for the sole purpose of giving effect to the Assembly's advice. At the same time the State or States which accept the Assembly's advice might receive financial assistance from an international fund built up by States Members of the League contributing, say, 1 per cent of their expenditure upon armaments.

CHAPTER 16

WELFARE AND ECONOMICS

Law and order are not the only concerns of government. Since the early days of the nineteenth century, the government of the United Kingdom has extended the range of its activities far beyond the defence of the realm and the maintenance of order within it. The list of British government departments functioning in time of peace now includes the Board of Education, the Ministry of Health, the Ministry of Labour, the Ministry of Agriculture and Fisheries, the Post Office, the Department of Scientific and Industrial Research, the Ministry of Transport. None of these existed when Queen Victoria came to the throne. The business of these new Ministries is to promote the welfare of each individual citizen by the co-operation of all.

We saw, in Chapter 4, that many of the tasks undertaken by these new Public Departments could not be properly handled without international co-operation. We observed how the unwilling nations were thus forced to create the beginnings of world government. The members of the human family have indeed many common interests which can best be served by a common government. Our hope is that it may eventually be provided by the evolution of the Commonwealth discussed in the preceding chapter. Meanwhile, the States uniting to limit armaments, to provide security and to settle disputes should make provision in their general settlement for their Commonwealth to cope with these other problems of international government.

It is true that the uniting States and their citizens have many interests which are not common to the whole world or even to the Commonwealth. With these interests the Commonwealth should not concern itself. For, all other things being equal, every human being enjoys most liberty when each group to which he belongs manages its own affairs in so far as they do not affect other persons outside the group.*

Thus the Commonwealth should only deal with those common interests which suffer if they are independently controlled by the several governments of the uniting States. The outline of our peace aims at the end of Chapter 14† showed what some of these common interests are. The Members of the Commonwealth will need to help one another in their handling of these problems. It would, perhaps, be wise, even at the outset and increasingly so as time goes on, to transfer the responsibility for some of them‡ from the national governments to the supreme authority of the Commonwealth itself. The Commonwealth would regulate matters so transferred just as it controls armaments, provides security and

---

* There might even be more liberty in England if some of the functions of government now exercised at Westminster were transferred to eight or ten provincial authorities. Such a transfer would give the Imperial Parliament more time to handle issues affecting the country as a whole with its colonies and dependencies. A beginning has been made with the creation of provincial authorities for the purpose of civil defence. The need for provincial authorities to assist in the administration of public education is discussed in *Knowledge and Character* by Maxwell Garnett (Cambridge University Press, 1939).

† See above, pp. 141 *et seq.*

‡ Governmental restrictions of trade, for example.

removes inter-State differences. But the question which, if any, matters over and above those discussed in Chapter 15 should be transferred at the outset from the uniting States to their Commonwealth can only be decided when the general settlement is made.

Meanwhile, the facts set forth in Chapter 4, as well as the experience of the League of Nations and of the International Labour Organization* sketched in Chapter 10, leave no room for doubt that there are many functions of government concerning economics, finance and human welfare generally which cannot be adequately performed by the independent action of separate States. In particular there are the vitally important economic problems indicated in the outline of our peace aims on page 144 above. They include the reduction and eventually perhaps the destruction of tariff walls within the Commonwealth. For all these purposes the co-operation of Members of the Commonwealth will be needed.

A broadsheet† issued by *Political and Economic Planning* points out that some of the issues here in question closely affect the problems of peace and war discussed in Chapter 15. Much harm has been done in the past by neglect of these issues. For example, there was

the failure of the democracies to bring about peaceful and orderly change at home and abroad and to organize for

* For further particulars of the work of the International Labour Organization reference may be made to *The International Labour Organization* by Dr. Harold Butler, its second Director (Oxford University Press, 1939, price 3d.). Dr. Butler's pamphlet records what has been done regarding Social Insurance, including Health Insurance, Hours of Labour, the so-called 'Seamen's Charter,' Protection against Accidents and Industrial Disease, and Forced Labour in Colonies.

† No. 154 of 7 November, 1939.

social ends power over finance, production and trade, and power over opinion. These were the failures which let loose the world slump of 1929-1932 and which allowed brutal methods of treaty revision not only to command great support in Japan, Italy and Germany, but to be widely condoned in more law-abiding countries.*

In many instances it may, indeed, be hard to distinguish between Commonwealth and national issues. The broadsheet just quoted asks:

What is a 'domestic' issue when . . . Germany's treatment of religious and political minorities can create stubborn refugee and other problems for Great Britain, while the existence of a free British Press is resented by a German government as incompatible with its own interests? Where also is the line to be drawn . . . when a British Import Duties Order can create a depressed area in, say, Thuringia or Honshu, and when British or transatlantic business men, by selling some key commodity to Germany, Italy or Japan, can unthinkingly aid in acts of aggression whose final reckoning has to be met by their fellow-citizens and fellow-taxpayers in blood and in money? Technical and economic advances have made all

* *Loc. cit.*, p. 4. Cf. also the following extract from *Labour's Peace Aims* (p. 15): 'Bold economic planning on a world scale will be an imperative necessity to meet the post-war situation, and to avoid in the future recurrent economic crises. . . . International institutions for this purpose must be created. It is of at least equal importance that the scope and authority of the International Labour Organization should be enlarged. It should be given the task of preparing international minimum standards of wages, hours and industrial conditions, in order that, by increased production, by a more just distribution and by the wealth released from expenditure upon arms, the standard of living of the workers shall everywhere be raised. For peace depends on social justice within States, no less than on political justice between States.' The pamphlet is written by the Rt. Hon. C. R. Attlee, M.P., and published by the Labour Party

countries so closely interdependent that the corresponding political advances can no longer be delayed.*

In cases of this kind the constitution of the Commonwealth should give each of the uniting States the friendly right to ask the supreme authority of the Commonwealth to decide whether any specified issue is a common concern of the Members. If the answer is 'yes,' then it is a matter for international co-operation between the uniting States and perhaps also for collaboration between them and other States outside the Commonwealth. Or the Commonwealth may decide that the issue should be referred, in the first instance, to such a 'regional group' as was described on pages 152 and 153 above. Where regional groups have been organized within the Commonwealth there is no reason why they should not form customs unions or areas of freer trade than the Commonwealth as a whole, or concern themselves in other ways with human welfare, as well as with political security. Indeed 'it is important that the European Powers should be left free, and even encouraged, to form regional groupings . . . for purposes of economic development.'†

We spoke in Chapter 10 of the success with which the Geneva machinery had handled many problems of international co-operation for human welfare and social justice. Nor has there been any breakdown in this machinery comparable with the League's failure to provide political security in recent years. There is no need to duplicate the Geneva instrument for work in this field. The constitution of the Commonwealth that figures in our peace aims is to be discussed in Chapter 19 below. If, as is possible, the Commonwealth takes the form of

* Loc. cit., p. 4.
† Broadsheet, No. 154, by *Political and Economic Planning*, p. 14.

restored, revitalized and reinforced* League of Nations, and if all the present Members of the League become Members of the Commonwealth, no question will arise of providing some alternative to the League's machinery for international co-operation in economics; finance; health and social services; questions concerning minorities, refugees and stateless persons; communication and transit; or colonial supervision. But if, at first, the Commonwealth is less universal than the League or the International Labour Organization, there will still be no need for the Commonwealth to duplicate effective machinery at Geneva. For if Germany or any other among the uniting States hesitates to join the League—for example, on account of its past† association with the Treaty of Versailles—that will no more prevent the Commonwealth from using the League's machinery for these purposes than America is prevented from using the International Labour Organization by her refusal to join the League. Or the Commonwealth might take over the League and provide for all its Members, whether they belong to the Commonwealth or not, and for Members of the International Labour Organization, all the services they now obtain from Geneva.

* 'The total sums subscribed to the League budget by the nations of Europe in recent years do not greatly exceed the annual expenditure of the London County Council on main drainage. . . . A common European development budget of substantial size—say of the order of £100 millions a year—could hardly be considered an excessive burden by States which have readily found far larger sums for non-productive armaments, and would do more to promote effective European unity than any number of unsupported pacts and redundant organizations. Such a budget might be raised by a percentage levy on national budgets which on recent figures for Europe west of Russia would need to reach only $2\frac{1}{2}$ per cent to find £100 millions' (*Political and Economic Planning*, Broadsheet, No. 154, p. 13).

† There would be no difficulty in severing the present formal links between the Covenant and the Versailles Treaty.

CHAPTER 17

COLONIES

★

The peace aims outlined at the end of Chapter 14 include a settlement of the problem of colonies. When, on 29 June, Lord Halifax described the dual policy of the British Government—first, resistance to aggression and then rebuilding world order*—he had a good deal to say about colonies. He reminded his hearers that

> There was a time when in the British Empire, as elsewhere, colonies were regarded merely as a source of wealth and a place of settlement for Europeans. You have only to read any of the colonial literature of those days to see for how little counted the rights and welfare of the natives. But during the last half century a very different view has gained ground, a view which has been finely expressed in Article 22 of the Covenant,† namely, that the well-being and development of 'people not yet able to stand by themselves under the strenuous conditions of the modern world' is 'a sacred trust of civilization.'

The Foreign Secretary went on to say that this 'trust has been steadily fulfilled . . . in the case of Mandated Territories,‡ on which the operation of the provisions of Article 22 of the Covenant has conferred 'immense benefits.' Then he put the question:

> Can we not look forward to a time when there may be agreement or common methods and aims of colonial

* See above, p. 124. † See above, p. 93.
‡ See above, p. 93.

development, which may ensure not only that the universally acknowledged purpose of colonial administration will be to help their inhabitants steadily to raise their level of life, but also that colonial territories may make a growing contribution to the world's resources?

There followed a declaration of the British Government's policy: 'On such an agreed foundation of purpose,' said Lord Halifax, 'we hope that others might be prepared with us to make their contribution to a better world. If so, I have no doubt that in the conduct of our colonial administration we should be ready to go far upon the economic side, as we have already done on the political side, in making wider application of the principles which now obtain in the mandated territories, including, on terms of reciprocity, that of the open door.'*

That speech was made before the outbreak of war and when the prospect of a general settlement that should begin the realization of British peace aims seemed further off than it does to-day. Before that settlement is negotiated by the belligerents in Hitler's War and as many neutrals as will help them to do so, consideration should be given to the question whether, so far as colonies are concerned, our peace aims ought not to go further than they did in June, 1939. In particular, since some sort of Commonwealth of nations will be needed for the purposes set forth in Chapters 15 and 16, may it not help to solve the colonial problem also?† Merely to apply 'the principles which now obtain in the mandated territories' to all the colonies of the uniting States would indeed provide a brighter future for the native inhabitants and lessen the

* The quotations from Lord Halifax's speech are taken from pp. 62–64 of *Documents concerning German-Polish Relations*, Cmd. 6106 (1939).

† *Cf.* the reference to colonies in the peace aims outlined at the end of Chapter 14, p. 145.

grievances of the Powers who would like to have colonies of their own. But it would leave Central Africa and some other non-self-governing parts of the world under the different administrations of rival colonial Powers. It would also leave most of the Members of the Commonwealth with a feeling that they had been treated unequally, if not unfairly. In the first place, the colonial Powers would actually *govern* colonies while the non-colonial Powers could only hope to share in *supervising* the colonial governments. In the second place, no equality of opportunity for equally capable persons would exist as between the young citizens of colonial Powers and those of the other States: the former might, while the latter might not, look forward to useful and well-paid careers in the administration and technical services of colonial territories

It is, of course, true that the sudden replacement by an untrained international personnel of the present British, French, Dutch and Belgian colonial services would be almost the worst thing that could happen to an African or Asiatic colony. The interests of the inhabitants require that the administrators should possess a tradition and an *esprit de corps*. The transition from the present régimes would therefore have to take place gradually over a period of years. During that time Scandinavians, Swiss, Germans, Poles, Czechs and others might gradually be introduced into the technical services and, more gradually perhaps, into the administrations until, after the lapse of some twenty-five years, the Commonwealth —with the help, perhaps, of its own Staff College— would have built up its colonial civil service, equal in personnel to the best that now exists but recruited from the most qualified young people in *any* of the uniting States. The evolution of such an international service has been proved possible by the efficiency of the League's Secretariat in its early years.

Let us look rather more closely at some aspects of 'the colonial problem' the solution of which is part of British peace aims. This time we will take the interests of the natives after we have glanced at those of the rest of the world.

The Former German Colonies

One of the grievances which the Commonwealth must, in any case, seek to remove by a process of peaceful change* is that felt by the Germans in the loss of their colonies after the World War. By the terms of the Armistice, the victorious Powers were bound to base their Treaty of Peace with Germany upon the fourteen points of President Wilson's address of 8 January, 1918, and his subsequent speeches. The fifth of the fourteen points provides for

> A free, open-minded, and absolutely impartial adjustment of all colonial claims, based upon a strict observance of the principle that in determining all such questions of sovereignty the interests of the populations concerned must have equal weight with the equitable claims of the Governments whose title is to be determined.

By Article 119 of the Treaty of Versailles, the title to the German colonies was transferred to the Principal Allied and Associated Powers as a body, and they handed over the government of these territories to some of their number as mandatories of the League of Nations.

It has sometimes been argued, for example by Mr. Gathorne-Hardy,† that Germany should not have felt

---

* See above, pp. 148 and 157 *et seq.*

† In *The Fourteen Points and the Treaty of Versailles*, Oxford Pamphlet, No. 6.

aggrieved by this decision. But national grievances stimulate the growth of armaments and make for war when they are *felt* as grievances, and not only when a dispassionate enquiry shows that they are unreasonable and ought not to be so felt. Many leading Germans certainly did regard the loss of German colonies in 1919 as unwarranted and unfair.* The sense of grievance was widespread, but not universal, in Germany.

The initiative in claiming possession of the former German colonies was taken in Paris by the British Dominions.† They were 'vitally interested in avoiding the re-establishment of potentially aggressive European sovereignties in their neighbourhood.'‡ But this and other strategic objections to handing over to possible enemies territories that could be used as bases for hostile submarines or aircraft would not apply to the transfer of colonies to the Commonwealth.

On the other hand, the transfer to the Commonwealth of *all* its Members' colonies, whether or not their sovereignty was affected by the World War, would make Germany's share of sovereignty§ over colonial territories equal to that of Britain and France. In 1914 it was far less. Although the satisfaction of many Germans in the attainment of equality with Britain and France would be impaired by the knowledge that this equality was also shared by other uniting States, more than ample resti-

* Cf. *German Colonization Past and Future* (1926), by Dr. Heinrich Schnee, the last Governor of German East Africa.

† Ray Stannard Baker in *Woodrow Wilson and World Settlement* (Vol. I, pp. 225 *et seq.*).

‡ *Colonies and Raw Materials*, by H. D. Henderson (Oxford Pamphlet, No. 7), p. 5.

§ The transfer to the Commonwealth of sovereignty over the former German Colonies would require the consent of all the Principal Allied and Associated Powers: the United States, Italy and Japan, as well as France and the British Empire.

tution would have been made for any unfair damage done to Germany by the Allies' refusal to restore her colonies in 1919. This particular grievance would then disappear.

Prestige

The same is true of the second German grievance we have now to notice. It concerns a matter of prestige. Germany and Russia are alone among the Great Powers in possessing no overseas empire. Worse still, from the German standpoint, some of the smaller States—Holland, Belgium, Portugal and Spain—are better off for colonies than Germany herself. If all the colonies belonging or mandated to the Members of the Commonwealth became Commonwealth colonies and were to be eventually administered directly by the Commonwealth this grievance also would become negligible, although it might not be entirely removed from the minds of those who felt with W. S. Gilbert that 'when everybody's somebody then no-one's anybody.'

Economic Benefits

The third grievance of the non-colonial Powers concerns the economic advantages to be got from the possessions of colonies. Mr. H. D. Henderson* has pointed out that these are far less than is commonly supposed; and that they are offset, to some extent, by the cost of subsidies to colonies which cannot pay their way.

The economic gains which the mother country is supposed to derive from her colonies are of three kinds: access to raw materials, opportunities for investments, and markets for exports. Let us consider them in that order.

* *Loc. cit.*

Raw Materials.—Colonies provide mankind with only about 3 per cent of all commercially important raw materials;* but this 3 per cent includes nearly all the rubber, half the tin, a quarter of the copper and much of the tea, sugar, bananas, coffee, oranges and grape fruit.† The supply of colonial products tends, however, to increase faster than the demand for them. Advances in the sciences of agriculture and entomology, more efficient technique in farming, better health conditions in the tropics, and the absence of birth control among the native populations, increase productive capacity and so tend to increase production. Meanwhile demand is held back by declining birth rates in Europe and America, by the policy of autarky‡ that results in the use of substitutes for rubber and other colonial products, and by the purchase of war materials instead of tea, coffee, cocoa or fruit. Consequently, all colonial territories are most anxious to sell to anyone who will buy, no matter whether the purchaser is a citizen of the mother country or belongs to some other State. Not even French colonies hinder exports by duties or administrative controls. In short, non-colonial Powers can buy raw materials of colonial origin on the same terms as the colonial Powers themselves.§

Moreover, because the latter have to assist indigent colonies by preferential duties, the inhabitants of colony-

* *Report of the League Committee on Raw Materials* (1937). League Document, A27, 1937, IIB.
† Henderson, *loc. cit.*, p. 10.   ‡ See above, p. 55.
§ It is possible to argue that if Herr Hitler's Germany possessed colonies of her own, without international restriction of her power over the native inhabitants, she would be able to exploit them to her great benefits and would derive from those territories greater economic benefits than any Colonial Power now obtains from colonies. But that is not an argument that could be reconciled with the peace aims of Britain and France.

owning countries often pay more for the products of those colonies than is paid by people who live elsewhere. In 1939, for example, sugar from British or French or American colonies could be bought in Sweden for £6 10s. a ton, while sugar from the British colonies cost £11 per ton in Britain, sugar from Puerto Rico cost £15 to £16 a ton in the United States and sugar from Martinique or Guadeloupe cost £18 a ton in France.*

On the other hand, the mother country can buy the produce of its colonies in its own currency, while other States have first to find the necessary foreign exchange. But this difficulty is often exaggerated. Mr. Henderson writes:

> A few years ago, when the different monetary systems were themselves linked together by the gold standard, it represented no difficulty at all. Even to-day† it represents an inconsiderable one in the case of most industrial countries; for foreign exchange can be purchased readily at reasonably stable rates. Even in the case of Germany it is not a really formidable difficulty. Germany carries on an export trade sufficient to equip her with large quantities of foreign exchange. She would have no difficulty in purchasing all the colonial raw materials that her people want to consume, if she were ready to use part of her foreign exchange resources for this purpose.‡

If, then, a general settlement were to remove or greatly lessen the danger of war, Germany would cease to buy vast quantities of war supplies from abroad and her people would be able to get all the colonial products they require. If, at the same time, the general settlement led to economic co-operation and freer trade, at least among the Members of the Commonwealth, many countries not possessing colonies would be able to obtain the foreign

* See Henderson, *loc. cit.*, p. 20.
† Just before Hitler's War began. ‡ *Loc. cit.*, p. 24.

exchange with which to buy whatever colonial products they required. And, if the general settlement followed the plan proposed in this chapter, not even a ghost of the *raw materials* grievance would remain.

Colonial Investments.—Here again the advantages of owning colonies are less than they are supposed to be or than once they were. Mr. Henderson mentions rubber, tea, sugar, tin and copper as the commodities which have represented the most profitable openings for British colonial investment in the past; and he adds that 'every one of these commodities is to-day the subject of an international restriction scheme.'* But whatever advantage the ownership of colonies does afford to investors from the mother country would be equally shared by all citizens of the Commonwealth if the proposal of this chapter were adopted.

Colonial Markets.—Once more, all the State Members of the Commonwealth would benefit from having equal access to the markets of all the Commonwealth colonies for their exports, provided that these exports were fairly produced—with wages, hours of work and conditions of labour regulated by international agreements.

Autarky

A fourth grievance felt by Germany and some other countries which do not now possess colonies of their own is that their lack of control over the sources of supply of some essential raw materials places them at the mercy of an economic blockade. This view ignores the fact that no conceivable colonial empire would supply all the raw materials needed by Germany. It is also apt to overlook the plain truth that, even if Germany possessed all the

* *Loc. cit.*, p. 18.

colonies in existence, she would not have access to them in war-time unless she were also mistress of the seas. What remains of this grievance when these facts have been understood would, however, vanish if a general settlement transferred to the Commonwealth all the colonies belonging to the uniting States.

Surplus Population

A fifth grievance due to lack of colonies is felt by some of those who imagine, or pretend, that a colonial empire offers a possible outlet for large-scale emigration from the mother country. In fact, however, no colonial empire however large would relieve any pressure of over-population (if and when a change from the present war-economy causes a surplus in Germany*) so well as the revival of German export trade. Not territorial expansion but industrialization, combined with free or freer markets, is the best remedy for over-population. Between 1800 and 1920 the inhabitants of Germany increased by thirty-six millions and the standard of living rose at the same time. But from 1816 to 1922 only four-and-a-half millions of Germans emigrated, and of these only a negligible proportion settled in German colonies. The total white population of all the German colonies in 1913 was only 28,000, of which some 10,000 were not German.

Careers in the Colonial Service

The sixth grievance felt in Germany as being due to her lack of colonies is that her young men have now no chance of honourable, useful and profitable employment

* At present Germany is suffering from a shortage rather than a surplus of labour.

in the colonial services. That grievance also, and it is substantial, would be gradually removed by the system of Commonwealth colonies suggested in this chapter.

The Interests of the Natives

The solution here proposed would benefit the native inhabitants of colonial territories. They would gain from more effective international regulation of colonial production. At the same time, restrictions of output would be less needed as demand increased. Nor is there any doubt that with less autarky, fewer substitutes, and a lower military expenditure in the countries which at present go short, there would be a substantially greater demand for food and raw materials from the colonies: the economic prosperity of the colonies would tend to revive with a wider and freer market for their products. During the transition period, however, some suffering might be caused to colonies by the loss of the preferential markets now provided for them by their mother countries. The Commonwealth would, however, be in a position to make good, and more than make good, any such loss of income from the savings of its Member States on preparations for war.

But native interests are by no means wholly economic. Our plan of Commonwealth colonies would have to be set aside if its material gains were offset by spiritual losses. There is, however, no sufficient reason to suppose that the introduction of individual citizens of totalitarian States into colonial services would damage the education of the natives or otherwise hinder their progress towards political maturity and independent status. Moreover, our plan would not be applied to territories—such as Ceylon, for example—which might be expected to attain self-government within twenty or twenty-five years and therefore before the plan could become fully operative. For other dependencies, our plan would increase rather than diminish their freedom to choose their own future—whether inside or outside the Commonwealth, and, if inside, whether as part of the British or some other group—when the tutelage should end and they should be able to stand alone. Any remaining risk of harm to the native population might be lessened if, should the Commonwealth to start with be less world-wide than the League of Nations, the Commonwealth's administration of colonial territories were placed, like the present mandates, under the League's supervision.

It remains to add that the solution of the colonial problem here suggested would mean that, as the Commonwealth gradually became world-wide and increased in strength, moral as well as material, so as to assert the necessary control, all colonial territories inhabited by backward peoples* not yet able to stand alone would come to be administered in their interests and with the ultimate goal of their self-government, by a central world authority.

* Such territories as Malta, Gibraltar, Panama and the Suez Canal zone form part of the problem of war prevention. See below, p. 183.

CHAPTER 18

THE FREEDOM OF THE AIR*

When, in Chapter 15, we considered the maintenance of law and order in the world, we reached the conclusion that the States uniting in a Commonwealth for this and other purposes neither would nor should pool their armies and navies but might be willing to combine their air forces. National air forces, we said, are not indispensable, although they may be convenient, for maintaining internal order. They might be abolished if other means could be found for aerial defence against aggression.

Suppose that the Members of the Commonwealth agreed to go without separate air forces of their own. It would be both practicable and desirable for them to create a Commonwealth Air Force (C.A.F.). Its functions would include joint action with contingents from the navies and armies of the uniting States to defend the Commonwealth against aggression from outside. It would also help to preserve law and order within the borders of the Commonwealth. In particular, the C.A.F. would prevent any Member State from being at the mercy of another which possessed a large number of civilian aircraft and a large personnel to fly them and which was prepared to ignore its promises not to use force against its neighbours.

* The substance of this chapter appeared under the above title in *The Contemporary Review* for May, 1933.

A Draft Convention presented by the British Government to the Disarmament Conference on 16 March, 1933, proposed that bombing from the air should be formally renounced by all States. If that were done and if, at the same time, national air forces were limited by treaty to fighting machines designed for intercepting such bombing raids as might be attempted by a covenant-breaking State, the danger from the air would be diminished. But paper promises are heavily discounted to-day as compared with 1933. So long as any national air forces are retained, people will have reason to fear that a would-be aggressor might surreptitiously acquire bombers for its air force; or that, without machines specially built for bombing, formidable raids might be made by civil aircraft escorted by fighters; or that the mere possession of a military air organization would enable an aggressively-minded State to collect, adapt and employ civil machines for bombing, even without escort.

The fear of a sudden devastating attack from the air would, however, become comparatively slight within the Commonwealth's borders if the uniting States abolished their air forces altogether, entrusted their defence against air attack to the C.A.F., and prevented the use of civil aircraft for bombing purposes by a central control of civilian aviation within the Commonwealth. This system of international control might perhaps be gradually extended over all the earth without waiting for the Commonwealth to become world-wide.

It is true that such changes as are needed to enable civil planes to carry and drop bombs can be generally made in a very short time and with very little trouble. These adaptations are, in certain cases, rendered all the easier by the subsidies with which some governments influence the design of civil aircraft.*

The use of civilian aircraft for bombing purposes would be made more difficult by general agreement upon such rules as were proposed in the British Draft Convention.† But so long as civilian machines are sufficiently powerful to carry an adequate number of bombs, or so numerous as to compensate for their small size, almost any machines could be used for bombing. Moreover, in the absence of any military machines to meet them, an attack could be made by civilian machines without much training. Unless, however, they came in very large numbers, untrained civilian pilots would have a very poor chance of carrying through an attack successfully against the opposition of fighter planes.

There remains the possibility that civil machines might be adapted for fighting sufficiently to deal with defence by military machines. Although, in many cases, a few days or even less might suffice to fit machine-guns in ring mountings, the training of the crews of civil machines for air fighting would occupy a considerable time, and that time would afford opportunity for many counter measures, both national and international.

It is clear, then, that military machines must be available to meet any air attack. If, however, these machines formed *national* air forces, they would themselves inspire fear in other nations. That is why the military machines which are needed to meet air attacks should be under international control. So far as the uniting States are

* In 1933, every important transport company maintaining regular air lines in Europe relied upon government subsidies for a substantial part of its total receipts. The proportion varied from some 30 per cent in the case of the Dutch air lines (K.L.M.) to over 85 per cent paid to some of the French companies.

† See Part II, Section II, Chapter 3, Annex II.

concerned, the controlling authority would be their Commonwealth. The machines would form the C.A.F.

Since, as we have seen, the C.A.F. would perform the double function of helping to defend the Commonwealth against aggression from outside and of acting as a police force inside the Commonwealth, the magnitude and composition of the C.A.F. would be determined by the size of the air forces that might threaten it from beyond its borders. As the Commonwealth gradually grew to worldwide dimensions, the threat from outside would become negligible and the composition of the C.A.F. would be defined by its police functions alone. For this purpose fighter planes alone would be needed. In particular they would suffice as a protection against air raids which, if no considerable national air forces were left in the world, could only be made by civilian machines. It would be contrary to the principles of our peace aims to equip the C.A.F. with bombing planes for the purpose of enforcing its will upon recalcitrant Member States or for punishing them for breaches of its constitution or other infringements of international law.

A difficult question for the uniting States to decide will be whether their C.A.F. should be made up of national units, like the Imperial German army before the World War or (in theory at least) the fleet of the British Commonwealth of Nations to-day,* or whether it should be constituted as a unified international service like the Secretariat of the League of Nations. To the present writer it seems that the latter plan would prove to be the better in the long run although it would have to overcome greater obstacles at the outset.

The principal bases of the C.A.F. and its training establishments should be located, so far as possible, in

* See the footnote on p. 148.

the smaller countries, or even in territory under international control. Such territory might eventually include not only the colonial lands discussed in the preceding chapter but also such strategic outposts of empire as Gibraltar, Singapore or (when America chooses to enter the Commonwealth) the fortified canal zone of Panama. But, in order to be ready when and where needed, detachments would be stationed in selected airports along the coasts or other frontiers of the uniting States. No doubt there would be some danger of these detachments being seized by a desperate nation determined on aggression. But no State would be able thus to capture more than a very small part of the C.A.F.

In order to see how such a system would operate to protect the people of the Commonwealth against a sudden air attack from one of its Member States, let us imagine that, some years after the peace settlement, the German Government decides to make a sudden bombing raid on France. (This hypothesis may seem foolish: if Herr Hitler abstained from trying to bomb Paris or London for many months after the outbreak of war in September, 1939, it is not easy to suppose that any future ruler of Germany would attempt anything of the kind in peacetime, and against far greater odds. But let the supposition stand and see what happens.) All national air forces having been abolished, the German army begins by seizing the contingents of the C.A.F., except such as make good their escape, in the airports of Germany. Civil aircraft are seized at the same time in the airports under German control. But the captured fighter planes of the C.A.F. might well be designed to fly but a few hundred miles; and they would not be able to carry bombs of large size suitable for attacking warships, fortresses or protected depots. Before they could be equipped with small bombs and sent to drop them on the industrial districts of north-eastern France, their seizure would be known and its purpose guessed. Time would be given for the assembling of C.A.F. contingents from France, Holland, Belgium, Switzerland and England. Damage from the German raid might then be negligible. Suppose, however, that the C.A.F. planes seized by Germany were used to escort civil aircraft. Again there would be ample warning; and the losses among the civilian planes would be so heavy as to render a repetition unlikely or impossible. The losses would be even greater if the raid were attempted without an escort.

Civil Aviation

International flying in Europe has hitherto been severely handicapped by the multifarious restrictions imposed by many separate governments. But in the United States, civil aviation does not suffer from this disadvantage, since control is exercised by a single federal government.

Some measure of public control over commercial air transport is, of course, indispensable.

The public is entitled to protection against ignorant, careless or wilful pilots and aircraft owners whose actions might bring destruction of life and property. Few will deny the wisdom of the State in requiring aircraft to be inspected in order to test their airworthiness, to be registered in order to establish their ownership and insure the responsibility thereof, and to require pilots to be examined and licensed in order to guard citizens against dangers arising from their inexperience and negligence.*

For similar reasons the British Mercantile Marine is

* Cf. *International Control of Aviation*, by Kenneth W. Colegrove, pp. 3 and 4. (World Peace Foundation, 1930.)

controlled by the Board of Trade under the Merchant Shipping Acts. But such public control as is necessary for international flying might well be exercised by a single, international authority*—at first in Europe and ultimately throughout the world.

An international authority of a sort was brought into existence by the Convention relating to the Regulation of Air Navigation, 1919. But the International Commission for Air Navigation (C.I.N.A.) then created does not suffice. It is, in fact, little more than a clearing-house for the interchange of information concerning the national control of civil aviation by the contracting States. This national control is of the essence of the Convention of 1919 under which C.I.N.A. works. For example, no aircraft may engage in international air transport unless it possesses the nationality of one State only and belongs wholly to nationals of the State or to a company of which the chairman and at least two-thirds of the directors possess the nationality in question.† Again, any aeroplane flying with mails and passengers and crossing several countries in the course of its journey, may not engage in an *entrepôt* trade, setting down and taking up passengers and goods at ports of call *en route*.‡ Finally, every State has 'complete and exclusive sovereignty over the air space above its territory;'§ and every aircraft, while it has the right to cross the air space of a foreign State without landing, must follow the route fixed by the State over which the flying takes place.||

---

* This aspect of the matter will become increasingly important to Great Britain when air transport develops so as to link Europe up more closely with America. The shortest air routes from New York to every European capital, except only Madrid and Lisbon, cross—or pass within a very few miles of—the British Isles.
† Article 7 of the Convention. ‡ Article 16 of the Convention.
§ Article 1 of the Convention. || Article 15 of the Convention.

Such restrictions as these are obstacles to the free development of international flying. The time has come to renounce in the interest of every nation, as well as in the general interest, some of these privileges hitherto associated with national sovereignty. The time has come to transfer the control of international flying—in western Europe for a start—to an international authority. If the general settlement leads to the creation of such a Commonwealth as we have envisaged, that authority (and not only for western Europe but for the whole Commonwealth) should be the Commonwealth itself. Its control might be exercised on its behalf by an 'Air Board of Control'* (A.B.C.) under its direction. The business of the A.B.C. would be to encourage international flying under conditions of free competition between international companies, national companies and privately owned air lines. Such regulation as might be needed for navigation in the free air above a territorial limit of, say, three thousand metres, would be undertaken by the A.B.C. with whatever help it might need from the C.A.F. The A.B.C. should also provide meteorological information, supervise the lighting of the principal international air routes within the Commonwealth, and have the right to inspect the airports of all the uniting States. The functions of the A.B.C. should also include the validation of certificates of air worthiness issued by some international registration society such as Lloyd's.

One further proposal deserves to be considered. The principal international airports of the uniting States, including every airport to or from which machines fly direct across an international frontier, might belong to the Commonwealth, be controlled by the A.B.C., and

* Cf. Mr. Rudyard Kipling's 'Aerial Board of Control' in *With the Night Mail*.

perhaps be extra-territorialized. Passengers and goods should be free to travel by the machines of any air line, in the free air above the territorial ceiling, between these Commonwealth airports. The A.B.C. might well provide hotel accommodation within its aerodromes so that it would be possible for a passenger, on a long journey by air, to sleep at night (and even get duty-free drinks and smokes) in these hotels without having his luggage or papers examined by, or being otherwise subjected to, national authorities between his starting point and his final destination. Even if he were a political refugee, or had been guilty of some minor offence against the government of the surrounding country, he would be free from arrest by the national police. On Commonwealth territory, as well as flying, he would enjoy the freedom of the air.

CHAPTER 19

INTER-STATE AND FEDERAL UNION

When the time comes for a general settlement such as was outlined in Chapter 14,* the negotiating Powers will have to decide what sort of a union of the negotiating Powers is needed to avert future wars between them, to protect them against aggression from outside, and to give each of their citizens a fairer chance of a useful and happy life.

It is not going to be easy to reach a general settlement of this kind. It may be impossible if some of the negotiators have the mistaken impression that nothing but some predetermined form of federal union will attain the end in view. Even a football match might be lost by the better team if handicapped by some preconceived notion of the only tactics by which to score.

The word 'federation' is used in popular speech with a variety of meanings. On the day that Great Britain and France went to war with Germany, an eminent American, Dr. Nicholas Murray Butler, delivered an address entitled *Toward a Federal World*. He said that the Statute of Westminster† 'applied the federal principle to legislatively independent members of a great empire scattered all around the world.' If the British Commonwealth of

---

* See pp. 142 to 145 above.   † See above, p. 38.

Nations is an example of federal union, so also, *a fortiori*, is the League of Nations: indeed the League's Covenant comes nearer than the Statute of Westminster to providing a written constitution for the British Commonwealth. But 'federal union' as it is generally advocated in the United Kingdom and in the United States to-day is essentially a system in which 'the central government is chosen by and is responsible to its citizens, and exerts its authority directly upon them, not through the machinery of the various State governments.'* That is the distinctive feature of the 'federal union' we are to discuss in this chapter, as it is also a feature of the federal Constitution of the United States of America.

In Chapter 3 we were reminded by the history of the English-speaking world that 'federal union' is not the only way of uniting States. Nor is it necessarily the best way when the States that have to be linked together are widely separated by geography or language or race or religion. It is, however, natural enough that the failures of the League of Nations in the 1930s should bring to mind the similar failures of the League of States or 'firm league of friendship' formed by the thirteen North American States when they had just torn themselves away from the first British empire. It would indeed be surprising if proposals had not been made to apply to the world the same remedy as proved so successful in

---

* Patrick Ransome in an article on 'Federal Government' in *The Fortnightly*, October, 1939, p. 418. Mr. Streit in *Union Now* adds the following essential conditions for the federal union which he advocates:
    a union citizenship
    a union defence force
    a union customs free economy
    a union money
    a union postal and communication system.

America. That remedy was the 'federal union' devised in Philadelphia in 1787.*

The British Commonwealth† adopted a different method of uniting States sufficiently for them to work smoothly together in matters of common concern while they remain otherwise free to govern themselves as they see fit. And when the Covenant of the League of Nations was being drafted in Paris under the joint leadership of both branches of the English-speaking world, it was to the representatives of the British Commonwealth, Lord Cecil and General Smuts, that the other members of the committee would commonly turn for advice. 'You already run a League of Nations,' they would say. 'Tell us from your practical experience how to meet the difficulty we have next to face.'

Thus the League is an inter-State system resembling the British Commonwealth in its political form but not, unfortunately, in its spiritual or psychological essence. We saw, in Chapter 11, how the efforts of the League of Nations Union and of its sister-societies abroad were not enough to form an 'invisible bond of ideals'‡ sufficiently strong to hold the League together.

That mistake must not be repeated. If the international Commonwealth created as part of the general settlement after Hitler's War is, in whole or in part, an inter-State system on the British model—a restored and revitalized League of Nations—it will not flourish or even survive unless it is rooted in a 'collective sentiment'§ or League loyalty so strong as to dominate and integrate the private interests of particular States. The individual citizens of

* See above, Chapter 3, pp. 36–37.
† See above, Chapter 3, pp. 38–39.
‡ See above, Chapter 3, p. 39.
§ See above, p. 97.

the uniting States must look upon themselves as citizens of the Commonwealth. They must be ready to obey the Commonwealth in all those matters in which its authority is to be supreme.*

It is sometimes said that this cannot happen unless the Commonwealth is a 'federal union'; and that, if the supreme authority of the Commonwealth were exercised by a body—like the League's Assembly on to-day's Supreme War Council of France and the United Kingdom—of representatives of State governments, it would be at the mercy of these governments and therefore incapable of effective control in its own sphere. But why should not the United Kingdom, for example, be represented on the Supreme Council of the inter-State Commonwealth by a Cabinet Minister who, so long as he has the backing of British public opinion, will preserve in his own person the continuity of his country's foreign policy? Why should he not retain his place, despite changes in the home government, both on the Supreme Council and in the Cabinet where he would keep the interests of the wider world before the minds of his colleagues? If he could not be dismissed by the Prime Minister except at the risk of a major political crisis, any doubt whether the British electorate supported him or the Prime Minister in the event of an irreconcilable difference between them would be settled by a general election. The issue would be decided as effectively as any direct election of the central government of a 'federal union' could possibly decide it.

A constitutional convention of this kind would ensure that the representatives of Great Britain, or of any other democratic country, on the Supreme Council were in as strong a position *vis-à-vis* their home government, as if they had been directly elected to the international body

* See above, p. 143, and Chapter 15.

by popular vote. Such was the position of Dr. Beneš when he represented Czecho-Slovakia at Geneva for a dozen years or more, and of M. Briand or Herr Stresemann for shorter periods. They continued to represent their countries at Geneva despite changes of government at home. If all the uniting democracies followed these examples, the central government of their Commonwealth would be almost as representative of their citizens as if the Commonwealth were a 'federal union.'*

Almost, but not quite. On the other hand, an inter-State Commonwealth might be of far wider extent than any 'federal union' that is likely to be formed in the 1940s. It would be difficult, if not impossible, for a State (like Italy, for example) without responsible government at home to join a Commonwealth which insisted upon the direct popular election of its federal government; and any one of the uniting States would afterwards have to leave the Commonwealth if, for domestic reasons, it passed temporarily under the rule of a dictator. Moreover, if no Commonwealth save a 'federal union' were capable of averting future wars and otherwise achieving the peace aims of the Allies, the form of Germany's internal government might have to be dictated by the Allies in order that she could enter the Commonwealth where, as we saw, her presence is indispensable. But, as we remarked in Chapter 14,† it is no part of our peace aims to interfere with Germany's internal political institutions so long as her internal government does not pursue an external policy injurious to her neighbours.

The extent of a 'federal union' would be further restricted if, as seems probable, some of the democracies

* The Dutch Government was generally represented on the League's Assembly by one member from each of three parties.
† On p. 139 above.

eligible for membership were unwilling to enter so close a federation. Great Britain and France do not seem likely to regard an Anglo-French parliament, or a large federal union parliament, as indispensable. And we have seen reason to suppose that an effective Commonwealth need not get rid of national armies and navies which would have no place in a 'federal union.'* Indeed, it may well be that no 'federal union,' except perhaps one of the Scandinavian States and another of States in the south-east of Europe, will come into being during the 1940s. The experience at Paris in 1919 and the replies of the twenty-six European governments to M. Briand's memorandum on *European Federal Union* in 1930 do not warrant a more ambitious view. And there is little prospect that any 'federal unions' of this limited scope would suffice to avert future wars.

All these obstacles to 'federal union' might perhaps be overcome if it were true that future wars could certainly be averted by a sufficiently large Commonwealth in the fashion of the United States but not by one on the model of 'Great Britain, Ireland and the British Dominions beyond the seas.' But the American Constitution did not save the United States from the War of Secession in which more men lost their lives than in any equal period of fighting up to that time; and no one can safely assert that a federal union, even if it included all the Great Powers, would be sure to avert a war of secession. It is not even possible to sustain the more modest claim that, although peace established by 'federal union' might be disturbed from time to time, it would always tend to return, while peace maintained by any other system would completely disappear upon the occurrence of the first international dispute. The evidence of the Geneva experiment makes that proposition untenable; for we

* See footnote on p. 189.

have seen* how, between 1920 and 1931, the League of Nations settled many international disputes of which a considerable number were serious. Nor has there been any likelihood of fighting between the States in the British Commonwealth since the creation of the present system of 'units within a larger Unity.' The view that 'federal union' alone can avert future wars in the next two decades is both mischievous and mistaken.

We come, then, to the conclusion that the effective working of the Commonwealth that is needed to stabilize peace and to make it constructive—so as to increase social justice, to raise the standard of living, to multiply the happiness and usefulness of human lives, and to open the way towards ever greater achievements by mankind—does not depend only or chiefly upon whether the Commonwealth is a 'federal union' on the American model or an inter-State system on the British model, or a mixture of both; and we have seen that they mix extremely well.† Rather does it depend upon whether the Commonwealth derives its authority from the thoughts and feelings, the sentiments and loyalties,‡ of individual men and women as well as from the promises made by their governments on their behalf.

We have already seen§ how the Members of the League of Nations failed in their attempt to bind the future by paper pacts and promises insufficiently supported by the peoples' loyalties and understanding. That is a lesson

---

* On p. 98 above. † See above, Chapter 3, p. 40.
‡ *Cf.* E. H. Carr: 'It is the embryonic character of this common feeling between nations, not the lack of a world legislature, and not the insistence of states on being judges in their own cause, which is the real obstacle in the way of an international procedure of peaceful change' (*The Twenty Years Crisis, 1919–1939*, p. 279).
§ On pp. 113–115 above.

INTER-STATE AND FEDERAL UNION

which the Members of the Commonwealth will do well to take to heart. It is no use trying to base a lasting peace on the doctrine that laws must be obeyed, that treaties must be respected, that *pacta sunt servanda*. It may or may not be true that an old catechism asked English children 'What are laws for?' and prescribed as the answer 'Laws are to preserve the rich in the possession of their riches and to restrain the vices of the poor.'* But that is how legal obligations are apt to appear to people who are bound by them without being either convinced of the justice of the law or conscious of themselves as its authors.†

Not even a fundamental law‡ forming part of the constitution of the Commonwealth and accepted by all the uniting States can take the place of a common purpose and a common loyalty in the mass of the citizens. For the Law is no Pole-star to guide the forward march of mankind. It has the humbler rôle of whipping in the laggards, so that the behaviour of men and women in

* Quoted by the Rev. Dr. Nathaniel Micklem in a recent broadcast. See *The Listener*, 14 March, 1940, p. 528.

† Cf. Lord Halifax's quotation from T. H. Green: 'That man is free who is conscious of himself as the author of the law which he obeys' (*Address to the University of Oxford*, 27 February, 1940).

‡ Mr. H. G. Wells, in his latest book, *The New World Order*, proposes some such fundamental law in the shape of a ten-article Declaration of the Rights of Man. Mr. Wells's draft should indeed provide the topic of 'a great debate' as he desires. In the end Great Britain may have to join in accepting the outcome of that debate. To agree to something of the kind may indeed be one of the 'sacrifices' (see p. 29 above) Britons will have to make in uniting with other States, including France at the outset and eventually America, which are accustomed to written constitutions and political declarations of abstract principles. But, to British minds, abstract principles and generalizations are better omitted from laws and constitutions. Even the Great Charter which King John signed at Runnymede was, as G. M. Trevelyan has pointed out in his *History of England* (p. 171), a 'technical' document, 'deficient in the generalizations with which the Declaration of Independence abounds' and 'totally ignorant of the "rights of man."'

their own country, as of nations in the world at large, will not fall too far behind the general sense of what is right and just. But it is only in so far as most of the citizens of the Commonwealth share a common purpose to seek its interest before all other political aims that they will be conscious of themselves as the authors of its laws and feel free—free to put their best into life and to get the best out of it. Liberty, as we said in Chapter 2, springs from harmony of purpose: a purpose which is superior to dictators, kings, parliaments, magnates, mobs and even majorities. Where that principle is rejected there is neither liberty nor peace, and men or nations have no choice but to fight for or against one of the partisans contending for supremacy.*

We have said that the citizens of the uniting States should learn, and be taught, to think of themselves as citizens also of the Commonwealth.† They should feel a loyalty to the Commonwealth stronger even than any of their national patriotisms. Sir Alfred Zimmern has written that 'nationality, like religion, is subjective . . . psychological . . . a condition of mind . . . a spiritual possession . . . a way of feeling, thinking and living.'‡ So it is with the Commonwealth. The sentiment for it in the public mind is of the very essence of the Commonwealth itself and the source of all its power.

On this understanding, the nascent Commonwealth which emerges from the general settlement that is to follow Hitler's War should include the 'federal union' of as many democracies as possible. Since, however, 'federal union' is hardly likely to unite a sufficient number of

---

* Cf. Walter Lippmann, *The Good Society*, p. 332.
† See above, p. 191.
‡ *Nationality and Government*, p. 51.

powerful nations to achieve our peace aims in the 1940s, the Commonwealth must bring together in an inter-State system many other States besides those in any 'federal union' or 'federal unions' which also belong to it. In this way many peoples who might not be ready to enter a 'federal union' would yet be able to take part in building a new world order. And this inter-State nut with its federal kernel might well be none other than the League of Nations* reconstructed, revitalized, perhaps renamed, and certainly enlarged so as to include at least Germany† from among the present non-Members of the League. If, however, some Members of the League did not enter the Commonwealth at the outset, the League should continue for the present as the whole fruit, with its fleshy husk outside the hard nut of the Commonwealth. Or, to change the simile, the Commonwealth should be a 'ginger group' within the League, always moving it to act upon the principles of the Covenant.

In any case we have to ask how the nascent Commonwealth is likely to be constituted, what States are likely to belong to it, within a few months of its emergence from the general settlement. We have seen that Great Britain, France and Germany must be among its first Members: without them there can be no Commonwealth capable of realizing our peace aims. Britons who are proud of being British subjects and of sharing this 'common status' with all citizens of the British Empire‡ will wish to see the United Kingdom remain at least as closely linked with the British Dominions as with France or

---

* See above, p. 143. † See above, p. 143.
‡ Inhabitants of a British protectorate or mandated territory are 'British protected persons' and are treated for some purposes as British subjects and for others as aliens.

Germany or other Members of the new international Commonwealth. If their wish is to be fulfilled, the Commonwealth will have to include the British Empire. It will certainly have to include the French Empire if it includes France. And the Poles and the Czechs are sure to want their new countries to be among its original Members.

It is also fairly safe to assume* that all the Scandinavian nations and indeed the whole Oslo group of Powers—Norway, Sweden, Denmark, Finland, Holland, Belgium and Switzerland—as well as Turkey and many of the Balkan States will wish to join. The 'Old Alliance' may be relied upon to bring in Portugal. This is perhaps as far as it is safe to go without risk of disappointment. But there is a balance of probability that Italy would not willingly remain outside a Commonwealth which embraced Germany as well as Great Britain and France, and indeed most of western and central Europe. Spain and Hungary may be expected to follow Italy's lead and even to press Italy not to hold aloof.

The nascent Commonwealth would then include the British and French Empires and all of Europe west of Russia.† The regional groupings suggested in Chapters 15 and 16 for defence and other purposes would make it easier for the Latin-American States to belong to the Commonwealth from the outset. Nearly all of them were among the original Members of the League of Nations. When the Commonwealth includes the Latin-American States, or at least so many of them as are now Members of the League, the remaining League Members in Asia—China, Iran, Iraq and Afghanistan, but not, perhaps,

---

* As we did on p. 152 above.
† Lithuania, Latvia and Estonia would only remain outside if compelled to do so by the U.S.S.R.

Siam—are likely also to come in; and that may quite well happen at the start. Japan's adhesion would doubtless be delayed. For the Membership of the United States the Commonwealth will probably also have to wait. Eventually, however, the American fear of entangling alliances will diminish as Americans grasp the truth that 'to keep out of horses' hoofs is good advice for a puppy, but not for an elephant.'*

Meanwhile the friendly co-operation of the Great Republic would enable the Commonwealth, long before it becomes world-wide, to act effectively in all the matters covered by its authority and gradually, no doubt, to extend that authority to some departments of government originally outside its scope. Nor would the absence of the U.S.S.R.† prevent the Commonwealth from functioning or continuing to evolve until at last the Russians could no longer afford to remain aloof. The Commonwealth would then become, to all intents and purposes, worldwide.

In any case, the Commonwealth of the general settlement must be only a beginning. From this nut, as we called it, there must grow a tree so tall and strong as to give shelter and security to all nations. Yet all the foresight of statesmen, all the skill of diplomats and all the science of economists will not make the tree grow unless it is rooted in the hearts and minds of common men. And, however great the economic and military power

* Don Salvador de Madariaga in *Elysian Fields* (George Allen and Unwin, 1937), p. 75, makes the spirit of President Washington speak these words in reply to a Senator of the 1930s who tried to hold the President to the terms of his Farewell Address.

† Mr. Litvinov told the Hague Conference of 1922 that 'it was necessary to face the fact that there was not one world, but two, a Soviet world and a non-Soviet world' (quoted by E. H. Carr, *loc. cit.*, p. 251). Mr. Litvinov's remark is still true of the world in 1940.

of the Commonwealth may become, however hard and tough the wooden heart of the tree, it will soon be stark and dead if it ceases to draw from these roots the life-giving sap that is world loyalty. As the rising sap surrounds the tree, so must the World Commonwealth of the future be held together by this world loyalty and the invisible bond of ideals. To foster all around the globe those thoughts and feelings that will put world-order and the welfare of mankind before selfish interests is a task that must commend itself as well to all believers in 'federal union' as to all who accept the principles of the League of Nations. It is a task of education, essential to the growth of lasting peace.

CHAPTER 20

EDUCATION FOR CITIZENSHIP*

Thirteen years ago, a memorandum was presented to the President of the Board of Education and the Secretary of State for Scotland by all the associations of schoolmasters and schoolmistresses in Great Britain. This *Declaration of the Teaching Profession* set forth some of the chief purposes of education. The first was 'to build up the coherent body of knowledge—the "single wide interest"—on which strength of character largely depends.'

Now there is no denying 'the radically untidy ill-adjusted character of the fields of actual experience.' These, Professor Whitehead† tells us, provide the starting point for scientific thought. He adds that its goal is 'a neat trim tidy exact world': an orderly and coherent whole built up, a bit at a time, by discoveries that link together all the separate branches of knowledge. So Rutherford linked chemistry with physics and Einstein made mechanics into an offshoot of geometry. Thus human experience is gradually arranged for handy reference, and loses much of its original untidiness.

Much, but not all. For the world of our experience includes mankind; and no amount of abstraction, analysis,

* The topic of this chapter is more fully discussed in *Knowledge and Character* by Maxwell Garnett (Cambridge University Press, 1939).
† Presidential Address to Section A of the British Association for the Advancement of Science, Newcastle, 1916.

synthesis or classification—no amount of effort spent in organizing thought—will get rid of man-made faults and discords. These constitute, in Whitehead's view, the problem of evil. If the goal of scientific thought is ever to be reached, men and women must help to complete the process of creation by seeking to eliminate this evil. They must bring order into the world itself, and not merely into their thoughts about the world.

Then scientific thought may go on towards its goal, linking up the whole realm of facts much as King Alfred made one realm of England out of the earlier heptarchy. The inspired guess of yesterday becomes the scientific theory of to-day, the accepted fact of to-morrow and the common sense of the day after. Helped by formal teaching, but by no means wholly dependent upon it, boys and girls learn to think of the world as it is commonly supposed to be. So the march of discovery towards the goal of scientific thought gets reflected in the minds of the younger generation. They see the process going on, and conceive that there can be no end to it until the world stands revealed as a single whole.

But the parts of the whole are not all of equal value. No man can know all that is knowable, and no man needs to. Even an omniscient God might waste energy in numbering the hairs of a head or the stones on Chesil Beach. Facts differ in value; and the same facts have different values for different people according to their several walks in life. For both these reasons, educational theory no longer echoes Mr. Gradgrind's 'What we want is facts.' Its quest to-day is for values even more than for facts.

What then ought a man to *know*, and what ought he to *feel* about the various facts that come to his knowledge?

For one thing, it is worse than useless to learn what is not true, or nearly true. My knowledge of the world is my chart by which I set my course and plan what I will do. If I think of the world as it is not, instead of as it is, I shall get into trouble. For instance, I have often had to cross Hyde Park Corner from Constitution Hill to an office in Grosvenor Crescent, next door to St. George's Hospital, one hundred yards of the most exciting roadway in London. I have sometimes wondered how far I would get if I were to think of the traffic as it used to be when I was a schoolboy and the push-bicycle was the fastest thing on the street. Probably no further than St. George's Hospital. Even so does disaster await all whose thought presents a grossly untrue picture of the actual world they walk or work in. Civilization itself may suffer shipwreck if civilized men persist in supposing that, in world affairs, the part can be greater than the whole; that *sacro egoismo* or *Deutschland über Alles* are practical politics; or that, in the long run, a nation can best serve its own interest if its chief concern is anything less than the welfare of mankind.

On the other hand, it would be a mistake to suppose that the facts we know are the very truth itself. My chart may tell me what I need to know of the sea I sail on. But it is not the sea: I could not swim in it. And most, if not all, facts are no more than statements that fit our experience, statements consistent with the bits of truth we think we know. There is no sharp line between the facts of science and those of religion.

Then, again, I shall waste my time in acquiring a number of disconnected fragments of information, such as fill the snappy paragraphs of many modern newspapers. Superficial knowledge of several separate subjects is almost equally easy to achieve. For that reason alone such studies provide but a poor substitute for a strenuous intellectual discipline, whether in school or at the university. But below the surface are other facts, more general and more abstract, harder to understand and much more worth learning. They are valuable, not only for being difficult, but also because they can be used so often. A regular conjugation covers a multitude of individual verbs: it is more general than they are and therefore of more value. Or, again, the very general (and very abstract) fact that twice two is four is much more useful than merely to know that two arms and two legs make four limbs. If God is everywhere and in all things, He is the most general fact of all; and it is better to know Him than to be acquainted with every science and every language under the sun.

Last, but not least important, a person's knowledge ought to hang together. It must not be stored in water-tight compartments. When Dido built Carthage on as much land as an ox-hide would cover, she made of it a leather thong a mile or more in length. In order to enclose as much land as possible, this giant bootlace would have to be laid on the ground in the form of a circle; and Dido did it near enough. But if she had cut her lace in halves and enclosed two separate circles with them, she would have got only half as much land for her city. In much the same way, knowledge that is linked together (like the language, literature and history of Greece and Rome taught by the form-masters in the old classical schools) is many times more useful than the same facts taught as separate subjects by independent specialists.

But what, we asked, ought a man to *feel* about the facts that come to his knowledge? To feel rightly about the world, to love what is good in it and to hate what is evil, to seek the highest when one sees it, is, for most people, at least as important as accurate knowledge or skill in one's own special line. The feelings or 'affects'—conations and emotions—belong to those instinctive processes which, as William McDougall taught, are the great driving forces of the mind, the prime movers of all human activity. Knowledge harnessed to instinct acquires far more influence over thought and conduct than facts that have no link with feelings.

When a fact is linked in my mind with some strong feeling, passion or emotion, it becomes the object of a *sentiment*; and the sentiment becomes an *interest* when a whole group of facts are linked together in the mind with feelings of emotion and conation (an urge to act). Thus, my interest in a group of facts consists in what I *know* of them and what I *feel* about them. And, according to the *Declaration of the Teaching Profession*, one of the chief purposes of educating anybody is to help him to form a single wide interest in the whole world of his experience, rather than several separate interests in different parts of it.

Single wide interests should not be all alike. One's knowledge, and one's feelings about it, should depend upon one's walk in life. Little Chinese girls in the schools of Singapore waste their time when learning the dates of the battles of the Wars of the Roses. And young Senegalese citizens of the French Republic do even worse when they recite in chorus, like the children of Normandy or Picardy, 'Our ancestors were tall fair men with yellow hair and blue eyes.'

Even the same subject should be differently studied by those who want to become expert in it and by those who are content to remain amateurs of that branch of knowledge. There is one knowledge by the expert and another knowledge by the amateur, and one amateur differs from another amateur in knowledge.

Even so, the single wide interests of different people ought to have much in common. It is not merely that, whatever a man's calling, he is also a citizen. But we all live in the same world, and all alike need to know and value its deepest truths. All alike need to think of that world as, potentially at least, an ordered and coherent whole: if it does not yet exist, it can and it shall.

But if we are to see it thus while scientific thought is yet far from its goal, we must guess at the links that have still to make all knowledge into one. That is the method of science. Such guesses—inspirations or revelations, if you will—led to the great generalizations of the past: to Newton's laws, to Maxwell's equations, to Rutherford's atoms and to Einstein's relativity. All these became discoveries when the original guesses were found to fit experience. Our hypotheses about the central truths, the supreme realities, of the universe have also to be tested by experience, our own and so much of other people's as we can disentangle from their accounts of it. And these supreme realities, facts of the future but hypotheses of the present, together with the sentiments formed round them, should be central in our single wide interests. Otherwise our charts will be wrong and our lives may lose their bearings.

That central place is, however, occupied already. We have seen that the value of a fact is enhanced by its frequent occurrence in the world of experience. General facts can be used so often that they are valuable on this account. But the importance of a fact to any particular person does not depend only upon how often he comes across it, and still less upon its generality in human experience as a whole. It depends chiefly upon the fact's influence upon his thought and conduct.

Every time I think of any fact, a neural record in my brain is deepened, and this makes my thought more likely to repeat itself. Here is the neurological basis of habit. And every time the thought comes back again, whether from habit, in day-dreaming, or because of incoming sense-impressions from my environment (including my own body), my neural record of the fact is made deeper still. If the fact is the object of a sentiment, so as to stir my emotions when I think of it, my thought is likely to be more intense and its recurrence will deepen my neural record, or neurogram, all the more on this account. My deepest neurograms have, as a rule, most influence over my thought and conduct.

No facts are more likely to present themselves to me from outside or from inside my body, or to occur to me while day-dreaming, or to stir my feelings when I think of them, than facts connected with myself, my family, my friends, my fellow-citizens, and our future. My neurograms of all these will be among the deepest in my brain. They form the neural counterpart of my self-regarding sentiment, a permanent possession of my mind. None of my other sentiments, or interests if I have several, is likely to have so great an influence upon my thought and conduct. If all my interests are joined in one, my sentiment of self-regard will still claim a central place in my mind and in my single wide interest.

How then is any man's single wide interest to be centred both in the supreme realities and in his own affairs, his sentiment for himself? An answer to this riddle is found in the Christian conception of God, who is both the supreme reality (the central fact in the universe, the first cause of it all) and the supreme good (the *summum bonum*) in the sense that to know Him is the highest good for every individual man and woman: 'This is life eternal, to know Thee, the only true God.'

But that is only half the text, and only half the story. If, instead of being driven by his self-regarding sentiment, with all the instincts belonging to it, to seek first his own personal welfare, a man is to seek first the kingdom of God, his sentiment for God—'the kingdom of heaven,' says Whitehead, 'is God'—must be as near to the centre of his interest as his sentiment for himself. Yet 'if he love not his brother whom he hath seen, how can he love God whom he hath not seen?' How can one's sentiment of love for God express itself in action except by acts of love and service to one's brother man? So it seems that some sentiment for all his neighbours, near and far, should lie, along with his sentiment for God, at the centre of each man's single wide interest.

Is it then possible, without sacrificing truth, to think of man as, next to God, the most valuable, significant and important of all the facts in the universe? Man is, from a material standpoint, but a tiny parasite on a diminutive planet of one of hundreds of millions of stars, and a very average one at that. Yet the Christian guess at the undiscovered centre of the realm of facts asserts that man does stand in a uniquely close relationship to God, that man has in him something of the Spirit of God, that he may even call God his Father, and that the most perfect Man of all was, in a special sense, not only Son of Man but also Son of God. So we complete our quotation from the Fourth Gospel: 'This is life eternal that they may know thee, the only true God, and Jesus Christ whom thou has sent.'

In this way the Christian hypothesis enables every man to organize his thought so that the most valuable and most central facts of experience in general are also the most important to him personally. They are then central in his single wide interest, linked with all his ordered thought, guiding his every considered act, part and parcel of his main purpose in life. If he takes this hypothesis and acts upon it in order to test it by experience, his religion becomes at one with his science. Theology, the queen of the sciences, should be, like the rest of them, experimental.

An education that aims at creating single wide interests centred in a sentiment of love for, and so in a purpose to serve, both God and man, adds the like-mindedness of all to the single-mindedness of each. Thus it makes for freedom from external as well as from internal conflict. For, if I want above all else to do what my neighbours wish me to do for all our sakes, then I am free to do as I like. Harmony of purpose, ὁμόνοια, to seek first the common goal is the root of liberty.* And the root of justice† is that feeling of comradeship, or ἀγάπη, which comes from having a sentiment for other people and for God (who, St. John says, is ἀγάπη) as near to the centre of one's single wide interest as one's sentiment of self-regard. An education that results in single wide interests of this kind will ensure for the people comradeship, liberty, justice, truth and unity.

But it will only ensure peace if the community thus educated is world-wide. Or, at least, the community must be so large as to leave no room in the world for any rival society that might bring upon it the catastrophe of modern war.

A world-wide Commonwealth may also bestow upon its members other blessings not to be found in smaller

* See above, p. 22.   † See above, p. 22.

self-contained societies. The larger the community, the more material wealth will it produce, other things being equal, for each of its members.* And more wealth per head means more men set free, or given more time free, from the task of producing or distributing material goods so that they can serve God in other ways: by discovery, or teaching, or governing, or otherwise ministering to the health and happiness of mankind.

A world-wide Commonwealth implies world-government. It also implies world loyalty as the only sure foundation on which that government's authority can rest. In a democracy, patriotism is the motive power of the State. That need not be so under a dictator. But even a dictator dare not rely only upon devotion to his person, admiration for his leadership or fear of his wrath. Herr Hitler, wishing to tighten his hold on Germany, seeks to intensify German patriotism and the sense of German unity as the bases of his authority.

World loyalty is a sentiment, akin to patriotism, for mankind as a whole. Such a sentiment should, we said, be at the centre of every single wide interest: a sentiment closely linked with a sentiment for God. Indeed, the fatherhood of God and the brotherhood of man are facts that belong together, like electricity and magnetism. So religion is brought into politics. 'Religion,' wrote Whitehead, 'is world loyalty.' Nor is this a modern doctrine. Pericles held that his dream of 'a united Greece with Athens as its eye,' if it were ever to come true, must have behind it a religious motive. Something of this kind has already happened in the British Commonwealth of Nations where, as we have seen,† there is not only a common kingship but also the 'invisible bond of ideals.'

Unless this kind of bond unites the world, or most of

* See above, pp. 44, 45.   † On p. 39 above.

it, and makes men *feel* for it as they now feel for their own nations, there will be no permanent union and no lasting world order. It is not enough for men to *understand* that the whole is greater than the part, that the world is greater than the nation, and that no nation can continue to live in isolation from the rest of mankind. It is necessary that the two consistent sentiments of patriotism and world loyalty should re-enforce each other, as a Scotsman's British patriotism is strengthened by his love for Scotland.

Thus the problem of building world order on a lasting basis belongs, in the long run, no less to psychology and education than to politics and economics.

But the immediate task, as we have repeated more than once, is to resist the aggression of any section of mankind that treats its own sectional interests as its supreme consideration. The nation that regards its collective egoism as sacred is indeed a menace to itself and to the world. Not much better is the nation that will never move to help the world unless its own national interest is directly at stake.

CHAPTERS ON THE BASIS OF GERMAN CO-OPERATION

by

H. F. KOEPPLER

CHAPTER 21

THE BASIC TRIANGLE

There can be no Anglo-German understanding without France. This country can no longer sit back and leave France alone in Europe. For the age of the aeroplane has made the safety of France and the French frontiers as vital to Great Britain as the independence of the Low Countries. Yet, after 1918 Great Britain resumed her rôle as referee. But because of her stake in the security of France she was now in the position of a referee who cannot afford to see one of the opposing teams beaten. The breakdown of the European order after the last war was partly caused by disregard for this new position of the three Great Powers: Great Britain, France and Germany. These chapters on Germany's place in a new world order may therefore fitly open with a brief reminder of Anglo-French relations in recent years.

France and Great Britain to-day form such a close unit in military, financial and economic affairs that we forget sometimes how their relations developed immediately after the last war. Only through a real understanding of Anglo-French relations in Europe since 1918 can we hope to avoid the mistakes which ruined Allied unity last time.

When the World War ended British interests were much concerned with the economic rehabilitation of

Germany.* The French did not share these interests. On the contrary, they were concerned above all with the security of the French frontier. This concern appeared to many people in this country exaggerated, misplaced, and an indication of an excessively nervous disposition on the part of the ex-Ally. When the French employed against democratic Germany draconic measures which culminated in the invasion of the Ruhr, they caused a storm of indignation in this country where people tended to forget that on 28 June, 1919, there had been signed at Versailles not one but three treaties.

Originally the French had demanded the Rhine frontier as the only sure shield of France. President Wilson could not allow that an era which was to bring self-determination to Europe should be ushered in by a denial of self-determination to millions of Rhinelanders. Thus the French demand was rejected. On the other hand, Wilson and Lloyd George did not forget, what British public opinion forgot for the next fifteen years, that the security of the French frontier was a vital interest not only of France but also of Great Britain. Since the Rhineland was to remain German, other means of protecting France had to be found. These means were provided by the two other treaties of Versailles. The first was signed between Great Britain and France, and the second between the United States and France.

In these two treaties this country and the U.S.A. agreed to come immediately to the assistance of France in the event of any unprovoked aggression against her by Germany. The second article of the Anglo-French treaty declared that Great Britain should only be bound if the United States ratified their promise to help France.

* *Political and Strategic Interests of the United Kingdom*, p. 73 (Publication of the Royal Institute of International Affairs).

The Franco-American treaty contained a corresponding provision.

President Wilson's mistake in coming to Europe as the representative of his party rather than of the whole American nation then began to show its terrible consequences. The result was that a matter of obvious national concern, the new world peace, was made an object of American party politics. We all know what followed. America's retreat from Europe not only robbed the League of a fair start, but destroyed one of the essential pillars of the new peace structure. For amongst the wreckage left behind in this great American retreat was that Versailles Treaty in which the U.S.A. guaranteed French security.

Ratifications of the treaty of security had been exchanged between France and Great Britain at Paris on the 20 November, 1919. When, on the next day, Mr. Bonar Law reminded the House of Commons that 'any obligation of this country . . . is contingent upon the United States Government undertaking the same obligation,' he might have had the foresight to declare that Great Britain would stand by France whatever happened to the Franco-American treaty.* He did not do so. If we are inclined to criticize him to-day, we must not forget that in 1919 nobody had foreseen Herr Hitler.

As it was, Britain had apparently disinterested herself in what had become her own vital interest: French security. It took some time for the full consequences to become visible. But one result was noticeable at once. Anglo-French relations deteriorated. The French felt that they had been let down. They had accepted as the final guarantee of their security two promises. Neither had come to anything. The French diehards were not

* *History of the Peace Conference*, ed. Temperley, III, 338.

now to be restrained from trying to get security by any other means they could.

They believed in the splitting up of Germany at almost any price. They financed the sporadic movements of separatists, men who desired to detach certain regions from the Reich against the wishes of the overwhelming majority of the inhabitants. For this purpose they paid the men round Hitler in Bavaria* and other down-and-out politicians in the Rhineland. The Rhineland became their great obsession.† It was their chief reason for the invasion of the Ruhr.

All this went right against British interests and the British desire to make things not too difficult for the young German democracy. Britain got more and more angry with the French, and finally Mr. Ramsay MacDonald told them so.‡ We had forgotten that there were three treaties signed at Versailles. The French felt under no obligation to listen. Since nothing had come of the treaty of French security signed at Versailles, Great Britain had lost her influence on the conduct of French foreign affairs.

This is a truth which must be remembered for the future. Only by sharing with France the burden of European security can this country claim a share in planning a common European policy.

Britain and France are bound to each other for better for worse. Neither country can pursue a European policy independent of the other. Both have to pay for it if they do. Look at the example provided by the results of the Ruhr invasion. France went her own way because Great Britain had not assured her of security. Britain tried to

* Heiden, *Hitler*, pp. 237 *et seq*.
† For the French argument see E. Driault, *La Paix du Rhin*, Paris, 1939. ‡ *The Times*, 3 March, 1924.

stop French foolishness, but she could not. As a result, the resentment felt in this country against France materially helped to ease Hitler's progress. For the increase of Nazi power was regarded, primarily, as a threat to the stability of the continental European system;* or, to put it more bluntly, as a threat to France. And over here there was a widespread feeling of 'Serve those Frenchmen right.' But we were soon to learn that it was a direct threat to Great Britain herself. After the Nazi occupation of the Rhineland, France and Britain were forced to realize that they must pursue the same European policy.

When their joint war effort has achieved its aim, the next great task of their common policy will to be to make a lasting peace. There must then be no quarrel and no misunderstanding between France and Britain.

It is safe to assume that the demand for the security of the French frontier will command the support of both countries. For we realize that it is a vital interest of France as well as Great Britain. However, the whole peace settlement hinges on the question how to achieve this security.

A false solution is preached by French diehards. It was expressed with admirable clarity by Jacques Bainville at the end of the last war. In his work on the results of the peace, written in 1920, he propounded with great skill the view that only the splitting up of Germany would help. All other conditions are to him but makeshifts, which will embitter but not really prevent the rise of yet another bellicose Germany. If Bainville were alive to-day, could he not say triumphantly: 'I told you so'? It seems so obvious that he was right, that we cannot be surprised if similar ideas make great headway on both sides of the

* *Political and Strategic Interests of the United Kingdom* (R.I.I.A.), p. 56.

Channel. In this country Mr. A. P. Herbert* has neatly summed up this feeling:

> We have no quarrel with the German nation,
> And Wagner's works are very good indeed:
> But if they *must* repeat this aberration
> It might be better if they did not breed.

In France, Bainville's friend, Professor Albert Rivaud, has told us what the new peace should be.† It implies total victory, an armistice signed in Berlin, and a Germany occupied by the victors. It implies further that Prussia should be 'chased out' of Germany, that a Great Austria should be recreated, and, above all, that the old divisions of Germany should be reintroduced and the old dynasties restored.

Any solution on these lines would be the ruin of Western civilization. It would not secure peace but destroy Europe. For it would run counter to the stream of historic development. The unity of Germany is now an historic fact. The world will have to accept this fact as it accepts the Reformation or the independence of the United States of America. We may well agree that German unity was bought too dearly: that the price of unity, which Bismarck exacted from the German people with his policy of force, was German internal liberty; and that at that price unity should not have been obtained. But it has come to stay.

German unity is now a unity of the German people, though it began as a union of German princes. The end of the World War showed this transformation quite conclusively. On the 6th of November, 1918, when the German

---

* In *Punch*, 20 September, 1939, p. 318.
† In his preface to an edition of Bainville's articles: 'L'Allemagne,' Paris, 1939, vol. I, p. xi.

people were beginning to glide into the revolution, Stresemann pleaded with all the power at his command for the maintenance of the Monarchy.* For in his view German unity, the most precious heritage of the German people, was bound to go if the Monarchy went. Events have proved him wrong. If the Bavarians, Saxons, Hanoverians and Rhinelanders had really desired to go their own way, nothing would or could have stopped them.†

The idea that Germany had become one bloc, one solid unit, had taken firm root. What broke down in 1918 in Germany was the Monarchical idea, not the unity of the country. We shall have to recognize that Germany is as much one unit as Great Britain. Scotland and England once were separate countries, and England once was divided between seven kings. We cannot imagine a return to the times of the Angles and Saxons.

It is, of course, true that the Allies could attempt by force to destroy this unit, to split up Germany. When the war has ended with a complete defeat of the Nazis, nothing which the Allies care to impose will appear impossible. But if we are right in believing that German unity has come to stay, then the enforced division of Germany will have to be maintained by force. This will necessitate large Allied armies of occupation for a considerable period, and even after that constant readiness on the part of Britain and France to pounce on the slightest attempt to restore German unity. Such attempts will be pretty frequent. Can anyone imagine the free democracies of France and Britain spending their time and

* In his paper *Deutsche Stimmen*.

† The collapse of Austria-Hungary is a good example of what did happen when various races had been forced to live together and wanted to separate. Italians, Czechs, Serbians, Croats and Roumanians just left the Austrian Empire.

money on a task so futile and repulsive? Fear and fury produced by prolonged fighting may indeed make such a solution appear tolerable for a while. But only for a while.

Nobody who remembers the attitude of the man in the street in 1936, when Germany reoccupied the Rhineland, can believe that this country will for ever sanction such a policy of suppression. As all can see to-day, the Rhineland provided an excellent case for not allowing the Nazis to 'get away with it.' And yet, people said, why should not Hitler put troops into his own territory? When the passions of this war have calmed down, public opinion will be strongly opposed to a system whereby peace is only assured by a permanent army of occupation.

We are driven to the conclusion that the destruction of Germany is a peace aim which could not be attained. It is unworkable because of the democratic control of policy in the Allied countries. Democracy is bound to be influenced in the long run by arguments of humanitarian wisdom and Christian charity. If France and Great Britain began a policy of destruction they would, therefore, be forced to stop it after some years. Such a policy if started and not proceeded with, obviously becomes the most dangerous and stupid undertaking. There is no grading of repression: it must either be all or none.

What then is the answer to our peace problem? So far we have established two basic facts.

(1) French security is vital for both France and Great Britain.

(2) United Germany has come to stay. Thus, French security, if it is to be permanent, cannot be achieved by destroying German unity. We have therefore to find a solution which will provide security for France and Great Britain and keep intact the unity of Germany.

CHAPTER 22

HOW TO APPROACH THE GERMAN PROBLEM

★

Germany, as well as Great Britain and France, must, as we have seen, be amongst the first members of that international organization or 'Commonwealth' without which there can be no lasting peace.

Nobody can foretell when the Nazis will fall, and who will succeed them. One thing is certain, the Nazis will go: the rest is in the hands of fate. It is most likely that civil war will follow the collapse of Hitler. The Western Powers had to go through a grim period of internal strife, England in 1648, France in 1789. It would appear that Germany's turn has come. It may be that the end of the civil war will see the rise of a Stalinist Germany. If so, we shall have to thank for that Herr Hitler and his dupes in Berlin and Vienna, London and Paris, in Warsaw, Rome and the Vatican City. They tolerated his methods, however abominable, his diplomacy, however deceitful, because they chose to believe that on one point he would not deceive them.* His claim to a mission was trumpeted abroad *ad nauseam*. His assertion that he was destined to protect Christianity and Western civilization from Russia, was somehow always accepted as sterling truth. There never was a chance, despite Herr Hitler's claims, for a successful communist rising in democratic Germany

* See Lord Lloyd, *The British Case*, pp. 54, 55.

during the years preceding the Nazi revolution. One who at that time was still an important Nazi official, has frankly admitted that 'nothing was more remote from the future of the Reich in 1932–1933 than a Bolshevist revolution or even a political revolt from the Left.'*

To-day we cannot be so certain. Even before the Reich and Russia entered into 'the pact of mutual suspicion,' Hitlerism had taken too many measures which might help Stalin at the end of the war. If Germany accepted Stalinism there could be no hope of peace in Europe as long as the West maintained its present structure of society. The problem of German co-operation with the Allies would not then arise. But the Reich is not likely to accept Stalin's domination. Even those Germans who are prepared to establish a proletarian dictatorship in order to prevent the recurrence of Hitlerism are hardly likely to join hands with the man who has done more to keep Herr Hitler and Hitlerism alive than any of his clandestine supporters in any capitalist country. Whatever the *social* structure of the new Germany, she will hardly look upon Soviet Russia as a *political* model.

There are many, and their number increases daily, who hold that, whatever the social structure of the new Germany, she will always believe in the old Prussian gospel of force and aggression. The Germans, it is said, are just built that way, and we had better face the facts.

What are the facts? Is it true that the Germans have been saddled by divine Providence with 'a double dose of original sin'? Such a charge is as monstrous as the Nazi claim to dominate the world because of the supposed superiority of the German race. Both deny the fundamental equality of man, the very basis of Christian teaching and democratic conviction. Those who bring

* Rauschning, *Germany's Revolution of Destruction*, p. 10.

this charge would have to provide convincing evidence. No such evidence has been forthcoming. For what some clever people have produced recently is not satisfactory evidence but an insult to the intelligence of their readers.

After struggling through some of the tangled mass of German philosophy these people announce triumphantly certain doctrines of certain German philosophers as proof positive of Germany's congenital wickedness. No doubt, even the hardest researcher cannot cope with more than one or two of these monumental treatises. But sympathy with these difficulties should not blind us to the failure of the political theorists to explore the whole of the material at their disposal. Why do they always quote certain passages from Fichte or Hegel, and seldom Kant or Wilhelm von Humboldt?

If people continue to quote the 'monstrous megalomania' of Hegel as representative of German political thought, is it fair to forget that at the same time the great Kant wrote a work entitled *Perpetual Peace*? We point to Fichte's 'Speeches to the German nation' as typically German, and, it is true, we find in them a source of that heretical abomination, the belief that the individual was made to live and die for the State, which has become one of the principal tenets of the Nazi creed. But Fichte's great contemporary, Wilhelm von Humboldt, wrote an essay on the limits of the State, asserting that the functions of the State must be restricted to the assurance of property and life, that the State should be considered simply as a law court, and that the individual will be inclined to shun war as the greatest conceivable evil. Why should this philosophy be less 'typically German' than Fichte's? The truth is, of course, that thinkers of the same nation have throughout the ages held opposed theories. And a scientific method of computing which of these theories is more typical of a nation has yet to be invented.

Until we find such a method it will not be possible to declare with conviction that Fichte's nationalism and Hegel's aggressiveness are more typically German than Kant's belief in a firm international order and Humboldt's belief in the State as the servant rather than the master of its citizens.

It is only too easy to overestimate the influence of philosophical theories on the practical politics of a nation. To divert the attention of the public from the real forces which shape the political activities of a nation, to bewilder them with the speculations of philosophers whose influence is at best very limited, is worse than misleading: it is dangerous. The Nazis of all people are most unlikely to have learned their technique and their doctrine from the vast tomes of German idealistic or romantic philosophy. They have always gloried in their furious dislike of all things intellectual. 'You only have to mention learning, and I reach for my gun!' Nothing sums up their attitude better than these words of a Nazi hero in a Nazi play. Most of their political theory is an afterthought, an ideological superstructure provided by careerists after the Nazis had gained power.

The claim that political philosophy is a sure guide to the understanding of political reality may thus be discounted. However, this method has at least a basis in the existence of such philosophical books. It is infinitely preferable to other attempts to explain German politics by means of bogus psychology. Here we are in the realm of pure speculation, and hard facts impose no restraint on the most fatuous phantasies. Yet, bogus psychological explanations of German politics appear in a never ending stream.

Hitlerism is declared 'to be acceptable to Germany, because the Germans *as a nation* are largely psychologically disordered,'* because 'at the heart of the German people there is a real neurosis.'† It would be interesting to know how the writers of these phrases can be so sure what is 'at the heart of the Germans.' Such words suggest that a representative sample of the nation has been analysed. No such task has, however, yet been attempted, let alone accomplished. It is dangerously anthropomorphic to suppose that a nation can suffer from diseases of the mind, or that the language of psychiatry is as applicable to a society as to a person.

Yet, it was the 'inferiority complex' of the German people which Herr Hitler had come to cure once and for all. Apparently he succeeded: Sir Nevile Henderson informed us‡ that 'it would be idle to deny the great achievements of the man who restored to the German nation its self-respect and its disciplined orderliness.' So there should have been no more talk of the complex. But, since the war, it has reappeared and surprised us by its marvellous adaptability. For we are told that there is nothing left for us to do but to resist the aggression that is now said to result from the inferiority complex. It is high time for serious students of international affairs to abandon such metaphors as 'the inferiority complex of a nation,' lest in the end they destroy the whole of political science.

Is there, then, no chance of explaining the German riddle? Unless we assume it is a mere coincidence, it becomes surely necessary to understand why Germany has hitherto always upset Europe's apple cart.

* Quoted from a letter to the *Spectator*, 29 December, 1939, p. 934.   † A. L. Rowse, in the *Political Quarterly*, January, 1940.
‡ In his *Final Report*, Section 5, Cmd. 6115.

There is, indeed, another approach to the problem. A survey of some essential points in German internal history can at least provide a clue, and perhaps even solve the riddle. It might appear odd to discuss internal history if what we really want to know is why Germany's external relations have been so unsatisfactory, why peaceful collaboration between her and other countries, particularly England and France, is seemingly impossible. But that there is an intimate connection between the internal and external policy of a country cannot be denied. One example will make clear the interdependence of the two and the need, in any study of international relations, for a good knowledge of the internal position of the countries concerned.

Since the last war amicable relations between France and Germany have been thwarted by the fact that Germany's government tended towards the Left when France had a Right wing government, and vice versa. The Right governments in France were suspicious of Germany and averse to close collaboration, although after 1925 most Frenchmen were in favour of such collaboration. But while every Frenchman's heart is on the Left, his purse is on the Right; and, since the parties of the Right appeared to provide a greater guarantee of financial stability than those of the Left, they received the votes of most Frenchmen, even of those in favour of better relations with Germany.

Thus French home affairs disastrously influenced Franco-German relations after the World War. Similarly, a review of internal German development will be most pertinent to the problem under discussion: what kind of Germany will be ready and eager to enter sincerely a new European order at the end of the present war?

CHAPTER 23

ENTER THE JUNKERS

★

It is misleading, to say the least, to speak of Germany as a country in love with force, and of the Germans as incurable addicts to militarism. There are Germans and Germans. Now it is, of course, true that in this country, also, people differ vehemently in their political outlook. But in Germany the difference is more fundamental because Germany has not yet solved the cardinal problem of all State organization, while this country has all but done so. This is the problem how to combine an efficient central government with respect for the liberty of the nation.

The story of the English constitution tells one tale, that of Prussian absolutism another. The strong centralizing measures of King Henry II and, three-and-a-half centuries later, the Tudor dictatorship were of benefit to the country; for they were followed, the one by Magna Carta and the other by the two English revolutions, timely reminders that firm government must not deteriorate into tyrannical absolutism. This success is largely due to the constant change in the composition of the governing class. The barons of King John had their part to play. They were superseded in time by new forces which shaped the constitution in their turn.

No such vital change took place in the dominant part of Germany. From the Middle Ages to Bismarck and the

World War the barons of Prussia, the Junkers, were the only people who counted politically. Thus while in Great Britain to-day, despite deep differences on questions of social justice, most people take it for granted that they share the same fundamental beliefs, this is not so in Germany. There exist two Germanies. One thinks as we do about the place of the individual in the State, but has no idea of power. The other cares little about popular rights, but possesses a keen appreciation of power. One is ready for international collaboration in the belief that this is the surest safeguard for the peace and well-being of the people. The other is bent on European hegemony in the belief that peace is a dream and not even a beautiful one.

We all know the second, the anti-European, Germany. It finds its most obvious expression in the Nazi dictatorship. And there are many who remember earlier manifestations of the same 'false, fleeting, perjured' Germany. They will almost certainly demand some solid evidence for the existence of the other Germany before they believe in it. If peace is to last it must be just; and, in order to be just, it must take the nature of post-war Germany into account. Conditions of peace which would be just to a Nazi Germany become a crying injustice if imposed on a European Germany.

But can there ever be such a Germany? Is it not true that 'generation after generation they choose a fool to govern them—and cheer'?*

Do they? No piece of Nazi propaganda has been more successful in this country than the story of Herr Hitler's inevitable rise to power. Most people here believe that he was swept into office by an ever-growing irresistible avalanche of votes. He was not.

* A. P. Herbert, *loc. cit.*

The inevitability of Hitler is a myth, a clever invention to saddle the whole German nation with a responsibility which properly belongs to an infinitesimal part of it, a part, however, possessing enormous influence and not afraid to use or to abuse it.

The responsibility for the Nazi régime, for the concentration camps, for the murder and rape of individuals and nations alike, the responsibility, if you prefer, for 'restoring to the German nation its self-respect and its disciplined orderliness,'* this responsibility belongs to the Junkers and the Junkers alone. Nazism is the true heir of Junkerdom, although not by legitimate succession. We can understand and even sympathize with the efforts so valiantly undertaken to-day to deny paternity; but the family resemblance is too obvious. Junkerdom may not like its bastard offspring, but cannot disclaim responsibility for it.

Who are the Junkers? Originally the term referred only to the relatively small class of big landowners in the eastern part of Prussia and Germany. *But it is appropriate to extend it now to all those who for economic or political reasons adopted the same attitude towards German affairs.* This essay will show how the original Junker policy succeeded in corrupting other groups of the German people. But what has all this to do with the rise of Herr Hitler?

It has this to do with it. So far from driving steadily towards its ultimate aim, the rule of the Reich, the Nazi machine was badly cracking and on the very point of final collapse at the end of 1932. In November, 1932, there had taken place yet another election to the German *Reichstag*.† For the first time since the great economic

---

* Sir N. Henderson, see above, p. 227.
† i.e. the German parliament.

blizzard had shattered much of Germany's economic structure in 1930, the Nazi poll failed to increase. On the contrary, it fell by a couple of millions. Worse still, from the Nazi point of view, this fall seemed to be the beginning of the end. For during the ensuing weeks the Nazis consistently lost votes at the local elections. It was apparent that their representation in the Reichstag would fall much lower still if another General Election were to take place in the near future.* This was the time when the newspapers announced, almost daily, that more Nazi leaders had left the party; when there were mutinies amongst the storm-troopers because the party, having lost its financial backers† as the result of its defeat at the polls, could no longer pay them.

During these critical winter weeks experienced people in Germany and in other countries generally agreed on one point: Herr Hitler was finished. Whatever the future government, it would not be led by him, nor would it have to rely on the support of his party.

For the German people, despite their terrible economic ordeal, despite their short experience of democratic self-government, had in their majority rejected the Nazis, even at the height of their distress. Now, at the beginning of 1933, when there were distinct signs of the tide turning, of unemployment going down while trade figures went up, it could reasonably be expected that the Nazis would never poll sufficient votes to get into power. It is quite true that no free election in Germany ever provided the Nazis with a majority. But votes are not the only weapons with which to obtain political power.

Those who at the end of 1932 predicted the inevitable

---

* J. W. Wheeler-Bennett, *Hindenburg, the Wooden Titan*, p. 415.
† For example, Herr Thyssen, who fled from Germany at the outbreak of war, has declared that he spent more than £5,500,000 on the Nazi Party (*The Times*, 23 December, 1939).

ENTER THE JUNKERS

decline and fall of the Nazi party and the triumphant resurrection of German democracy, forgot that there existed other forces no less hostile to popular freedom and social justice. The Junkers had no love for law and liberty, no respect for the will of the people. Up to the end of 1932 they had despised the Nazi leaders as mean agitators, low born and ill bred. They might support them secretly against the common enemy, the liberal Republic, but so far they had not been prepared openly to collaborate with Herr Hitler. Nor had he shown any desire to collaborate with them.

However, the election of November, 1932, with its defeat of the Nazi party, and subsequent events affecting the Junkers, changed their mutual antipathy to willing if cool co-operation. The new government formed after the elections by General Schleicher decided on certain measures which were exceedingly unpopular with the Junkers. They implored President Hindenburg, who shared their political outlook, to ask the Schleicher government to resign; whereupon Schleicher retaliated by threatening to publish the report of the Commission set up to inquire into alleged scandals in connection with a great scheme of agricultural subsidies, the *Osthilfe*. This financial 'help for the East' had been intended to save the farmers in the districts of the Reich bordering on Poland, and it had been proclaimed a great patriotic undertaking. The enquiry had disclosed scandals from which 'the mud splashed even to the steps of Hindenburg's palace.' Only the smallest percentage of the subsidy had reached real peasants; it had chiefly helped the big landowners, the Junkers. Some of them had squandered the public money, yet had received more of it, since their names had been for centuries coupled with their estates.*

* For a fuller account see Wheeler-Bennett, *loc. cit.*, pp. 423 *et seq.*

If these scandals became known, even the long-suffering German taxpayer might revolt and at last destroy the privileged position of the Junkers. This had to be prevented, even at the cost of a revolution. And so the Junkers decided to combine with Herr Hitler in order to overthrow Schleicher who had dared to threaten them. There was to be a coalition Nazi-Junker government. The Nazis would be freed from their financial embarrassment caused by their defeat at the last election, and the Junkers from their political embarrassment caused by the *Osthilfe* crisis. Both would triumph over the hated liberal State.

As to the future, the Junker leader, Papen, and the Nazi leader, Hitler, promised each other loyal collaboration. Papen was convinced that he could cope with the Nazis and that he could get rid of them when they had done the task he had allotted to them.* Hitler thought the same about the Junkers. To-day we know who was right. As Papen had the confidence of the aged President Hindenburg, he succeeded in persuading him to let Hitler form the government. So it was that Herr Hitler became Chancellor on 30 January, 1933.

These facts concerning the rise of the Nazi State have important consequences for the future of Europe. For they answer the question whether the German people in giving all power to Hitler have not proved themselves incapable of ever becoming good Europeans. We have to acquit the German people of this charge. We have even seen that a majority of Germans showed a true appreciation of what a Nazi régime would entail for the world by barring its way to power with their votes, their only weapon. We are therefore justified in declaring that there are within the German people no fundamental obstacles

* Rauschning, *loc. cit.*, p. 107 *et passim*.

to their collaboration in a peaceful Europe or in the new Commonwealth.

However, we cannot escape one obvious and just comment: It is all very well to say the Germans did not put Hitler into power. But the Junkers did, and for Europe that comes to the same thing. Even if the large majority of Germans are all right, what about the Junkers? Why were they allowed to continue in their privileged position? If, at the end of the war, the Allies make a decent peace with an apparently decent German government, what guarantees have we got that the Junkers will not again play the same trick on Europe?

All these questions are fully justified and demand a full answer. But this answer cannot be given in one sentence. If we want to understand how the Junkers gained their position and managed to keep it, even in democratic Germany, we must look into the historical origins of their power.

CHAPTER 24

WHO THE PRUSSIANS ARE

The problem of the Junkers is related to, but not identical with, the problem of Prussia. Most Junkers are Prussians, but most Prussians are far from being Junkers. Many writers have declared that the Prussians are the bad Germans, anti-liberal, anti-democratic, opposed to everything that is treasured by Western civilization. The Bavarians, Württembergers, Badeners, all the Southern Germans and even the Saxons, they assert, are very much like the British or the French; only the Prussians are the trouble. Hence the wish 'to chase Prussia out of Germany,' to form a new gentle Reich out of the South Germans and the Austrians. But is it true that the Prussians are the disturbers of the peace? No, it is not.

To repeat, it is not the Prussians, but the Junkers, the ruling caste of Prussia, who are the trouble. If all the Prussians were bad Europeans the outlook would be bleak indeed. For almost forty out of the sixty-five millions of pre-Nazi Germany are technically Prussians, and three-fifths of German territory belongs to Prussia.

But the Prussian people have shown during the short life of the German Republic that they are not behind the other Germans in their appreciation of democratic institutions. On the contrary, the Prussians readily elected within the democratic Germany of 1919 a more progressive government, and kept it in power longer than any other Germans. And the first step of the Junker reaction of 1932 was to abolish this government by force.

The heart of the Prussian State is the March of Brandenburg, that flat country of sand, pine forests and lakes which formed the border between medieval Germany and her Eastern neighbours, the Slavs. It was a district on the very outskirts of civilization. It was colonial territory, lately conquered from the Slavs. This explains its constitutional development. In the early Middle Ages, when central government was weak and the menace from raiding neighbours strong, kings and rulers were everywhere content to hand over most of their power in outlying regions to marcher lords as the only means of protecting the frontiers of their realm. These marcher lords thus achieved a position of almost royal importance. But, while in France and England the central government grew steadily more powerful, until its writ would run even in the remotest corners of those countries, the central government of Germany, the Holy Roman Emperor, had lost almost all his power by the end of the Middle Ages.

Into the constitutional vacuum created by this collapse stepped the various German princes whose rule now became untrammelled from the restrictions imposed by a superior authority. Now, in most German countries there existed an internal system of checks on the power of the prince, a body of customary privileges for the inhabitants, which was the result of historic development. No such limitations prevailed in the marches of the East. They had been conquered by the sword, and the conquerors were not obliged to acknowledge any ancient rights of their Slav inhabitants.

As Brandenburg, the future Prussia, was won by the sword, so it was maintained by the sword. Not only was it maintained, but it expanded throughout the centuries until finally it engulfed all Germany in 1871. This position was reached not by the collaboration of the people, but by their subordination; not by a free constitution, but by the best drilled army and civil service in the world.

This, rather than the belated coming of Christianity or the lack of Rome's imperial influence, must account for the rise of Prussian absolutism. It has been pointed out often enough that only the western and southern fringes of Germany were included in the Roman Empire. But it was from these very districts that the ruling class of Prussia came to conquer the East and to establish its absolute rule. Also, as regards the belated conversion of the Germans to Christianity, it was only two hundred years after St. Augustine had rekindled Christianity in the south of England that most parts of Germany were Christian too. Since then, over a thousand years of Christianity could surely have removed the initial difference between the two countries.

No, the solid facts of Prussian constitutional history, of Germany's internal structure, are really a safer guide to the solution of our problem.

A new period in the history of the region begins in 1417, when a nobleman from south-western Germany became ruler or 'Elector' of Brandenburg. He was Frederick I, and with him begins the long rule of the house of Hohenzollern in Brandenburg-Prussia. It came to an end only in 1918, when the Kaiser left for Holland.

The Hohenzollerns fully accepted the old-established system of their predecessors,* to run the country in

* See Marriott and Robertson, *The Evolution of Prussia*, p. 42. The best English account of early Prussian history is still Th. Carlyle, *History of Frederick II of Prussia*, 1858, Vol. I, pp. 67–377.

collaboration with a small and dominant group of local nobles, the squirearchy of the Junkers. This collaboration of Monarch and Junkers became the cornerstone of Prussia. It was of great benefit to prince and Junkers alike, for every increase in his dominions brought an increase in the privileged position of the Junkers. But this result was achieved at the expense of everybody else.

The end of the Middle Ages saw the rise of the towns in Northern Germany. Even in Brandenburg the towns succeeded in gaining a measure of independence. They tried to preserve it by refusing to allow either their prince or his Junkers to enter their gates without permission. Berlin was the leader of these towns. And on Berlin the new Hohenzollern rulers concentrated their efforts to re-establish their absolute power. At last the Elector succeeded. He entered Berlin, demanded and obtained the Charters which guaranteed the liberties of the town, and himself tore off the seals. Thus ended one of the few attempts to resist absolutism in Brandenburg. Thereafter Berlin remained submissive. What a different story London has to tell!

The greater power of Brandenburg's ruler was acknowledged in 1701, when, in return for the loan of some regiments, the Holy Roman Emperor bestowed on him the title of King in Prussia. It was appropriate that the change from Elector to King should have been achieved with the help of the Prussian army.

The most powerful of Prussian kings was Frederick the Great. At home he reorganized the country till it was covered with a close network of bureaucracy which thereafter hampered all free development. Frederick turned his army into his most successful instrument of policy. The necessary revenue was provided by merciless taxation, and a special corps of 'coffee smellers' was embodied to prevent the evasion of the new coffee tax. Here is a precedent for 'guns instead of butter.'

His internal measures gave him the basis for his startling foreign policy. By force of arms and deceitful diplomacy he conquered Silesia. He obtained more territory from the first partition of Poland. He became the apostle of a political faith which centred in the belief that the actions of a State were to be guided solely by narrow expediency.

The great personal qualities which Frederick undoubtedly possessed cannot be pleaded in mitigation. His brilliant brain, and his incredible tenacity when faced with the most fearful odds, only added to the corrupting influence of his success. Men were dazzled by his gifts and thereby prevented from seeing the destructive results of the policy to which these gifts were devoted.* No wonder, then, that an account of his internal and foreign policy reads like a description of modern Nazi methods, or that the worship of Frederick is a popular pastime with the Nazi élite.

Now it may be said that all this only goes to justify those who maintain that German history is a continuous tale of bad faith, force and aggression which prove that the German people are by nature incapable of any more civilized conduct. If this were a fair criticism, then, indeed, all hope for a new and European Germany should be abandoned. However, the people had no say in the matter. Frederick had made Prussia into a first-class Power, but his subjects were bled white for the greater glory of a monarchy in which there was no place for a free citizen. The absolute King, supported by his army

* This blindness was not restricted to Germans, witness Carlyle.

WHO THE PRUSSIANS ARE 241

and bureaucracy, thought of everything and acted for everybody. The people had no stake in the country. They had only to pay their taxes, serve in the army, and keep their mouths shut.

The collapse of Prussia which Napoleon brought about in 1806 was the inevitable consequence. The people of Prussia watched with utter indifference, even with malicious joy, the complete collapse of a society in which only the interests of the State counted; and the State meant the king and his privileged supporters, the Junkers.

The total ruin of the country made it clear to everybody that nothing but the most far-reaching reforms could resurrect Prussia. The period which immediately followed the defeat at Jena deserves the special attention of those concerned with Germany and the chances of her co-operation in Europe. For in the history of that period we find sufficient evidence for the belief that there does exist a better Germany, a Germany animated by those ideas which make for liberty and social justice at home and for willing collaboration abroad. We can learn that Germany's anti-European attitude is not inevitable, that this attitude which is the result of her internal structure can be cured at the root, and that she can produce great statesmen who, unlike Frederick or Bismarck, are not a menace but an asset to Europe.

Such a statesman was the Ritter vom Stein. He was a member of the German nobility, but not a Junker. His education, too, did much to make him see beyond Prussian absolutism. He went to the University of Göttingen, at that time the most advanced university in Germany. Göttingen was the creation of the Electors of Hanover, who were then also Kings of England. The political ideas which English parliamentary history had to teach came as a revelation to Stein who saw round him nothing but the most rigid absolutism.

There was one little oasis in that desert of despotism called Prussia. The Hohenzollerns had acquired certain small territories in Westphalia in the West of Germany. Here there remained a good deal of the self-government which had developed through the centuries before the territory became Prussian. Stein was fascinated by Westphalian self-government, and delighted to see that it extended to the organization of the Church. Luther had separated most Germans from the Pope only to push them under the yoke of their princes. Here in Westphalia the Protestant Church had preserved its freedom from royal control.

Stein was convinced that the Westphalian way was better than the Prussian. He saw the dangers of the Prussian methods, and since he had become a high official in the Prussian administration, he felt it his duty to warn the King. The result was his dismissal from the King's service. But the collapse of the old Prussia forced the King to reconsider his decision. The reorganization was entrusted to Stein; and Prussia, Germany and Europe would be in a better state to-day if all his reforms had been carried through.

'The number of free men must be increased'; this sentence from Stein's great plan served as the basis of his liberating ideas. He began his work with the emancipation of the peasants and Jews: serfdom was abolished. In view of what the Nazis are doing in Poland it is worth while to recall that Stein wanted to give full autonomy to the Poles living in Prussia. But personal freedom was not enough. The whole people had to be interested in the running of the country, and the deadening influence of a gigantic Junker-ridden bureaucracy had to be suppressed. Local self-government, followed later by central self-government, was the great creative idea which Stein gave to German history. Self-government was better than bureaucratic monarchy.

Stein realized, better than the men of the Weimar Republic, that you cannot entrust a nation with the running of its own affairs if its people have had no previous experience of political responsibility. Men should obtain that experience in local self-government before being called to national assemblies and entrusted with the government of the country. Nobody knew better than Stein that education in citizenship is a prime necessity for the well-being of a democracy.

Criticism of Stein's plans was not lacking. There were many who pointed out that so far the people had never governed themselves, that they did not want to govern themselves, and that, even if they did, they could not be trusted. How familiar all this rings to-day. But Stein was not perturbed; he was convinced that the nation was 'reasonable, moral and trustworthy'; and he looked forward to a Prussian and even a German parliament. Stein always felt that a free Prussia would attract the other German States and thus achieve a united Germany. It is the great tragedy of the German people that their union was brought about by Bismarck's policy of blood and iron and not by Stein's liberating ideas.

Stein's reforms went even further. He saw that the liberation of the people would remain a hollow sham unless it was accompanied by a severe reduction in the privileges of the ruling caste, the Junkers. Thus his most daring reform was concerned with the most Prussian institution of all, the army. Here his work was carried through by two generals of genius, Scharnhorst and Gneisenau. They wanted a democratic army, an army which was a part of the State, not outside and above it. That is why they desired general conscription and the control of the army chiefs by the civil administration.

But from the beginning there was a furious opposition led by the Junkers* and supported by the King. It was only the desperate position of Prussia which induced the King to accept these reforms. They were not to last very long.

Only the most elementary of Stein's reforms survived the war against Napoleon. Some were never introduced. Neither the abolition of feudal jurisdiction nor the creation of parliament was attempted. The army became again the preserve of the Junkers. The Prussian monarchy had no reason to show the people the true greatness of Stein. The real meaning of his intended reforms was twisted until it almost looked as if his sole object had been to provide the absolute king and his Junkers with more efficient subjects. And the official historians turned into a loyal servant of His Prussian Majesty the great reformer who had endeavoured to free the people from the oppression of the Prussian ruling caste and to entrust the key position in Europe to the care of responsible citizens rather than to a small group of narrow-minded reactionaries.

* When a statue of Scharnhorst was erected in Berlin, one of the Junkers objected to it on the ground that the sculptor had made this son of a N.C.O. look too much like a gentleman: 'He certainly did not have such splendid calves in life; in fact, his calves were quite common.' What did it matter that he had organized the people's army and so enabled the King of Prussia to win the war?

CHAPTER 25

UNITY, LAW AND LIBERTY

★

Even the few reforms of emancipation and local self-government which were carried through after Prussia's defeat in 1806 changed the outlook of the Prussian people. At last it seemed as if Prussia was going to be their country as well as that of the Junkers. The hour for the defeat of Napoleon struck in 1813. The Prussian King had renewed his promises of a constitution and representative assembly—which Stein had intended as the crowning achievement of his reforms. And the people of Prussia went to the war with an enthusiasm which was as conspicuous as its complete absence during the war of 1806. The fearful sacrifices which the untrained levies suffered were borne in the belief that this was a war not only for the liberation of Prussia from Napoleon, but for the liberty of the Prussian people.

However, they were to be cruelly disappointed. True, between 1810 and 1820 the King promised his people a representative parliament no less than five times. They never got it from him. Instead they got further promises from his successors for another century, up to 1918.

On the other hand, most of Stein's and Scharnhorst's reforms were discontinued or hampered during the nineteenth century. The old privileges of the Junkers were renewed whenever possible. The Prussian people were cheated out of the fruits of their victory.

The new Western provinces, gained after the war with Napoleon, could not assert themselves. So far from driving Prussia towards freedom, they were themselves subjected to the colonial type of administration which permeated the whole Prussian State from the East.

Outside the big towns there was no official movement towards self-government, no possibility for the people to take a share in the running of the country. The omnipotence of bureaucratic government by the Junkers was re-established, the reforms of Stein forgotten. The nation was treated as a child whose guardians were the civil service and the army. This obedience to an all-embracing bureaucratic tutelage was spread systematically throughout the country with such efficiency that it became deeply ingrained in the people. The liberal democracy of 1918 had only fourteen years in which to eradicate this well-established pernicious principle. Most of these years were filled with international and economic anxieties. It was not enough time to give the people a fair chance.

The nineteenth century saw a demand for liberty everywhere in Europe. In Italy and Germany this desire for popular liberty was coupled with a struggle for that national unity which the British and the French had achieved long ago. The Congress of Vienna had established Germany as a loose confederation of two big Powers, Austria and Prussia, and thirty-seven other States, some of them tiny. There had been some timid attempts to give Germany a closer unity. They could not succeed, since neither German nor foreign governments desired it.

The policy of the foreign Powers has been aptly put: 'For the sake of the peace of Europe, German unity, that most dangerous idea, must not be achieved.' German governments did not want German unity either, since it went against the very basis of their existence; for all German rulers claimed to rule by divine right and not by the support of their nations. But divine right was a splendid cloak for both absolutism and disunity. That is the reason why those Germans who wanted more liberty also wanted national unity.

The dual struggle for internal liberty and German unity went on steadily up to the revolution of 1848. The year 1848 saw revolutions everywhere on the Continent. In Germany they completely failed to achieve unity and they brought only a small amount of liberty.

Not that people did not know what they wanted. The basic demands were formulated for the whole of Germany in the so-called March claims:

(1) A people's army with promotion from the ranks.
(2) Absolute freedom of the Press.
(3) Juries to assist in trials as in England.
(4) Immediate convocation of a German parliament.

The literature of the revolutionary radicals was brilliant and impressive in its clarity. Magnificent manifestos were published, comprehensive constitutions drawn up. The King of Prussia, as usual, made great promises when it looked like danger, only to break them when the danger passed. Within a year the revolutionary effort, fired by all that is best in the German character, had ignominiously collapsed. Why?

The vast majority of those who wanted the changes had no sense of power, and were afraid of fighting. There was a democratic minority who knew what power meant and were prepared to fight for it. But this minority was something on which the liberal majority looked with uneasiness and alarm. The situation was repeated in 1918.

In order to gain political power you must be prepared

to employ force if your opponent is not open to persuasion. This principle has always been understood in this country: it was force from Simon de Montfort to Cromwell, and persuasion from the Reform Bill to the Statute of Westminster. We can only hope that experience of the Hitler régime has taught the German people this lesson.

But in 1848 they had not yet learnt it. And so, after a short interval of fright and indecision, the rulers who understood the importance of power so much better than their people, everywhere set their troops in motion, and another period of reaction followed. However, the German people were awaking. The enormous changes in the social and economic structure of Prussia helped the progressive movements. Prussia was no longer exclusively agricultural. Her industrial development was rapid. Thus the influence of the agricultural Junkers was lowered; the new type of Junker, the industrial, did not fully develop until the end of the nineteenth century. The pressure on the King to grant a constitution in fulfilment of so many royal promises proved irresistible. On 6 February, 1850, Prussia got her constitution, though not before the King had broken his pledges twice again.

The Prussian constitution of 1850 did, of course, provide a parliament, but what a parliament it was! The people could elect only the lower house. Here the vote was public and unequal. It was based on a complicated system dividing the electorate into three classes according to their payment of income-tax. This meant that a few rich people had as much voting power as the rest of the population. Since voting was in public, the rural population at least could be intimidated so as not to oppose their lords and masters. This monstrous method was defended because it corresponded to the 'god-given realities of life,' as Bismarck put it.* Public and unequal voting was bad enough, but even worse were two other features of the constitution. The control of the budget was severely curtailed by the fact that the government could continue to levy those taxes which had been agreed to without a time limit. Thus the government could obtain the greater part of its income without annual parliamentary sanction. And, finally, the Prussian Prime Minister and his colleagues could not be forced to resign by a parliamentary vote of No Confidence. They were dependent solely on the goodwill of their King.

It was not much of a constitution. But, although it could hardly be considered more than a very timid step in the right direction, it displeased the Junkers. They felt the King had been lamentably weak in giving it at all. But as it was now in existence they worked hard to make it serve their purpose. Again they showed the quality so typical of them and their disciples, the Nazis: complete lack of respect for the law of the land. Political power alone mattered to them, not how they got it.

But in the middle of the nineteenth century all the might of the Junkers could not stem the tide now running very strongly towards parliamentary control. The new parliament of 1861 had an enormous progressive majority, which was determined to safeguard the few popular rights guaranteed by the constitution but restricted by the Junker administration. But the people wanted more than that: they wanted, in accordance with countless royal promises, a full parliamentary monarchy or its equivalent in a system of constitutional government.

A situation was rapidly approaching which shows a striking similarity to the great conflict between Charles I

* *Reflections and Reminiscences*, Vol. II, p. 64.

of England and the House of Commons. Had the Prussian conflict ended like the English with the defeat of royal absolutism, it is unlikely that we would have to fight Herr Hitler to-day. But, again, the story of the conflict shows quite clearly that there was nothing inevitable in the victory of reaction, that it was not achieved because of the inherent characteristics, the moral and mental 'make-up' of the people.

The battle-cry of the Prussian parliament* was the old English slogan of no taxation without representation: that is, effective representation. The constitutional conflict came to a head over that peculiarly Prussian institution, the army. In principle, parliament agreed with the government that a reorganization of the army was necessary. But parliament wanted to keep the *Landwehr*, the territorial militia, because it was a reminder of the democratic reforms of Scharnhorst, and because it had sympathized with the revolutionaries of 1848. For this very reason the King wanted it abolished. He also wanted to keep the conscripts for three years with the colours, admittedly for reasons of home politics rather than for purely military considerations. Of course, parliament objected; and it was dissolved.

The new elections increased the power of the parliamentary opposition. Apparently there was complete deadlock. The language of the deputies grew more menacing. The King had visions of Charles I and the scaffold outside Whitehall, and he drafted his abdication.

We might well pause here to consider what would have happened if he had signed and published it. He would have been succeeded by his son, Queen Victoria's son-in-law, the future Emperor Frederick III and the only

* i.e. the *Abgeordnetenhaus* or Lower House.

progressive and enlightened monarch whom the house of Hohenzollern produced in five centuries. Frederick would then have reigned for twenty-six years instead of ninety-nine days; and nobody to-day would accuse the German people of ingrained lawlessness in foreign policy.

But the King did not abdicate. Instead of Frederick III, Bismarck, the greatest of the Junkers, became the ruler of Prussia and of Germany for the next generation. When he began he found the Junker monarchy near collapse. When he resigned the Junkers were not only re-established in Prussia, but they had conquered Germany and were beginning to conquer Europe.

> So much one man can do
> That does both act and know.

On the very day of Bismarck's appointment, parliament rejected the budget which contained the army reforms of the King. The issue was clear. The most decisive moment in the history of the Prussian people had arrived. If parliament had won, a great step would have been taken towards a European Prussia. The parliamentary demands tried to achieve what budget control and the annual Army Act have done for British democracy - to allow to the government no income which parliament has not sanctioned, and to prevent unconstitutional methods of obtaining money by keeping a sharp control over the standing army.

Bismarck opposed parliament with his notorious *Lückentheorie*, the theory of the gap in the constitution. He declared that the constitution did not say what should be done if parliament rejected the budget. Since, however, the government of the country could not simply stop, the King and his ministers were entitled to carry on as they pleased. This was clearly a breach of the spirit of the constitution, and parliament retaliated by declaring, in February, 1863, that the ministers would have to answer with their person and property for all expenditure not sanctioned by the constitution. But that was as far as they would go; and Bismarck knew it. He calculated that opposition would be confined to resolutions in parliament, and that there would be no refusal to pay illegal taxes or to serve in an illegal army.*

Still, he could not be certain. Neither the suppression of the liberty of the Press which he ordered in June, 1863, nor the cruel persecution and vexation of his opponents inside and outside parliament were measures which would make the success of his policy a certainty. Despite all oppression the opposition grew.

In this situation Bismarck showed his great, though evil, political genius. The issue on which he was quarrelling with parliament concerned only one of the two great German problems: liberty and unity. Before Bismarck's rule in Prussia both those most potent ideas of the century were weapons in the hands of the parliamentary liberals. Bismarck transformed this position.

The Junkers had opposed the offer of the German national assembly of 1848, which had wanted the King of Prussia to become Emperor of Germany by the will of the nation. They had seen in this offer a danger for a King who wanted to be King by the grace of God alone. True, the Junkers did not take the offer very seriously then, because the national assembly had no force at its disposal with which to back up its demand for unity. Yet for them it remained a potential danger after 1848.

Prussian liberals could say that they were fighting the battle of the whole German people in trying to unify

* Grant Robertson, *Bismarck*, p. 127.

Germany under a democratic constitution. They could declare that of all the constitutions of the smaller States, which were far in advance of Prussia's, could only be made secure if the greater part of Germany, if Prussia herself, were made safe for democracy. They might well maintain that the day which would see a liberal, a truly German, Prussia, would break down the barriers between the German States and establish a free, united and therefore a peaceful Germany. The Prince Consort wrote to the future Queen of Prussia: 'The Germanizing of Prussia is the condition of her greatness and power and of bringing peace to Germany.'

But what if German unity were achieved, not by a union of the free people of Prussia with the free people in the rest of Germany, but imposed with blood and iron on Germany by an unfree Junker Prussia? With one stroke this would ruin the parliamentary opposition within Prussia and for ever establish the power of reaction by Prussianizing the whole of Germany!

This was Bismarck's bold idea. He would achieve German unity at the expense of German liberty. Nobody, least of all his political opponents, can deny that he showed an extraordinary imaginative and inventive capacity in the choice of his means. With supreme disregard for all principles save that of expediency he succeeded in unifying and Prussianizing Germany, and in poisoning her political outlook by the doctrine of *Realpolitik*. By his achievement Bismarck gave the best proof that a political victory is barren if it has no moral basis, and he left a legacy of corruption and anxiety from which Europe has not yet recovered.

CHAPTER 26

THE PRICE PAID FOR UNITY

★

This success left the political leadership of Germany to the exponents of Junker ideas. They became so firmly entrenched that one half-revolution in 1918 has not been sufficient to dislodge them. And Europe has to pay for this in yet another war.

Ever since 1815 various governments had prepared and submitted plans for the greater coherence and efficiency of the German confederation. All these efforts were now crowned by Bismarck himself with a sudden demand for a German parliament based on manhood suffrage and secret ballot. Here was a change indeed! The Junker Bismarck had been the leader of the diehard Prussians in their fight against a constitution. Later, when this constitution had to be granted, he supported all the measures intended to stunt the growth of popular liberties. And now he came forward as the champion of the most cherished of all the popular demands, a free and powerful parliament for the whole of Germany!

The change was too sudden. Many knew that his demand for a free parliament was simply intended to embarrass Austria. For Bismarck had realized that, if he wanted to achieve German unity in the Prussian way, he had first to get rid of Austria. Austria had to be chased out of Germany lest she prevent her Prussianization. What better method than to put on the shining armour of progressive demands and make Austria appear the only prop of reaction! Bismarck deceived the liberals, for though they were not wholly convinced of Bismarck's change of heart, they were beginning to waver.

And he certainly fooled Europe. Lord A. Loftus, the British Ambassador, continued sending reassuring despatches. More important still, for it concerned them more, Bismarck fooled the French. The Emperor Louis Napoleon listened to and believed in all the same arguments that we have heard recently. Bismarck did not disguise his forthcoming acts of violence, but he assured the Emperor that they were strictly limited.

Four years later Louis Napoleon paid at Sedan for his folly in believing the assurances of a Junker politician. He could have learnt the principles which dominated Bismarck's policy from Bismarck's attitude to the Prussian constitution. The conviction that the law of the land put restrictions only on those who did not appreciate the over-riding influence of armed force had brought victory to Bismarck at home. Since these principles had proved so successful, was he likely to abandon them in his foreign policy? The French Emperor believed he would, and the mistake lost him his throne. He was not the last to pay the price of wishful thinking.

Having forestalled all opposition, Bismarck was able in 1866 to march the Prussian army, illegally recruited and illegally equipped, to Königgrätz and victory. Bismarck told his King that Austria and the rest of Germany looked with hungry eyes at innocent Prussia and plotted her destruction. The King believed him, and the royal proclamation, announcing to the Prussian people that they were to fight Austria, first embodied the myth of encirclement. 'Wherever we look in Germany,' declared the manifesto of the Prussian King, 'we are surrounded by enemies and their battle-cry is the humiliation of Prussia.'—Substitute 'the world' for 'Germany,' and 'Germany' for 'Prussia,' and you have the ever-recurring theme of Nazi propaganda.

Bismarck proved his true genius by the political measures which he took after the decisive battle of the Austro-Prussian war. He was opposed by the King and the Junkers who did not realize that only by his methods could their privileged position survive. Without Bismarck both King and Junkers would have been brushed aside by the forces of progress. Yet, he was attacked with such vehemence by the blind Junkers, that he would assuredly have fallen, had not the majority of liberals, equally blind, supported him just at this critical period.

Here Bismarck showed once more his political flair. He held elections in the middle of the war with Austria, and so defeated his liberal opponents. For the victory of Königgrätz, though won illegally, was victory still. We can see here the first-fruit of that political corruption which Bismarck's successful methods achieved. The final collapse of popular resistance to his policy was brought about by another of his astute moves.

The exclusion of Austria from German affairs was the price she had to pay for her defeat. It made the unity of the rest of Germany only a question of time. Thus the great dream of Prussian and German progressives would be realized. People forgot the measures by which the first step to unity had been achieved: that it had not been brought about by willing co-operation of free men, but imposed by Junker armies and Junker statesmanship. Thus the liberals were already wavering, and, when Bismarck built for them a golden bridge, they rushed over it into a Germany built and controlled by the Junkers. The golden bridge was Bismarck's Bill of Indemnity.

THE PRICE PAID FOR UNITY

In this bill his government asked parliament to approve *after the event* all expenditure incurred without parliamentary sanction. Thereby Bismarck made a cheap concession to the opposition, which he could well afford.*

The victory at Königgrätz, the energetic attempts at achieving German unity with Junker methods, and the indemnity bill, all helped to bring about the most decisive victory for Bismarck and the Junkers. The progressives split. It will suffice to say that they split into those who put unity before liberty and those who put liberty first. Here is the key to an understanding of German history since Bismarck.

Great numbers who ought to have been fighting for a true parliament, for popular participation in government, were doped and corrupted by the picture of German unity which Bismarck presented to them. The new party, the national liberals, became Bismarck's strongest supporters. No doubt economic considerations influenced many liberals in favour of Bismarck. Also, they thought that the man who had brought about German unity deserved their support. Little did they realize that they were being given the shadow for the substance. For a Junker Germany was not the Germany for which their predecessors had died. Those progressives who saw that liberty had been lost when unity was won, continued the struggle. They were always in a minority.

Had a united liberal opposition endured there would have been no party to support Bismarck. The Junkers had not yet realized that he had in fact re-established their position after its bad shaking by the constitutional conflict of the early 'sixties. To them it appeared that

* See his *Reflections and Reminiscences* for his cynical reasons for demanding a German parliament and an indemnity (Vol. II, p. 64 and pp. 76–77).

Bismarck had forgotten Junker principles when he made too many concessions to the progressives in his constitution of the new German Empire. For was there not now a German parliament which differed from the Prussian in that every man had a direct and secret vote irrespective of his income?

Yet, the importance of this vote was negligible. In this country it is often pointed out that, if the Germans were really ready to govern themselves, they had their chance in the new parliament, the Reichstag, from 1871 onward. This is a fallacy. The power of this Reichstag was extremely limited. The government of Germany was not dependent on the confidence of the majority of Reichstag members. Nothing mattered in Germany from 1871 to 1918 save Prussia, and in Prussia nothing had been done to destroy the privileged position of the Junkers. The Prussian constitution* had not been changed when German unity was achieved.

Bismarck had wrested the banner of German unity from the astonished liberals. He had unfurled it in front of the conquering armies of the King of Prussia and finally hoisted it over a Germany united by blood and iron. He had thereby saved Junker Prussia. The army remained their stronghold, and the Junker bureaucracy maintained its grip over the country, and especially over the rural districts where the local Junker combined his private position of big landowner with his official position of magistrate.

Thanks to Bismarck's victories, the spirit of Junkerdom spread over the whole of Germany. For Prussia wielded a hegemony which was not less powerful because it was indirect.

* Described on p. 248, above.

Prussia's hegemony was apparent in the economic field. It had been so ever since the formation of the *Zollverein*, the customs union, in 1834. In military matters, too, Prussia dominated Germany. For in his capacity of German Emperor the King of Prussia was the supreme commander of the German army and navy.

In this same capacity the Prussian King was the head of the Reich administration. He represented Germany in international relations, and he had, in practice, the unrestricted right to declare war or make peace. In all the branches of administration which remained with the former independent States such as Bavaria, Saxony, Württemberg and Baden, Prussian influence was powerful enough to make itself felt, despite the nominal right of these States to regulate their own internal administration. Their laws, and their education, showed the impact of Prussian preponderance. In fact, Prussian hegemony was made easier by its indirectness. Outright annexation of all Germany would have called forth more resistance.

It is vital to remember that all this is not ancient history. Prussia kept her semi-absolute constitution until 1918. The Prussian Government was now the real ruler of Germany. Thus we must not forget that the German people left a state of political bondage less than twenty-five years ago. In other countries, too, the first attempt at responsible self-government was not an immediate success. We have therefore no right to make the glib assumption that the German wants to be ordered about by his Junkers or that he feels happy only when under their heel.

When, in 1888, William II began his reign, he could already stress his imperial rather than his Prussian office; for Prussian principles had permeated the German body politic in all its essential parts. The Prussian King, his soldiers and his bureaucrats now governed all the Germans. This was inevitable, since the German people had not won unity, but had been beaten into it by the Prussian ruling caste.

The most powerful economic interest behind this caste was still the big landowners. In February, 1893, they founded the *Bund der Landwirte*, or Farmers' Union. This organization catered solely for the big estates, to such a degree that small farmers had to found their own group.

The end of the nineteenth century brought a severe crisis in agriculture. For centuries the Junkers had increased their lands by forcing free peasants to give up their holdings. The political power wielded by the Junkers had facilitated this task. But by the end of the last century the big estates had ceased to be a profitable business; for the industrialized West of Germany could now buy grain from overseas countries more cheaply than from the German East. However, the political influence of the Junkers was so strong that, instead of having to abandon their traditional position, they were able to force the whole country to pay more for its bread.

A still better example of their all-pervading influence in the new Germany and of the complete impotence of the representatives of the people is the dismissal of Caprivi, Bismarck's successor. Caprivi was no Junker. On the contrary, he was most unpopular with the Junkers because of his economic policy. Furthermore, he had made attempts to deal reasonably with the ever-growing Social Democratic party, the chief representative of the German workers.* He finally undermined his own position by attempting to restrict the political influence of the army. His fall was therefore brought about by all that was

* See first footnote on p. 271 below

powerful at the imperial court: the big landowners, the Junker party and the army. Parliament had no voice.

The new course pursued in economic policy resulted in a close alliance between the original, or agrarian, Junkers and those industrialists who came to share the political outlook of the Prussian squirearchy and whom, as was explained in Chapter 23,* we find it appropriate to describe as industrial Junkers.

In all countries the period from 1890 to 1914 was on the whole one of unparalleled prosperity. Yet, in Germany, most people became convinced that this prosperity was solely due to Bismarck's great achievement of German unity. People had desired unity for idealistic reasons. Now it seemed also to have brought great economic advantages. It was not surprising that a good number of the middle class whose ancestors had been passionately opposed to Bismarck's methods now came to regard them with respect and even with affection.

The political consequences of such an attitude were disastrous. The great majority of the German people felt helpless to oppose the machinery which governed them. It was an all-powerful machinery controlled by the Junkers in army, bureaucracy, agriculture and industry. The most important agent of the Junker influence became the army.

The personality of the Emperor William II contributed to this influence. 'When the diplomatists failed to bring about a political agreement with England, the Kaiser felt confirmed in the (to him) congenial belief that the military had better judgment even in political matters, and that the civilians were really no use whatever.'† This belief was so absurdly self-confident that he could say in 1908 to Sir Charles Hardinge, British Under-Secretary for

* See p. 231 above.
† Brandenburg, *From Bismarck to the World War*, p. 416.

Foreign Affairs: 'Your material is all wrong! I am an Admiral of the English Fleet which I know very well and understand better than you who are a civilian.'*

This attitude of mind had its fatal significance for the peace of the world. It has been established that neither the Kaiser nor his advisers deliberately planned a world war.† The fact remains that theirs was an outlook which made all international confidence and collaboration difficult, if not impossible. It was as true of the period before 1914 as of the anxious years through which we have just passed that there had to be either confidence or war.

The Kaiser and his advisers did nothing to establish confidence. Nor could they as long as they followed the Junker principles which had brought about German unity under Prussian hegemony. These principles forbade them to look with favour on any plans for restrictions of armaments and international arbitration. General Bernhardi acted as mouthpiece of the German rulers when he declared that

'a peaceful decision by an Arbitration Court can never replace in its effects and consequences a warlike decision, even as regards the State in whose favour it is pronounced. . . . It was war which laid the foundations of Prussia's power. . . . The military successes and the political position won by the sword laid the foundation for an unparalleled material prosperity. It is difficult to imagine how pitiable the progress of the German people would have been had not these wars been brought about by a deliberate policy.'‡

* Official German Documents, *Grosse Politik*, No. 8226, Vol. 24, p. 126.

† For the evidence see Gooch, *Germany*, p 110, and his *Recent Revelations of European Diplomacy*, p. 2.

‡ *Germany and the Next War*, popular edition (1914), pp. 33, 34, 43.

A ruling class which remembered that it had kept its internal position in 1862 only because of its hold over the armed forces, was not inclined to approve sincerely of any international agreement for the limitation of armaments. Thus when President Theodore Roosevelt suggested in 1906 a limitation in naval armaments the Kaiser commented: 'To be refused. Every country builds as much as it likes. It is the concern of nobody else.'*

These views were not those of Germany, nor of a majority of the German people. But they were the views of that group which led the country to war and to defeat. As an acute American observer put it in 1913: 'We shall have war when the German Kaiser touches a button and gives an order, and the German people will have no more to say in the matter than you and I.'†

Was there, then, no opposition at all to this policy? There was. And it was exceedingly vociferous; but, since it lacked all material power, it was not taken very seriously. Perhaps the most brilliant attack on the régime came from outside parliament. It was undertaken by a Professor of History and took the form of a biographical study of the Roman Emperor Caligula.‡ It was a seditious libel on the Kaiser, William II, but since it was all dressed up as ancient history the Public Prosecutor could do nothing. Yet the parallels were obvious. Seldom can a learned work have enjoyed such a sale!

The Caligula affair was not the only attack. The German Reichstag continuously complained; that was all it could do. Popular feeling against the Junker State

* *Grosse Politik*, No. 7820, Vol. 23, 1; p. 90. See also the Kaiser's comments on similar suggestions of Grey and Lloyd George in 1908 (*ib.*, No. 8217, Vol. 24, pp. 99–104).

† Collier, *Germany and the Germans* (1913), p. 104.

‡ Quidde, *Caligula; Eine Studie über römischen Cäsarenwahnsinn* (1906).

increased. In the last election before the war, in 1912, the opposition parties had a clear majority. But what was the good of a majority that had no real power! The Reichstag could neither force the government to resign if the government had the support of the Emperor; nor could it stop vital supplies, for the budget was largely outside its control. Many voted socialist not because they approved of socialism, but because they were discontented with the Junker rule. But nobody ever thought that a change was possible.

The army and the bureaucracy seemed much too firmly established. A voter in the 1912 election was warned of the awful things that would happen did the socialists come into power. 'Ah,' he replied, 'but the government would not permit that.' This pathetic answer expressed the feeling of the disgruntled majority. It also taught the tiny minority who ruled the country that they had nothing to fear from the people.

CHAPTER 27

LESSONS FOR A LASTING PEACE

The military collapse of Germany in 1918 entailed the complete collapse of Junkerdom. It is not unimportant to remember the order of events. It was the breakdown of the army led by Ludendorff, who had been, in fact, both military and civil dictator since 1916, which caused the revolution of 1918. As in the Allied countries, there was plenty of unrest on the home front before that date; but there is no evidence for the notorious 'stab in the back,' i.e. the theory that all was well with the fighting forces and only bolshevist agitation at home caused the collapse.

If there was 'a stab in the back' it was administered by Ludendorff; and the victim was the new parliamentary monarchy which had just been established at last, but too late. For, although the new government was strongly against an immediate armistice, the Higher Command insisted on the inception of the negotiations which led to the armistice, and it did so because of its view of the military situation.* Stresemann, who at that time was still a firm supporter of Junker foreign policy, himself admitted† that this request of the army for an

* *History of the Peace Conference*, Vol. I, p. 113.
† In his paper *Deutsche Stimmen*, 6. XI, 1918.

immediate armistice was considered by friend and foe alike to be a conclusive proof of Germany's downfall.

Military defeat was followed by the rapid outward disappearance of all the forces which had supported the Hohenzollern monarchy. Red flags flew everywhere, voluntarily hoisted even by members of the Imperial family. Within two days of the revolution the Journal of the Junkers, the *Kreuzzeitung*, voluntarily suppressed its heading: 'With God for King and Country.' If anything killed the monarchical idea in Germany for ever, it was this disappearance of the Empire without a blow being struck in its defence by those who had enjoyed all its privileges!

This utter failure of army and bureaucracy meant that the forces which had been kept in impotent opposition were called upon to save the country by making peace. The German people had been forbidden to have a say in the affairs of their country. Now suddenly they had to manage them entirely themselves. Thus power was thrust into the hands of politicians weakened by years of opposition and without any practical experience of government.

The legacy left to them was appalling. Starvation at home, troops flowing back from the front, the possibility of a bolshevist rising, and the severe demands of the Allies, all these were enough to confound the greatest statesman. Thus it became the chief concern of the new social democratic government to keep the old machinery going in order to avoid a complete breakdown.*

Nobody can blame them for this patriotic endeavour. Yet, as we can see to-day, it proved the downfall of Democracy in Germany. For it meant that the astonished Junker officers and bureaucrats in hiding for fear of

* *History of the Peace Conference*, Vol. I, p. 100.

revolutionary justice found themselves entrusted by the new government with the task of maintaining law and order.

The all-powerful machine of imperial government with its control of every aspect of the political life had brought the whole population to an enfeebled social and political condition. The people thought that they could do nothing by themselves. The urgent desire of the new rulers to restore things to normal as quickly as possible was responsible for their fatal decision not to 'purge' the administrative and judicial bureaucracy. In later years the Republic had to pay heavily for its mistakes. The Law Courts, steeped in the doctrines of Bismarckianism, effectively sabotaged the young democracy.

The most disastrous consequences for Germany and Europe were produced by the attitude of the new rulers to the old army. Within a year from the outbreak of the revolution the old officer-class was again firmly ensconced in the German body politic, and it was soon to become a State within the State. Here is a lesson to be learned by all those who are striving for a lasting peace.

There were two reasons for the re-establishment of the Junkers within the army of the Republic. The first was the fear of bolshevism, a quite unfounded fear as was soon to be realized. It was true that the workers of Berlin had become very radical, but even amongst these the bolshevists were in a hopeless minority. In most other districts of the Reich their numbers were even smaller. But the Social Democratic government had before its eyes the fate of the mildly Left government of Kerensky in Russia: it had been short-lived and ousted from power by Lenin and Trotsky, leaders of a small minority group.

The functionaries of the labour movement who were

now the rulers of a chaotic Germany, had been brought up in an almost pathological detestation of anything which was connected with the army; for they saw in it, quite rightly, the main prop of the Junker system. But this made them forget that no government which finds itself faced with a revolutionary situation can dispense with force.*

There was indeed some realization amongst the Labour rank and file that, during a revolution, political power needs military power to defend itself. Thus a few corps of volunteers were formed, almost exclusively of trade unionists. When the bolshevik minority attempted a rising early in 1919, these democratic volunteers were mainly responsible for its failure. Yet the new leaders of Germany felt that only the old officers really knew how to deal with armed risings. Any doubts they might have had as to the political reliability of former imperial officers were smothered by their declarations of loyalty to the democratic Republic. This loyalty was not to last. But it resulted in the acquiescence of the Republican government in the re-establishment of the army under the old officers.

The other reason which allowed reaction to creep back into the armed forces was the bitter disillusionment over the terms of the peace. The forces of progress in Germany had genuinely believed that the disappearance of Junkerdom would procure a peace of justice and reconciliation. They had a passionate faith in the ideas of the League of Nations, which would establish a new era for humanity. All the hopes that German democracy would be granted generous terms and could thus establish a happier future were doomed to disappointment.

* A detailed account of the Republic may be found in A. Rosenberg, *A History of the German Republic*, 1936. See also Daniels, *The Rise of the German Republic*; and R. T. Clark, *The Fall of the German Republic*.

It is quite easy to understand the feelings of the Allies at the end of four years of frightfulness. Yet, political wisdom should have shown them that their own self-interest demanded the strengthening of German democracy in order to prevent the recurrence of Junker aggression.

By failing to distinguish between democratic and Junker Germany they played into the hands of the very people whose policy had led Germany to destruction. German democrats remembered with bitterness President Wilson's promises of fair play for a Germany which had overthrown the Kaiser and the Junker régime. As soon as the old ruling group realized that it was safe to proclaim their views, they began to declare that the collapse was due to Leftist propaganda, and that the chaos in which Germany found herself was the fault of the new Republic.

There had been such a time-lag between the victory of Bismarckianism and its inevitable consequence, between the creation of united Germany by Prussia and the World War, that people failed to see the direct connection between the two. Instead they looked back on the golden days of prosperity under the semi-absolute Monarchy, and compared them with their terrible distress under the young Republic. They did not realize that the distress was the legacy of the Monarchy. Thus within a year of the revolution the old ideas had gained a considerable following, and as a result the re-establishment of the old officer-class was not opposed by the whole nation.

From 1919 the nation was anti-socialist in its majority, and since the socialist leaders believed in democracy they did not establish the socialist State which they had advocated for so long. Democracy in Germany did not even use the moderate powers given it by the new republican constitution of Weimar to take over private businesses. It did make use of the power to enforce amalgamation, and by doing so helped to create a small class of strong industrial magnates, who became the greatest economic power in the State.* The old alliance between agricultural and industrial Junkers revived, and found its terrible expression in the catastrophe of the inflation.

It was inevitable that as a result of the defeat there should be an inflation in Germany. But that it was allowed to develop for four years until it ruined the whole middle class was solely due to the interest which the industrial, agricultural and financial Junkers took in its prolongation.†

The democratic Republic never really recovered from this blow. Its supporters were weakened, while Junkerdom strengthened its position. On the surface there was much that seemed to give reason for hope. After 1923 the economic situation improved. The elections of December, 1924, and May, 1928, showed a steady increase in the votes of the democratic parties.

This was the period of Locarno and of Germany's entry into the League of Nations, the era of Stresemann, who would appear to have changed his wartime opinions and sincerely desired collaboration with the West. The enemies of peace and of the Republic felt that their time was not yet.

However, the way in which Stresemann's own party, the representative of the Junker mentality in industry and the higher bureaucracy, opposed its leader on many crucial issues, did not promise well. Large numbers of

* R. Muir, *The Political Consequences of the Great War* (1932), p. 118.

† Rosenberg, *loc. cit.*, p. 150 and pp. 182 to 184; Rauschning, *loc. cit.*, English edition, p. 116.

the middle class could not forget the military collapse and the inflation, for which they blamed the Republic, since nothing was done to tell them who was responsible. Thus the main support for democracy had to come from Labour. But there were three different parties among the workers.*

The split in the working-class vote enabled the Junkers to score their first great democratic triumph. They cleverly exploited the Hindenburg myth by running the old Field-Marshal for the Presidency of the Reich. Hindenburg was elected on a minority vote in a three-cornered fight, since the communists had refused to support the democratic candidate.

The election of the aged soldier, who for all his charm and dignity was yet the very embodiment of the Junker army, brought no immediate danger to the Republic.† The Weimar constitution placed the President in a position of great elevation without much political influence. According to this democratic constitution, the country was ruled by a government which was dependent on the support of the Reichstag.

This constitutional situation was changed by the political results of the great economic crisis which began in 1929. Germany was hit worse than most other countries, because her apparent prosperity had been built on short-term loans, mainly from America. These were now withdrawn. And Germany's economic fabric, which had

---

* As in other industrial countries there were the socialists and the communists; but a great part of the German working class was Roman Catholic, and they formed the left wing of the Centre Party, the representative of Roman Catholicism.

† However, many of the future Nazi leaders were free to start their activities again thanks to an amnesty which Hindenburg promoted. They had been imprisoned or had left the country after the failure of Hitler's *Putsch* in Munich in 1923.

hardly recovered from war and inflation, was utterly shattered.

The first elections held after the beginning of this disaster in September, 1930, increased the representation of the Nazis, up till then an insignificant minority, from 12 to 107 members in a total of 577. They were now the second strongest party after the socialists. Great numbers of Germans untrained in civics and the responsibilities of democratic self-government, in despair because of yet another economic catastrophe, fell for the brilliant demagogic tactics of the Nazis. But although in the next two years the Nazis further increased, until they were by far the strongest single party, the dam built by the good sense of the German people just managed to stand the strain—the Nazis never got their majority.

We have seen* how the flood of Nazism which had failed to break through this dam and was beginning to recede, was let into the land because the Junkers opened the gates. What enabled them to kill German democracy and European peace by handing both over to Herr Hitler, was the change in the constitutional position of the President.

After the elections of 1930 the Prime Minister, Brüning, decided not to resign, although his government had no longer a real majority in the Reichstag. His stay in office was made possible by the desire of the Social Democrats to keep Hitler out and therefore to tolerate Brüning as the lesser evil. Furthermore, at that time Brüning enjoyed the confidence of President Hindenburg, and thus he decided to base his government on presidential rather than parliamentary support.

This was a return to the Bismarckian constitution with

* In Chapter 23 above, p. 231 *et seq.*

Hindenburg in the place of the Kaiser. It cannot be doubted that these tactics certainly 'dented' the democratic Weimar constitution, even if they did not actually break it. What is still doubtful for the historian is the real intention which animated Brüning. Did he hope to steer democracy safely through desperate times by these desperate means and to return to the constitution as soon as possible?

His intentions were not put to the test. For he lost Hindenburg's confidence, or rather that of Hindenburg's Junker entourage; and, since Brüning's government was based on this confidence, it fell. Herr von Papen became the new Prime Minister.

There is no better representative of Junkerdom alive than this charming, incompetent, unprincipled and lawless gentleman. He combines Junkerdom in industry, agriculture and bureaucracy, for he is a wealthy industrialist and landowner, and a diplomat of notorious reputation. His sabotage in America during the last war, and the criminal negligence with which he betrayed his confederates, are well known. Less well known is his claim to have influenced the Vatican to sign the *Concordat* of 1933 with Herr Hitler despite the warnings of the German episcopate. This treaty gave Herr Hitler in the eyes of the world the respectability so badly needed at the outset of his rule. It induced people in many countries to accept the Nazis as the Christian bulwark against bolshevism.

Papen showed his true spirit in the *coup d'état* by which in July, 1932, he forced the democratic government of Prussia to resign. His rule of reaction was cut short by the famous election of November, 1932, in which the great drop in the Nazi poll reflected the improvement in the economic situation and the return of common sense to millions of Germans. But it was too late for democracy to reassert itself. The Junkers were determined not to let go the hold over the country which they had gradually regained since 1918, even at the price of a pact with Herr Hitler.

To-day the meaning of Nazism in international relations is recognized; that is why we are at war. But the defeat of Nazism will not solve the German problem. For the Allies will still be faced with the urgent question: Can we trust their successors to play their part in the new Europe? Last time Clemenceau refused to make concessions to the young German democracy, because he felt he could not be certain that the revolution of 1918 had produced a lasting change in Germany.* The same uncertainty will exist this time.

It would be unwise and indeed fatal for this country and France to impose a certain type of government on the defeated Reich. But, in the interest of their own countries and of the whole world, it will be the duty of the Allied governments thoroughly to scrutinize the real forces behind any new German government. Mr. Chamberlain has said that in the new Europe 'each country would have the unfettered right to choose its own form of internal government, so long as that government did not pursue an external policy injurious to its neighbours.'†

The plain lesson which history has to teach us is that a resurrection of Junkerdom in all its aspects must be prevented if the new peace is to last. We ought to be grateful to the Nazis for having made this danger quite

* In his note of 16 June, 1919; quoted by D. Hunter Miller, *The Drafting of the Covenant*, Vol. I, p. 542.
† In his broadcast of 26 November, 1939.

clear. Their foreign policy, their attitude to international co-operation, is only a coarsened version of Junker politics, as our survey has shown us.

Yet we might see the Junkers creep back into power unless we are determined that they shall not. The Nazis have crushed the Junker parties like all others. But Junkerdom, although somewhat subdued, has remained in existence on the land, in industry and particularly in the army, where the old Junker tradition is still alive in many important officers. All other political groups had to disappear underground when their party organizations were smashed. The Junkers alone have survived as a group, without a party, only too ready to replace National Socialism. Thus they appear to be the obvious alternative to the Nazis; and there are many who, out of a praiseworthy longing for peace and because of an honourable determination not to meddle in the internal affairs of other countries, might welcome a Junker government. Their long tradition of ruling and their fearless use of force might be regarded as an assurance of the early restoration of law and order.

It must also be realized that the Junkers, thanks to their influential positions, have frequent opportunities of coming into contact with the leaders of other nations. In these contacts they have appeared as the charming and well-mannered human beings a great number of them are. But the tenets of their political faith never became apparent to their British friends, who were apt to mistake for conservative gentlemen people whose politics were neither conservative nor gentlemanly, but destructive and treacherous.

There has never been a full realization that Germany's internal development has been so utterly different from that of Britain and France. In Germany true conservatism ceased to exist long ago; there has remained only a belief in the omnipotence of lawless force. It is much to be regretted that this fact, which has been stated with such admirable clarity in Herr Rauschning's book, has been omitted from the English translation.*

Superficial similarities in the social background have deceived many people. Few in this country realized the deep significance for the future of Europe of the Prussian constitutional struggle in 1862. There was no appreciation of the fact that victory for parliament would have given it control over Prussia and would have defeated Junkerdom. The similarities between Hitler's and Bismarck's policy have been overstressed. There are profound differences. But it is tragically true that both were able to do too much before Europe awoke. The complete initial misunderstanding of Bismarck's and Hitler's policy in both England and France is frightening in its likeness. 'The English ambassador in Berlin must write to his minister much more nonsense than I imagine,' wrote Bismarck. 'Neither at the Foreign Office, nor in Parliament, not even in the office of *The Times* . . . did they know the truth about Prussia and Germany, and it is doubtful whether they wished to know.'†

Yet knowledge of the forces which collectively we have called Junkerdom is vital. If a resurrection of their power be permitted, the future peace of Europe will be murdered while still in the womb of time. Relief from Hitler by means of a government of so-called 'gentlemen and moderate generals' would be like the use of some patent medicine which eases the pain but does not cure the

---

* Rauschning, *Revolution des Nihilismus*, 2nd edition, pp. 33 and 179. English translation, *Germany's Revolution of Destruction*; but see pp. 118 *et seq.*

† Grant Robertson, *Bismarck*, p. 114.

disease. On the contrary, such a course is fatal in the long run; for it encourages the neglect of proper treatment until it is too late.

The resurrection of Junkerdom could only result in the revival of 'that aggressive bullying mentality which seeks continually to dominate other peoples by force ... and in the name of the interests of the State justifies the repudiation of its own pledged word whenever it finds it convenient.' But, as the Prime Minister has so rightly said,* this is the very thing we are determined to defeat.

If, then, we are agreed that in the interest of a lasting peace the danger to guard against is the reintroduction of Junkerdom in Germany after Herr Hitler's fall, a final problem arises. How can we be certain that a new German government will be bent on international co-operation and therefore opposed to Junker principles?

The answer may be found in a study of the internal measures which such a new German government would undertake at once. Three are particularly essential, as they deal with the three strongholds of Junkerdom. The *first two* concern the economic structure of Germany. They are *a thorough land reform in the East*, and a *close supervision of the key industries*.

It must be emphasized that these measures have more to do with democracy than with socialism. We must not consider them from their economic, but rather from their political aspect. Seen in their political significance these measures prove to be the only sure way by which any new German government can effectively lay the danger of Junkerdom for ever.

This struggle against Junkerdom is nothing new; it is the German equivalent of the fight against the 'over-

* In his broadcast of 26 November, 1939.

mighty subject' to which centuries of English constitutional development were successfully devoted. The late Pope acknowledged that such measures are not socialism, when he stated in his famous encyclical *Quadragesimo Anno*, that they are an attack on

> a form of social authority which property has usurped in violation of all justice. This authority in fact pertains not to individual owners but to the State. . . . For it is rightly contended that certain forms of property must be reserved to the State, since they carry with them a power too great to be left to private individuals without injury to the community at large. Just demands of this kind contain nothing opposed to Christian truth; much less are they peculiar to socialism.*

The splitting up of the uneconomic large estates besides breaking down one Junker stronghold would have another effect equally beneficial to Germany and Europe. For in them may be found the *Lebensraum*, the living space, for great numbers of Germans. This might entail State support and supervision. But Germany would then only follow the example of such democracies as Holland, where the farmer has got used to the organizations which control production, or Switzerland, where economic planning in agriculture has also been a success.†

More important even than these two steps in the economic sphere is the *third* which would have to be taken by any German government genuinely anxious for a lasting peace. If there is room in the new international order for national armies, then *the new German army will have to become a real people's army* modelled on

---

* Printed in *Modern Political Doctrines*, edited by Sir A. Zimmern, pp. 142-3.

† See *Proceedings of the Third International Conference of Agricultural Economists*, 1935, pp. 91 *et seq.* and 56 *et seq.*

the ideas of Stein. We have seen the baleful influence of the Junker army throughout history. It shows that the importance of this third reform cannot be overstressed.

When these three measures have been carried out, the key positions in Germany will no longer be held by a ruling class who believe in the uselessness of collaboration and the omnipotence of force, or who are convinced that any legal obligation ceases to be binding with the benefits derived from it. The Junkers have always based both their internal and their external policy on these principles. In their dealings at home and abroad they have thereby set aside all Justice, and 'when Justice has been set aside what are kingdoms but great bands of brigands?'*

A Germany which will prove by her measures that she has banished the Junker spirit in her internal affairs will be a Germany whose readiness for international collaboration can be trusted. It will then not matter whether the Germans prefer a Republic or a Monarchy. The new German State should be welcomed into the new Commonwealth, and the victorious Allies should show their political wisdom by the magnanimous treatment of a Germany reborn for willing co-operation in building a lasting peace.

* St. Augustine, *De Civitate Dei*, IV, 4.

INDEX

Abgeordnetenhaus, Prussian, 250
ABYSSINIA, 86, 105, 107–109, 115, 117
Achilles, H.M.S., 148
ADAMS, Quincy, 33
Admiral Graf Spee, 126
ADRIATIC, 89
'Affect,' 202, 204, 205, 207, 210
AFGHANISTAN, 155, 198
AFRICA, 26, 43, 169, 171. *See also* South Africa
Aggression, 17, 19, 29, 57, 61, 65, 71, 73, 74, 79, 81, 84, 103, 104, 107, 109, 113, 114, 118, 119, 120, 122, 124, 125, 129, 130, 131, 136–141, 148–156, 164, 179–184, 188, 211, 216, 224, 226, 227
Agriculture, 173, 260, 261, 278
Alabama, 34, 52
ALBANIA, 86, 105, 124
ALBERT, Prince Consort, 253
ALFRED, King, 202
Air—145, 157, 179–187
 Board of Control, 186, 187
 Force, 80, 147, 148, 155, 157, 179–184. *See also* Commonwealth Air Force
ALEXANDER the Great, 22
ALEXANDER I, Tsar, 32
Amateur, 205
AMERICA, 21, 36, 37, 40, 41, 42, 43, 44, 48, 59, 67, 72, 74, 82, 83, 95, 97, 107, 114, 122, 152, 153, 155, 164, 166, 174, 183, 185, 188, 194, 195, 199, 216, 217, 220, 263, 271, 273. *See also* UNITED STATES
Anger, 62, 65
Anglo-Saxon, 26, 65, 67, 80, 113. *See also* English-speaking world
ANNE, Queen, 37
Appeasement, 53, 115–126, 130
Arbitration, 29, 34, 52, 72, 102, 144, 262
ARCTIC, 89
ARGENTINE, 43
Armaments, 17, 34, 35, 61, 62, 65, 72, 73, 75, 80–82, 91, 93, 98, 107, 112, 115, 141, 144, 146–148, 160, 162, 163, 171, 180, 262, 263
Armed Force. *See* Force
Armistice, 77, 141–142, 220, 265, 266
Army, German, 259, 261, 264–268, 271, 278, 279
Army, Prussian, 239, 240, 241, 243, 244, 246, 247, 250–252, 255, 258, 260

Army Act, British annual, 251
ASIA, 48, 169, 198
ASQUITH, H. H., Earl of Asquith and Oxford, 66
Assembly of the League of Nations, 93, 94, 95, 97, 105, 106, 109, 110, 113, 158–160, 191
Assembly, German National (1848), 252
Assistance, Draft Treaty of Mutual (1923), 113
Assistance, Mutual. *See* Defence
ATHENS, 29, 104, 210
ATTLEE, C. R., 164
AUGUSTINE, Saint, 30, 279
AUSTEN, Jane, 43, 58
AUSTIN, John, 85
AUSTRALIA, 38, 43, 48, 148
AUSTRIA, 32, 48, 55, 86, 90, 101, 126, 127, 129, 136, 138, 142, 220, 221, 236, 246, 254–256
AUSTRIA–HUNGARY, 34, 101, 221
Autarchy, 55
Autarky, 55, 173, 175, 177
Aviation, Civil, 157
Axis, Berlin-Rome, 125, 132

BACH, J. S., 23
BADEN, 236, 259
BAGHDAD, 42
BAINVILLE, Jacques, 219, 220
BAKER, Ray Stannard, 68, 75, 171
BALFOUR, A. J., Earl of, 39, 71, 97, 101
BALKAN STATES, 152, 153, 193, 198
BALTIC SEA, 127, 128, 132
BASRA, 42
BAVARIA, 218, 221, 236, 259
BELGIUM, 114, 134, 150, 152, 156, 169, 184, 198, 215
BENEŠ, Edouard, 119, 192
BERCHTESGADEN, 134
BERLIN, 122, 123, 134, 220, 223, 239
BERNE, 48
BERNHARDI, F. von, 262
Birth-rate, 44, 173
BISMARCK, O. E. L., von, Prince, 123, 220, 229, 241, 243, 248, 251–258, 261, 269, 276
BLACK SEA, 132, 158
BLENHEIM, Battle of, 58
BLÜCHER, G. L. von, 58
Bolshevist, 224, 265–268, 273

BONO, Emilio de, 108
Bootlegger, 40
BORAH, Senator, 114
BOSTON, 36, 37
BOURGEOIS, Léon, 66
BRANDENBURG, 237-239
BRANDENBURG, E., 261
BRAHE, Tycho, 27
BRAZIL, 43, 44, 91
BREST-LITOVSK, Treaty of (1918), 76
BRIAND, Aristide, 104, 114, 192, 193
BRIAND-KELLOGG Pact. *See* Pact of Paris
BRIERLY, J. L., 31
BRITAIN, 17, 20, 21, 32, 34, 42, 45, 47, 49, 52, 58, 63, 64, 66, 71, 75, 79-83, 86, 87, 95, 96, 98, 102-126, 130-143, 147-157, 161, 164, 167-175, 180-185, 188-198, 201, 215-223, 228, 230, 236, 237, 246, 261, 274-276
British Commonwealth of Nations, 21, 36, 38-40, 41, 85, 86, 112, 148, 188-190, 193, 194, 210
British Empire, 36, 38-40, 82, 125, 167, 171, 197, 198
BRÜNING, Heinrich, 272, 273
BRYCE, Viscount, 37, 67
Budget, Prussian or German, 249, 251, 264
BULGARIA, 90, 103, 104, 105, 131
Bureaucracy. *See* Officialdom
Prussian and German, 239, 240, 242, 246, 258, 260, 261, 264, 266, 267, 270
BUTLER, Harold, 98, 163
BUTLER, Nicholas Murray, 188

CALAIS, 51
CALIFORNIA, 43
CALIGULA, Emperor, 263
CANADA, 38, 40, 43, 52, 96, 148, 152
CANNING, George, 33
CANTERBURY, Archbishop of (Dr. Lang), 154
CAPE TOWN, 39
CAPRIVI, Count L. von, 260
Career (in Colonial service), 169, 176, 177
CARLYLE, Thomas, 238, 240
CARR, E. H., 194, 199
Cartel, 51
CARTHAGE, 54, 140, 204
CASTLEREAGH, Viscount, 32, 33
Catholic, 30, 111, 132, 271
CECIL, Viscount, 66, 67, 71, 78, 79, 83, 98, 190
Celt, 26
CEYLON, 177

CHAMBERLAIN, Sir Austen, 113, 114
CHAMBERLAIN, Neville, 56, 121, 122, 123, 132, 134, 135, 138, 139, 142, 144, 274, 277
Character, 201
CHARLEMAGNE, 54
CHARLES I, 249, 250
CHARLESTON, 37
CHESTERTON, G. K., 109
CHICAGO, 43, 120
CHINA, 86, 100, 106, 107, 115, 152, 156, 198, 205
Christianity, 22, 30, 32, 109, 207, 208, 222, 223, 224, 238, 273, 278
Church, 30, 111
  of England, 111, 154
  Free, 111, 154
  Protestant (in Germany), 242
CHURCHILL, Winston, 59, 123, 125
Citizen, 25, 33, 40, 99, 100, 145, 161, 169, 175, 177, 189, 191, 192, 196, 201-211
Civil aviation, 184-187
Civilization, 24, 28, 30, 32, 41, 157, 167, 203, 220, 233, 236, 237
CLARENDON PRESS, 99
CLARK, R. T., 268
CLAUSEWITZ, General von, 54
CLEMENCEAU, Georges, 72, 73, 80, 82, 83, 274
'Coffee smellers,' 239
COLEGRAVE, K. W., 184
COLLIER, P., 263
Colonies, 18, 21, 78, 79, 145, 164, 166, 167-178, 183
COMMONS, HOUSE OF. *See* Parliament, British
Commonwealth, 143-200, 209, 210, 223, 235, 279
  Air Force, 157, 179-184
Communications, Transit and, 37, 42, 52, 100, 145, 161, 166, 181, 184-187
Comradeship, 209
Conation, 205
Concentration Camp, 125, 230
Concordat, Nazi-Vatican (1933), 273
Conduct, 206, 207
Confederation, 36
  German, 254
CONSTANTINE, Emperor, 85
CONSTANTINOPLE, 51
Constitution—
  Bismarck's, 258, 259, 272
  Commonwealth, 188-200
  English or British, 189, 190, 229, 241
  Prussian (1850), 248-250, 258, 259
  of United States, 37, 189, 193
  Weimar, 243, 270, 271, 273

INDEX

Constitutional Convention, 191
Contemporary Review, 118, 179
COOPER, Duff, 125
COPERNICUS, 27
CORFU, 105
Corridor, Polish. *See* Polish corridor
COSTA RICA, 91
Council of the League of Nations, 93, 94, 102–104, 110, 149, 150, 158, 159
Coup d'état, von Papen's (1932), 273
Covenant of the League of Nations, 54, 69, 72, 77–79, 83, 84, 88–98, 108, 109, 110, 113, 115, 117, 120, 121, 125, 146, 149, 150, 157, 159, 166, 167, 189, 190, 197
CRETE, 155
CRIMEA, 62
CROATIA, 221
CROMWELL, Oliver, 248
CROWE, Sir Eyre, 66
Cruelty, 140
CZECHO-SLOVAKIA, 43, 55, 72, 86, 105, 113, 121–123, 126, 129, 130, 139, 142, 150, 152, 169, 192, 198, 221

DALADIER, E., 122
Dane. *See* DENMARK
Dane-geld, 53, 54
DANIELS, H. G., 268
DANZIG, 78, 127, 128, 129, 130, 133
DAVIES, Lord, 147
DAVIS, Norman, 75
Dawes Report (1924), 75
Declaration of the Teaching Profession (1927), 201, 205
Defence, Power of, 57, 61
 Collective, 21, 61, 109, 115, 118, 119, 122, 126, 131, 147, 148–157, 160, 180–184
DEFOE, Daniel, 26, 27
Demobilization, 144
Democracy, 22, 37, 39, 163, 191, 192, 210, 222, 224, 243, 253, 277
 German, 218, 223, 233, 235, 243, 246, 266–272
DENMARK, 26, 27, 43, 139, 142, 198
DICEY, A. V., 85
Disarmament. *See* Armaments Conference (1932), 107, 115
Discipline, 204
Discovery, 41, 201, 202, 206, 210
Disgust, 62
Disputes, International, 17, 33, 34, 40, 52–57, 60, 61, 65, 79, 84, 92, 98, 99, 102, 103, 114, 144, 148, 157–160, 162, 163
Dominions, British, 38, 39, 89, 125, 171, 197

DRESDEN, 49
DRIAULT, E., 218
DRISCOLL, Joseph, 122
Drugs, 79, 93
Dual Policy (1939), 17, 118, 124–127, 137, 142, 167
DURHAM, Earl of, 38, 52
Dutch, 31, 32, 65, 69, 70, 152, 156, 169, 181, 192. *See also* Netherlands
Dynasties, German, 220

Economics, 18, 41, 55, 98, 99, 100, 101, 102, 106, 107, 144, 150, 152, 153, 160, 161–166, 168, 173–177, 199, 211, 215, 232, 246, 248, 259, 260, 270, 271, 273, 277, 278
Economist, The, 82
EDEN, Anthony, 109, 110, 119–122, 125, 126, 159
Eden, Garden of, 42
EDENBRIDGE, 78
Education, 18, 25, 100, 111, 112, 162, 177, 200, 201–211, 243, 259
EDUCATION, BOARD OF, 161, 201
EGYPT, 43, 108
EINSTEIN, Albert, 27, 201, 206
EIRE, 38, 151. *See also* Ireland
Elector (of Brandenburg), 238, 239
Elector (of Hanover), 241
Emigration (to Colonies), 176
Emotion, 205, 207
Emperor. *See* Empire
Empire, British. *See* British Empire
Empire, French. *See* France
Empire, German. *See* German Empire
Empire, Holy Roman, 127, 237, 239
Encirclement, 62, 133, 255
ENGLAND, 26, 27, 33, 46, 56, 58, 67, 68, 70, 102, 106, 128, 154, 162, 184, 195, 202, 221, 223, 229, 241, 249–250, 277
English-speaking world, 35, 39, 41, 65, 67, 189, 190
ENOCK, Arthur, G., 35
ENSOR, R. C. K., 119
Entomology, 173
Epidemic disease, 48, 49, 52, 60
Equilibrium (in Europe), 61, 62, 157, 193
ERITREA, 108
ESTONIA, 198
EUROPE, 21, 22, 27, 29–35, 37, 39, 41, 48, 49, 53–57, 61–64, 87, 89, 90, 94, 98, 100, 114, 115, 116, 128, 130, 132, 137, 142, 146, 149, 152, 157, 166, 167, 181, 184, 193, 215–222, 224, 227, 228, 230, 234, 235, 241, 242, 244, 246, 253, 254, 255, 267, 272, 274, 276, 278
Europe, Concert of, 34

INDEX

Evil, 202
Export, 205
Extra-territorial (aerodromes and air), 187

Fact, 202–208
Faith, 76
Fear, 35, 61, 62, 65, 67, 80, 221
Federation (or Federal Union), 36, 37, 40, 41, 85, 86, 188–197, 200
Feeling. *See* 'Affect.'
FEISAL, King, 42
FICHTE, J. G., 225, 226
Finance, 18, 50, 98,101, 106, 107, 144, 149, 160, 163, 164, 166, 215, 228
FINLAND, 21, 198
Fleming, 27
FLETCHER, C. R. L., 54
Flood relief, 100
FOCH, Marshal, 73
Food, 42, 43, 44, 52, 55
Force, armed or military, 39, 73, 74, 144, 150, 152–155, 179, 199, 220, 221, 224, 229, 255, 263, 268, 276, 279
FOREIGN OFFICE, 66, 79, 102, 276
Form-master, 204
'Fourteen Points' (1918). *See* Woodrow Wilson
FRANCE, 17, 20, 21, 26, 32, 36, 47, 54, 56, 66, 67, 72, 73, 74, 80–83, 86, 87, 102, 103, 104, 105, 108, 113–125, 131, 132, 136–143, 147–153, 155, 169, 171, 173, 174, 181, 183, 184, 188, 192, 193, 195, 197, 198, 205, 215–223, 228, 236, 237, 246, 255, 274–276
Franco-Soviet Treaty (1936), 115
FREDERICK I, of Brandenburg, 238
FREDERICK the Great, 238, 239, 240, 241
FREDERICK III, Emperor of Germany, 250, 251
Free Church. *See* Church
Free Trade. *See* Trade; *see also* Tariffs
Freedom. *See* Liberty
FREUD, Sigmond, 52, 53
FRICK, Dr., 27

GALILEO, 27
GATHORNE-HARDY, G. M., 170
GENEVA, 76, 97–99, 103, 106, 112, 113, 115, 130, 131, 150, 158, 159, 165, 166, 192, 193
Protocol (1924), 113
GEORGE III, 36, 53
GERMANY, 17, 20, 21, 25–27, 32, 48, 54, 56, 57, 70–82, 90, 91, 98, 105, 107, 108, 114–143, 147, 150, 151, 155, 164, 166, 169–177, 183, 184, 188, 192, 197, 198, 210, 215–279

German-Polish Agreement (1934), 129, 130
German Empire, 72, 252, 258, 259
German Republic, 72, 79, 107, 236, 267–272
GIBRALTAR, 178, 183
GILBERT, W. S., 172
GLADSTONE, W. E., 34
GNEISENAU, N. von, 243
GOOCH, G. P., 27, 28, 30, 32, 262
Good, supreme, 207
GÖTTINGEN, 241
GREAT BRITAIN. *See* Britain or United Kingdom
GREECE, 22, 27, 29, 30, 103, 104, 105, 124, 131, 204, 210
GREEN, T. H., 195
GREY, Viscount, of Fallodon, 35, 66, 263
Grievance, 61, 74, 118, 148, 157, 159, 169–177
GROTIUS, Hugo, 31
GUADELOUPE, 174

Habit, 207
HAGUE, The, 34, 66, 95, 158, 199
HAILSHAM, Viscount, 103
HALIFAX, Viscount, 17, 124, 130, 133, 134, 137, 138, 142, 143, 144, 151, 154, 167, 168, 195
HAMILTON, Alexander, 22
HANOVER, 156, 221, 241
HARDINGE, Sir Charles, 261
HARTE, Bret, 59
Hatred, 61, 65, 67–70, 76, 80, 154
Health, 25, 48, 49, 79, 98, 100, 145, 161, 163, 166, 173, 210
Hebrew, 22
HEGEL, G. W. F., 225, 226
HEIDEN, K., 218
HENDERSON, H. D., 171–175
HENDERSON, Sir Nevile, 131, 133, 134, 227, 231
HENRI IV, 31
HENRY II, 229
HENRY VII, 57
HERBERT, A. P., 220, 230
Herd Instinct, 70
HERTZ, H. R., 27
Hibbert Journal, 68
HINDENBURG, Paul von, 232, 233, 234, 271, 273
HITLER, Adolf, 17, 20, 25, 27, 28, 43, 70, 74, 115, 116, 117, 119, 121–138, 173, 183, 210, 217–223, 227, 230–235, 248, 250, 271–277
HOARE, Sir Samuel, 109
HODSON, H. V., 148
HOHENZOLLERN, 238, 239, 242, 251, 266

HOLLAND. *See* Netherlands *and* Dutch
Holy Alliance, 32
Holy Roman Empire. *See* Empire
Hours of Work. *See* Labour, Hours of
HOWARD-ELLIS, C., 68–71
Huguenot, 27, 31
HUMBOLDT, W. von, 225, 226
HUNGARY, 43, 90, 198
Hypothesis, 206, 208, 209

Iberian, 26
Ice Patrol, North-Atlantic, 156
Ideal, 33, 39, 40, 86, 111, 190, 200
Immortality, 23
Imperial Conference, 39
Indemnity, Bill of, 256, 257
INDIA, 38, 42, 43, 96, 148, 155
'Industrial Junker,' 248, 261, 270
'Inferiority Complex,' 227
Inflation, German (1923), 270, 271
Inspiration, 206
Instinct, 205, 208
Interest, 205
International Authority, 19, 47, 61, 62, 63, 65, 84, 86, 142, 185, 186, 191. *See also* Commonwealth
International Cartel, 151
International Chamber of Commerce, 49
International Commission for Air Navigation (C.I.N.A.), 185
International Conference, 33, 49, 50
International Federation of Trades Unions, 49
International Government, 46–51, 55, 56, 161, 162, 210
International Labour Organization, 18, 69, 72, 79, 91, 93–96, 98, 145, 163, 164, 166
International Trust, 51
Inter-Parliamentary Union, 49
Inter-State, 40, 41, 85, 188–197
Investments, Colonial, 172, 175
IRAN, 198
IRAQ (or Iraqui), 42, 198
IRELAND, 27, 38, 112, 128. *See also* Eire
ITALY, 27, 81, 94, 105, 107, 108, 114, 115, 117, 118, 119, 120, 122, 125, 132, 136, 150, 155, 164, 171, 192, 198, 221, 246

JAPAN, 43, 81, 91, 106, 107, 110, 114, 115, 117, 132, 149, 150, 155, 164, 171, 199
JAY, John, 22
JENA, Battle of, 241, 245
Jew, 27, 125, 242
JOHN, King, 195, 229

JOHN, Saint, 207, 208, 209
Junker, 229–279
 Definition of, 231, 248, 261
 Political principles of, 233, 240, 249, 255, 262, 279
Justice, 22, 31, 41, 60, 73, 74, 79, 89, 91, 92, 93, 95, 99, 154, 158, 159, 195, 209, 230, 268, 278, 279
 Permanent Court of International, 89, 94, 95, 102, 103, 110, 158

Kaiser WILHELM II, 18, 68, 69, 70, 71, 238, 259, 261–263, 269
KANT, Immanuel, 23, 32, 225, 226
Kellogg Pact. *See* Pact of Paris
KEPLER, Johann, 27
KERENSKY, A. F., 267
KEYNES, J. Maynard, 75
KIPLING, Rudyard, 53, 54, 186
Knowledge, 201–206
KÖNIGGRÄTZ (or Sadowa), Battle of 255, 256, 257
Kreuzzeitung, 266

Labour, Conditions of, 93, 144, 163, 164, 175
Labour, Hours of, 25, 144, 163, 164, 175
Labour International. *See* International Labour Organization
Labour's Peace Aims, 164
LANCASHIRE, 43
Landwehr, Prussian, 250
Landwirte, Bund der, 260
LATIN AMERICA, 132, 198
LATVIA, 198
LAUSANNE, 158
LAVAL, Pierre, 108
Law, 25, 29, 31, 39, 47, 56, 59, 60, 63, 85, 88, 91, 92, 95, 98, 99, 102, 103, 116, 118, 146–160, 161, 179, 182, 195, 245–253, 255, 259, 267, 275, 279. *See also* Justice
LAW, Bonar, 70, 217
Law Courts, German, 267
LEAGUE OF NATIONS, 18, 21, 31, 32, 54, 55, 66, 67, 72, 76–120, 125, 128, 130, 131, 143, 145, 146, 148–151, 157–160, 163, 166, 170, 173, 178, 189, 190, 194, 197, 198, 200, 217, 268, 270. *See also* Assembly, Council, Covenant and Secretariat of the League of Nations
LEAGUE OF NATIONS UNION, 43, 67, 78, 99, 111, 112, 126, 190
LEAGUE TO ENFORCE PEACE, 67
Lebensraum, 14, 44, 278
LENIN, W. I., 267

Liberty, 22, 25, 41, 125, 138, 162, 196, 209, 220, 229, 233, 241, 242, 245–253, 257
LIPPMANN, Walter, 196
LISBON, 185
LITHUANIA, 198
LITVINOV, M. M., 131, 199
LIVERPOOL, 43
Living, Standard of, 144, 164, 176, 194
LLOYD, Lord, 123, 223
LLOYD GEORGE, David, 68, 71, 83, 216, 263
Local Education Authority, 111
Local self-government, 162, 239, 243
LOCARNO, Treaty of (1925), 114, 116, 150, 270
LOFTUS, Lord Augustus, 255
LONDON, 42, 122, 135, 183, 223, 239
   COUNTY COUNCIL, 166
   Naval Conference (1930), 81
LOUIS XIV, 54, 57
LOUIS NAPOLEON, 255
Love, 22, 208, 209
LOW COUNTRIES. *See* NETHERLANDS
Loyalty, 19, 28, 33, 82, 83, 86, 109, 111, 113, 190, 194, 195, 196, 200, 210, 211
Lückentheorie, 251
LUDENDORF, Field-Marshal E., 265
LUTHER, Martin, 242
LUXEMBURG, 117

MACDONALD, Ramsay, 80, 82, 108, 111, 218
MCDOUGALL, William, 205
MACHIAVELLI, Nicolo, 30, 31
MADARIAGA, Don Salvador de, 23–25, 199
MADISON, James, 22
MADRID, 185
MAGINOT LINE, 117
Magna Carta, 195, 229
MALTA, 102, 108, 178
MALTHUS, Thomas, 44
MANCHURIA, 105–107, 149, 150
Mandate, 93, 167, 168, 170, 178, 197
Manœuvres, Naval and military, 156
Maps, 90
'March Claims' (1848), 247
Marcher Lords, 237
MARCONI, G., 27
Markets, 51, 52, 55, 56, 172, 175–177
MARLBOROUGH, Duke of, 57
MARRIOTT, Sir J. A. R., 238
MARTINIQUE, 174
MARVIN, F. S., 28
MAXWELL, James Clerk, 27, 206
MEDITERRANEAN, 29, 43, 109, 120, 155, 158

MELBOURNE, Lord, 34
MEMEL, 123
MICKLEM, Nathaniel, 195
Middle Ages, 30, 127, 229, 237, 239
Militarism, 229
MILLER, David Hunter, 274
Minorities, 72, 78, 99, 145, 164, 166
MONROE, James, 33
Monroe Doctrine, 33
MONTFORT, Simon de, 22, 248
Montreal Daily Star, 122
MONTREUX Conference (1936), 158
MOROCCO, 102, 119
MOSCOW, 132
MUIR, Ramsay, 270
MUNICH, 122, 129
   Putsch (1923), 271
MUSSOLINI, B., 25, 107, 108, 109, 118, 124, 134, 150

NANKING, 101
NAPOLEON I, 32, 42, 46, 56, 58, 241, 244, 245, 246
NAPOLEON III. *See* Louis NAPOLEON
Nation, 24, 196
Nationalism, 31, 155
National Socialism, 21, 27, 125, 129, 132, 155, 219, 221, 223–227, 230–234, 256, 271–275
Nature, 27
Navarino, Battle of, 155
Navy, Royal, 39, 63, 81, 109, 146, 148, 155, 182, 262
Navy, German, 64, 259
'Nazi.' *See* National Socialism
Nazi-Soviet Pact. *See* Russo-German Agreement
NEBRASKA, 44
NEBUCHADNEZZAR, 26
NETHERLANDS, 69, 134, 172, 184, 198, 215, 238, 278. *See also* Dutch
Neurogram, 207
Neurosis, 227
Neutral, 28, 65, 84, 142, 154, 168
NEW YORK, 42, 105, 185
NEW ZEALAND, 38, 43, 148
NEWFOUNDLAND, 43
NEWTON, Sir Isaac, 23, 27, 206
NICOLSON, Harold, 72–74, 77, 122, 128
Nordic, 27
NORMANDY, 26, 205
NORWAY, 40, 139, 142, 198
NYON, 120

Occupation, armed (of Germany), 221
Officialdom (British and French), 83, 86, 112. *See also* Whitehall
OKLAHOMA, 42

INDEX

Opinion. *See* Public Opinion
Opium. *See* Drugs
ORANGE, WILLIAM OF, 26
OSLO, 198
Osthilfe, 233, 234

Pacifism, 153
PANAMA, 178, 183
Pan-America, 152
PAPEN, F. von, 234, 273
PARIS, 71, 74, 76-88, 104, 146, 183, 190, 193, 223
    Pact of (1928), 54, 92, 114, 129
Parliament, British, 36, 38, 72, 85, 162, 217, 241, 249, 276
    German, 231-233, 254, 257, 258, 261 263, 271. *See also Reichstag*
    Prussian, 243, 245, 248-253, 257, 276. *See also Landtag*
Patriotism, 97, 196, 210, 211
Pay. *See* Wages
Peace Aims, 138, 139, 140, 142-145, 162, 165, 167, 168, 170, 173, 182, 192, 197
    Front (1939), 33, 124, 131, 132
    Terms, 17. *See also* War Aim *and* Peace Aims
Peaceful change. *See* Revision of treaties
PEEL, Sir Robert, 42
PENN, William, 32
PENNSYLVANIA, 32
PERICLES, 210
PHILADELPHIA, 37
PHILLIMORE, Lord, 66
Philosophers, German, 225, 226
PICARDY, 205
PIERRE, Abbé St., 32
Plebiscite, 142
POLAND, 17, 27, 55, 72, 87, 113, 124-136, 139, 142, 150, 152, 169, 198, 233, 240, 242
Police, Air, 179, 182
Polish Corridor, 127, 128, 129, 130
Political and Economic Planning, 163-166
Political Quarterly, 227
Population, 44
PORTUGAL, 132, 172, 198
Post, 47, 49, 57, 161. *See also* Universal Postal Union
PRAGUE, 123, 130, 136
Prince Consort. *See* ALBERT
Propaganda, 18, 56, 61, 112, 154, 230, 256, 269, 272
Prosperity, 110, 111, 140, 262, 269, 271
Protestants, German, 242
Province, 162

PRUSSIA, 32, 127, 220, 224, 229-231, 236, 262, 269, 276
    EAST, 127, 128, 129, 130
Psychology, 39, 52, 56, 67, 71, 140, 141, 190, 196, 211, 226, 227
Public opinion, 33, 71, 73, 76, 80, 83, 86, 88, 89, 92, 99, 111, 112, 113, 117, 125, 136, 141, 156, 191, 216, 222
PUERTO RICO, 174
Punch, 220
Punishment, 68, 69, 71, 154, 182
Purpose, 22, 195, 196, 209
Putsch, Hitler's (1923), 271

Quadragesimo Anno, 278
Quarantine, 48, 100
QUIDDE, L., 263
Quintuple Alliance, 32, 33, 46

Radio. *See* Wireless
RADIO-TELEGRAPHIC UNION, 47
RANSOME, Patrick, 189
RAUSCHNING, Hermann, 26, 224, 234, 270, 276
Raw materials, Colonial, 172-175, 177
READING, Marquess of, 102
Reality, 206, 207
Realpolitik, Bismarck's (1863), 253
Red Cross, 93
Reform Bill (1832), 248
Reformation, 30, 220
Refugees, 98, 145, 164, 166, 187
Regional Groups of States, 152, 153, 156, 165
Regional Pacts, 114
Reich. See GERMANY
Reichstag, 129, 130, 231, 232, 254, 257, 258, 261, 263, 264, 271, 272
Religion, 196, 203, 209, 210
Renaissance, 30
Reparations (1918), 72-75
Republic, German. *See* German Republic
Responsible government, 38, 189, 192
Revision of treaties, 79, 92, 93, 110, 118, 144, 157-160, 164, 170
Revolution, German—
    (1848), 247, 248, 250, 252
    (1918), 221, 265 *et seq.*
REYNAUD, Paul, 44
RHINE, 73, 113, 116, 117, 121, 216
RHINELAND, 116, 121, 129, 136, 216, 218-222
RICHMOND, Sir Herbert, 147, 155, 156
'Rights of man,' 195
RIVAUD, Albert, 220
RIVER PLATE, Battle of, 126, 148

INDEX

ROBERTSON, Sir Charles Grant, 238, 252, 276
Robinson Crusoe, 26
ROME, 22, 26, 29, 30, 42, 54, 85, 204, 223, 238
ROOSEVELT, Franklin D., 113, 120, 134
ROOSEVELT, Theodore, 263
ROSENBERG, A., 268, 270
Roses, Wars of the, 57, 205
ROUMANIA, 124, 131, 221
ROWSE, A. L., 227
ROYAL INSTITUTE OF INTERNATIONAL AFFAIRS, 124, 216, 219
RUMBOLD, Sir Horace, 104
RUHR, 216, 218
RUSKIN, John, 76
RUSSIA, 32, 76, 81, 98, 106, 111, 115, 119, 121, 124, 127, 131, 132, 133, 136, 155, 172, 198, 199, 223, 224, 267
Russo-German Agreement (1939), 131, 132, 133
RUTHERFORD, Lord, 201, 206

SAAR, 78
Sacrifice, 29, 47, 48, 60, 86, 88, 89, 139, 195
SALISBURY, Marquess of, 34
SALTER, Sir Arthur, 76, 84, 141, 151
SALVATION ARMY, 111
Sanitary Convention, 48, 49, 57
SAUDI ARABIA, 91
SAXONY, 221, 236, 259
SCANDINAVIA, 43, 65, 152, 169, 193
SCHARNHORST, G. J. D. von, 243, 244, 245, 250
SCHLEICHER, General, 233, 234
SCHNEE, Heinrich, 171
SCHUSCHNIGG, Kurt, 119
Science, 201, 202, 203, 206, 209
SCOTLAND, 27, 29, 32, 85, 154, 201, 211, 221
Secession, 193
Secretariat of the League of Nations, 93, 95, 170, 182
Security, 62, 82, 89, 91, 92, 107, 109, 115, 124, 138, 147, 152–155, 162, 163, 165, 215–222. *See also* Defence, Collective
SEDAN, Battle of, 255
Self-determination, 89, 116, 216
-government, 17, 177, 178, 232, 242, 243, 245, 246, 259, 272
-regard, Sentiment of, 207–209
SENEGAL, 205
Sentiment, 61, 97, 109, 190, 194, 196, 205–210
Separatist, 218

SERBIA, 221. *See also* Yugoslavia
SETON-WATSON, R. W., 27, 121, 122, 123
Settlement, General, 19, 124, 125, 139, 141, 142, 146, 147, 162, 163, 168, 174, 175, 176, 186, 188, 190, 199, 219
Settlement of international disputes. *See* Disputes
SEYMOUR, Charles, 72
SHAKESPEARE, William, 23
SHANGHAI, 107
SHOTWELL, James T., 114
SIAM, 199
SILESIA, 240
SIMON, Sir John, 108, 109
SIMPSON, Sir John Hope, 98, 100
SINGAPORE, 183, 205
'Single wide interest,' 201, 205–210
SLAVS, 127, 237
SMUTS, Jan Christian, 39, 66, 67, 79, 89, 98, 190
Social Insurance, 163
Social Justice, 18, 79, 88, 89, 93, 95, 145, 164, 165, 194, 230, 233, 241
Social Service, 99, 145, 166
SOFIA, 131
SOUTH AFRICA, 38, 39, 43
SOUTHAMPTON, 42
Sovereignty, 29, 30, 31, 36, 39, 47, 51, 56, 57, 83–86, 88, 145, 170, 171, 185
SPAIN, 26, 86, 94, 119, 132, 172, 198
SPANISH AMERICA, 33
SPARTA, 29
Spectator, The, 227
'Split-up' (of Germany), 218, 221
'Stab in the back' (1918), 265
STALIN, J. V., 25, 223, 224
State, 25, 225, 229
Stateless persons, 145, 166
STEIN, Ritter K. vom, 241–246, 278
STIMSON, Henry L., 107
STREIT, Clarence, 189
STRESA, 108, 109
STRESEMANN, Gustav, 114, 192, 221, 265, 270
STRUMA, 104
SUDETENLAND, 123, 129, 136
SUEZ, 178
SULLY, M. de B., 31
Super-State, 83–86
SUPREME WAR COUNCIL, 16, 191
SWEDEN, 40, 45, 46, 104, 174, 198
SWITZERLAND, 152, 169, 184, 198, 278

Tariff, 56, 163, 165
Taxes (in America), 36
(in Prussia), 249–252
Teach, 111, 201, 202, 210

INDEX

Telegraph, 49
TEMPERLEY, H., 217
TESCHEN, 130
TEUTONIC KNIGHTS, 127. *See also* Marcher lords
Theology, 209
Thought, 202, 206–210
THYSSEN, Herr F., 232
Times, The, 17, 19, 118, 137, 138, 142, 151, 218, 232, 276
Trade, 162, 164, 165, 174, 176, 185
TRADE, BOARD OF, 185
Trade Union, 125, 268
TRADES UNION CONGRESS, 111
Traffic in arms, 93
Traffic in women. *See* White Slave Traffic
Treaty Revision. *See* Revision of Treaties
TREVELYAN, G. M., 36, 38, 57, 195
TROTSKY, L. D., 267
TROTTER, W., 70, 71
Trust, 51
Truth, 203, 206, 208, 209
Tudor, 229
TUNIS, 102
TURKEY, 21, 78, 124, 131, 152, 153, 155, 158, 198

UKRAINE, 132
Unanimity, Rule of, 110, 159
Unemployment, 102, 105, 113, 232
UNITED KINGDOM, 38, 75, 89, 106, 111, 112, 117, 125, 135, 152, 161, 189, 191, 197. *See also* Britain
UNITED STATES, 33, 34, 36, 37, 40, 44, 52, 60, 66, 75, 81, 85, 90, 97, 98, 106, 113, 114, 115, 132, 134, 137, 152, 171, 174, 184, 189, 193, 199, 216, 217, 220
Unity (of civilization), 20–30
(of creation), 22
German, 220–222, 243, 245–264, 269
World, 30, 210
Units within a larger. *See* British Commonwealth
Universal Postal Union, 47, 48
U.S.S.R. *See* Russia
Utopia, 19, 76
UTRECHT, 32

Value, 204, 206, 208
VATICAN, 223, 273
VELASQUEZ, 23
VERSAILLES, 18, 69, 70, 73, 77–80, 95, 107, 116, 128, 139, 166, 170, 216, 217, 218
VICTORIA, Queen, 34, 250
VIENNA, 32, 34, 55, 101, 119, 123, 223, 246

VILNA, 105
VISTULA, 127, 128
VÖLKERBUND, LIGA FÜR, 78

Wages, 25, 144, 164, 175
Wagons-Lits, Compagnie Internationale des, 51
WALES, 154
War aims, 17, 136–145
'War-guilt clause' (of Versailles Treaty), 18, 73
WARSAW, 127, 133, 134, 223
Warships, Maximum size of, 80, 147
WASHINGTON, 40, 81, 97, 120
WASHINGTON, George, 199
WATERLOO, Battle of, 32, 58, 156
Wealth, 44, 45, 144, 164, 209
WEBSTER, C. K., 32, 33, 65–67, 77, 78, 83, 96
'WEIMAR, 243, 270, 271, 273
Welfare, 56, 88, 93, 98, 100, 145, 161–166, 167, 203
WELLINGTON, Duke of, 58, 156
WELLS, H. G., 195
WEST INDIES, 43
WESTMINSTER, 36, 71, 162
Statute of, 38, 39, 41, 188, 189, 248
WESTPHALIA, 242
WHEELER-BENNETT, J. W., 232, 233
WHITEHALL, 83, 250. *See also* Officialdom
WHITEHEAD, A. N., 201, 202, 210
White Slave Traffic, 79, 93
WILLIAM II. *See* Kaiser
WILSON, Woodrow, 66, 67, 72, 73, 77–79, 88, 89, 97, 128, 170, 216, 217, 269
Wireless telegraphy, 42, 47, 49
WOOLF, Leonard, 45–51
Work. *See* Labour
World authority, 178, 185
World government. *See* International government
World loyalty. *See* Loyalty
World settlement. *See* Settlement, General
World War, 18, 34, 41, 58–60, 64–75, 82, 128, 141, 145, 146, 155, 170, 171, 215, 220, 228, 230, 269
Worship, 25, 85
WÜRTTEMBERG, 236, 259

YANGTSE, 100
Young Plan (1929), 75
YUGOSLAVIA, 100, 105, 113

ZELIGOVSKI, General, 105
ZIMMERN, Sir Alfred, 63, 76, 84, 86, 197, 278
Zollverein (1834), 259

For Product Safety Concerns and Information please contact our EU
representative GPSR@taylorandfrancis.com
Taylor & Francis Verlag GmbH, Kaufingerstraße 24, 80331 München, Germany

www.ingramcontent.com/pod-product-compliance
Lightning Source LLC
Chambersburg PA
CBHW071809300426
44116CB00009B/1254